THE DIVINE COMEDY
PURGATORIO

DANTE ALIGHIERI

THE JOHN CIARDI
TRANSLATION

THE MODERN LIBRARY
NEW YORK

1996 Modern Library Edition

Biographical note copyright © 1996 by Random House, Inc.
Copyright © 1954, 1957, 1959, 1960, 1961, 1965,
1967, 1970 by John Ciardi
Introduction copyright © 1970 by The New American Library, Inc.

Acknowledgment is made to *Venture, The Italian Quarterly,
The Saturday Review, Between Worlds, The Massachusetts Review
New World Writing,* and *Arbor,* in which excerpts
from the present work first appeared.

Canto I was first published in *Italian Quarterly*, 1965.
Canto VIII was first published in *Arbor*, 1961.
Canto XXI was first published in *Hartwick Review*, 1967.
Canto XXXIII was first published in *The Rarer Action: Essays in Honor of
Francis Fergusson*, ed. Alan Cheuse and Richard Koffler, 1970.

This edition published by arrangement with
W. W. Norton & Company, Inc., N.Y.

Jacket painting: *Dante*, Florentine School (sixteenth century),
courtesy of The Granger Collection, N.Y.

LIBRARY OF CONGRESS CATALOGING-IN-PUBLICATION DATA
Dante Alighieri, 1265–1321.
[Purgatorio. English]
Purgatorio/Dante Alighieri: the John Ciardi translation.
p. cm.
ISBN 0-679-60210-0
I. Ciardi, John, 1916–   . II. Title.
PQ4315.3.C5   1996
851'.1—dc20   96-17277

Random House website address: http://www.randomhouse.com/

Printed in the United States of America on acid-free paper ∞

2 4 6 8 9 7 5 3 1

DANTE ALIGHIERI

Dante Alighieri, the Italian poet whose great allegory *The Divine Comedy* has exerted a profound effect on Western literature and thought, was born in Florence in May 1265. He came from a noble though impoverished family, descendants of the city's Roman founders. Relatively little is known with certainty about Dante's early life, but it is noteworthy that he grew up during the restless period that followed decades of bloody rivalry between two opposing Florentine political groups, the Guelphs and the Ghibellines. His childhood was doubtless colored by stories of this partisan strife from which, as Machiavelli later wrote, "there resulted more murders, banishments and destruction of families than ever in any city known to history."

Dante probably received his early schooling from the Franciscans and the Dominicans; later, he studied rhetoric with the Guelph statesman and scholar Brunetto Latini. Another significant mentor was the aristocratic poet Guido Cavalcanti, who strongly influenced his early work. For the young Dante, writing poetry became an important expression of his passion for art and learning, and of his abiding concern with the nature of love and spiritual fulfillment. A Florentine woman of exceptional beauty, Beatrice Portinari, provided a powerful stimulus to the poet's artistic development. Dante idealized her as the "bringer of blessings," a beatific guide capable of pointing him toward the inner perfection sought by every noble mind. Following her untimely death in 1290, Dante, overcome with grief, celebrated her grace and virtue in *La vita nuova* (1292–1294), a small "book of memory" written in verse and prose. He then sought renewal in an extensive study of theology and philosophy.

In 1295 Dante entered public life and within a few years emerged as a prominent figure in Florentine politics. By then he had entered into an arranged marriage with Gemma Donati, a gentlewoman by whom he had several children. In the summer of 1300 Dante was named one of the six governing magistrates of Florence. During this time he was involved in the clash between two hostile factions of the Guelph party, the Whites and the Blacks. Aligning himself with the White Guelphs, Dante campaigned to preserve the independence of Florence and repeatedly opposed the machinations of Pope Boniface VIII, who was attempting to place all of Tuscany under papal control. In 1301, however, the Black Guelphs seized power, and Dante was banished at once on trumped-up charges of graft, embezzlement, and other transgressions. Later sentenced to death by fire if he returned to Florence, Dante never entered his native city again.

Dante's remaining years were spent with a series of patrons in various courts of Italy. Two uncompleted works date from his early period of exile. *De vulgari eloquentia* (1303–1304), a scholarly tract in Latin on the eloquence of the Italian vernacular, is generally acknowledged to be the key to Dante's artistic inquiries. *Il convivio* (1304–1307), a glorification of moral philosophy, is viewed as the cornerstone of his investigations into knowledge and wisdom. Perhaps as early as 1306, Dante began to compose *The Divine Comedy,* the greatest poem of the Middle Ages and the first masterpiece of world literature written in a modern European language. The Latin treatise *De monarchia* (1312–1313), a practical guide calling for the restoration of peace in Europe under a secular ruler in Rome, is a statement of the poet's political theories. In his final years Dante was given asylum in Ravenna, where he completed *The Divine Comedy* shortly before his death in September 1321.

PURGATORIO

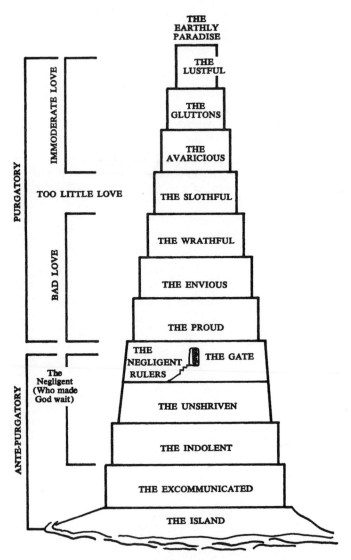

Diagram of Purgatory

CANTO I

The Poets emerge from Hell just before dawn of Easter Sunday (April 10, 1300), and Dante revels in the sight of the rediscovered heavens. As he looks eagerly about at the stars, he sees nearby an old man of impressive bearing. The ancient is *Cato of Utica,* guardian of the shores of Purgatory. Cato challenges the Poets as fugitives from Hell, but Virgil, after first instructing Dante to kneel in reverence, explains Dante's mission and Beatrice's command. Cato then gives them instructions for proceeding.

The Poets have emerged at a point a short way up the slope of Purgatory. It is essential, therefore, that they descend to the lowest point and begin from there, an allegory of Humility. Cato, accordingly, orders Virgil to lead Dante to the shore, to wet his hands in the dew of the new morning, and to wash the stains of Hell from Dante's face and the film of Hell's vapors from Dante's eyes. Virgil is then to bind about Dante's waist one of the pliant reeds (symbolizing Humility) that grow in the soft mud of the shore.

Having so commanded, Cato disappears. Dante arises in silence and stands waiting, eager to begin. His look is all the communication that is necessary. Virgil leads him to the shore and performs all that Cato has commanded. Dante's first purification is marked by a miracle: when Virgil breaks off a reed, the stalk immediately regenerates a new reed, restoring itself exactly as it had been.

For better waters now the little bark
    of my indwelling powers raises her sails,
    and leaves behind that sea so cruel and dark.   3

Now shall I sing that second kingdom given
    the soul of man wherein to purge its guilt
    and so grow worthy to ascend to Heaven.   6

Yours am I, sacred Muses! To you I pray.
  Here let dead poetry rise once more to life,
  and here let sweet Calliope rise and play   9

some far accompaniment in that high strain
  whose power the wretched Pierides once felt
  so terribly they dared not hope again.   12

Sweet azure of the sapphire of the east
  was gathering on the serene horizon
  its pure and perfect radiance—a feast   15

to my glad eyes, reborn to their delight,
  as soon as I had passed from the dead air
  which had oppressed my soul and dimmed my sight.   18

The planet whose sweet influence strengthens love
  was making all the east laugh with her rays,
  veiling the Fishes, which she swam above.   21

I turned then to my right and set my mind
  on the other pole, and there I saw four stars
  unseen by mortals since the first mankind.   24

The heavens seemed to revel in their light.
  O widowed Northern Hemisphere, bereft
  forever of the glory of that sight!   27

As I broke off my gazing, my eyes veered
  a little to the left, to the other pole
  from which, by then, the Wain had disappeared.   30

I saw, nearby, an ancient man, alone.
  His bearing filled me with such reverence,
  no father has had more from any son.   33

His beard was long and touched with strands of white,
   as was his hair, of which two tresses fell
   over his breast. Rays of the holy light   36

that fell from the four stars made his face glow
   with such a radiance that he looked to me
   as if he faced the sun. And standing so,   39

he moved his venerable plumes and said:
   "Who are you two who climb by the dark stream
   to escape the eternal prison of the dead?   42

Who led you? or what served you as a light
   in your dark flight from the eternal valley,
   which lies forever blind in darkest night?   45

Are the laws of the pit so broken? Or is new counsel
   published in Heaven that the damned may wander
   onto my rocks from the abyss of Hell?"   48

At that my Master laid his hands upon me,
   instructing me by word and touch and gesture
   to show my reverence in brow and knee,   51

then answered him: "I do not come this way
   of my own will or powers. A Heavenly Lady
   sent me to this man's aid in his dark day.   54

But since your will is to know more, my will
   cannot deny you; I will tell you truly
   why we have come and how. This man has still   57

to see his final hour, though in the burning
   of his own madness he had drawn so near it
   his time was perilously short for turning.   60

As I have told you, I was sent to show
  the way his soul must take for its salvation;
  and there is none but this by which I go.   63

I have shown him the guilty people. Now I mean
  to lead him through the spirits in your keeping,
  to show him those whose suffering makes them clean.   66

By what means I have led him to this strand
  to see and hear you, takes too long to tell:
  from Heaven is the power and the command.   69

Now may his coming please you, for he goes
  to win his freedom; and how dear that is
  the man who gives his life for it best knows.   72

You know it, who in that cause found death sweet
  in Utica where you put off that flesh
  which shall rise radiant at the Judgment Seat.   75

We do not break the Laws: this man lives yet,
  and I am of that Round not ruled by Minos,
  with your own Marcia, whose chaste eyes seem set   78

in endless prayers to you. O blessed breast
  to hold her yet your own! for love of her
  grant us permission to pursue our quest   81

across your seven kingdoms. When I go
  back to her side I shall bear thanks of you,
  if you will let me speak your name below."   84

"Marcia was so pleasing in my eyes
  there on the other side," he answered then
  "that all she asked, I did. Now that she lies   87

beyond the evil river, no word or prayer
  of hers may move me. Such was the Decree
  pronounced upon us when I rose from there.   90

But if, as you have said, a Heavenly Dame
  orders your way, there is no need to flatter:
  you need but ask it of me in her name.   93

Go then, and lead this man, but first see to it
  you bind a smooth green reed about his waist
  and clean his face of all trace of the pit.   96

For it would not be right that one with eyes
  still filmed by mist should go before the angel
  who guards the gate: he is from Paradise.   99

All round the wave-wracked shore-line, there below,
  reeds grow in the soft mud. Along that edge
  no foliate nor woody plant could grow.   102

for what lives in that buffeting must bend.
  Do not come back this way: the rising sun
  will light an easier way you may ascend."   105

With that he disappeared; and silently
  I rose and moved back till I faced my Guide,
  my eyes upon him, waiting. He said to me: 108

"Follow my steps and let us turn again:
  along this side there is a gentle slope
  that leads to the low boundaries of the plain."   111

The dawn, in triumph, made the day-breeze flee
  before its coming, so that from afar
  I recognized the trembling of the sea.   114

We strode across that lonely plain like men
  who seek the road they strayed from and who count
  the time lost till they find it once again.   117

When we had reached a place along the way
  where the cool morning breeze shielded the dew
  against the first heat of the gathering day,   120

with gentle graces my Sweet Master bent
  and laid both outspread palms upon the grass.
  Then I, being well aware of his intent,   123

lifted my tear-stained cheeks to him, and there
  he made me clean, revealing my true color
  under the residues of Hell's black air.   126

We moved on then to the deserted strand
  which never yet has seen upon its waters
  a man who found his way back to dry land.   129

There, as it pleased another, he girded me.
  Wonder of wonders! when he plucked a reed
  another took its place there instantly,   132

arising from the humble stalk he tore
  so that it grew exactly as before.

NOTES

4. *that second kingdom:* Purgatory.

5. *to purge its guilt:* (See also line 66: *those whose suffering makes them clean.*) There is suffering in Purgatory but no torment. The torment of the damned is endless, produces no change in the soul that endures it, and is imposed from without. The suffering of the souls in Purgatory, on the other hand, is temporary, is a means of purifica-

tion, and is eagerly embraced as an act of the soul's own will. Demons guard the damned to inflict punishment and to prevent escape. In Purgatory, the sinners are free to leave off their sufferings: nothing but their own desire to be made clean moves them to accept their pains, and nothing more is needed. In fact, it is left to the suffering soul itself (no doubt informed by Divine Illumination) to decide at what point it has achieved purification and is ready to move on.

8. *dead poetry:* The verses that sang of Hell. Dante may equally have meant that poetry as an art has long been surpassed by history as the medium for great subjects. Here poetry will return to its classic state.

7–12. THE INVOCATION. Dante invokes all the Muses, as he did in *Inferno* II, 7, but there the exhortation was to his own powers, to High Genius, and to Memory. Here he addresses his specific exhortation to Calliope, who, as the Muse of Epic Poetry, is foremost of the Nine. In *Paradiso* (I, 13) he exhorts Apollo himself to come to the aid of the poem.

Dante exhorts Calliope to fill him with the strains of the music she played in the defeat of the Pierides, the nine daughters of Pierius, King of Thessaly. They presumed to challenge the Muses to a contest of song. After their defeat they were changed into magpies for their presumption. Ovid (*Metamorphoses* V, 294–340 and 662–678) retells the myth in detail.

Note that Dante not only calls upon Calliope to fill him with the strains of highest song, but that he calls for that very song that overthrew the arrogant pretensions of the Pierides, the strains that humbled false pride. The invocation is especially apt, therefore, as a first sounding of the theme of Humility.

17. *the dead air:* Of Hell.

19–21. *The planet whose sweet influence strengthens love:* Venus. Here, as morning star, Venus is described as rising in Pisces, the Fishes, the zodiacal sign immediately preceding Aries. In Canto I of the *Inferno* Dante has made it clear that the Sun is in Aries. Hence it is about to rise.

Allegorically, the fact that Venus represents love is, of course, indispensable to the mood of the *Purgatorio*. At no time in April of 1300 was Venus the morning star. Rather, it rose after the sun. Dante's description of the first dawn in Canto I of the *Inferno* similarly violates the exact detail of things. But Dante is no bookkeeper of the literal. In the *Inferno* he violated fact in order to compile a perfect symbol of rebirth. Here, he similarly violates the literal in order to describe an ideal sunrise, and simultaneously to make the allegorical point that Love (Venus) leads the way and that Divine Illumination (the Sun) follows upon it.

23. *four stars:* Modern readers are always tempted to identify these four stars as the Southern Cross, but it is almost certain that Dante did not know about that formation. In VIII, 89, Dante mentions three other stars as emphatically as he does these four and no one has been tempted to identify them on the star-chart. Both constellations are best taken as allegorical. The four stars represent the Four Cardinal Virtues: Prudence, Justice, Fortitude, and Temperance. Dante will encounter them again in the form of nymphs when he achieves the Earthly Paradise.

24. *the first mankind:* Adam and Eve. In Dante's geography, the Garden of Eden (the Earthly Paradise) was at the top of the Mount of Purgatory, which was the only land in the Southern Hemisphere. All of what were called "the southern continents" were believed to lie north of the equator. When Adam and Eve were driven from the Garden, therefore, they were driven into the Northern Hemisphere, and no living soul since had been far enough south to see those stars.

Ulysses and his men (*Inferno* XXVII) had come within sight of the Mount of Purgatory, but Ulysses mentioned nothing of having seen these stars.

29. *the other pole:* The North Pole. The Wain (Ursa Major, i.e., the Big Dipper) is below the horizon.

31 ff. CATO OF UTICA. Marcus Porcius Cato, the younger, 95–46 B.C. In the name of freedom, Cato opposed the policies of both Caesar and Pompey, but because he saw Caesar as the greater evil joined forces with Pompey. After the defeat of his cause at the Battle of Thapsus, Cato killed himself with his own sword rather than lose his freedom. Virgil lauds him in the *Aeneid* as a symbol of

perfect devotion to liberty, and all writers of Roman antiquity have given Cato a similar high place. Dante spends the highest praises on him both in *De Monarchia* and *Il Convivio*.

Why Cato should be so signally chosen by God as the special guardian of Purgatory has been much disputed. Despite his suicide (and certainly one could argue that he had less excuse for it than had Pier delle Vigne—see *Inferno* XIII—for his) he was sent to Limbo as a Virtuous Pagan. From Limbo he was especially summoned to his present office. It is clear, moreover, that he will find a special triumph on Judgment Day, though he will probably not be received into Heaven.

The key to Dante's intent seems to lie in the four stars, the Four Cardinal Virtues, that shine so brightly on Cato's face when Dante first sees him. Once Cato is forgiven his suicide (and a partisan could argue that it was a positive act, a death for freedom), he may certainly be taken as a figure of Prudence, Justice, Fortitude, and Temperance. He does very well, moreover, as a symbol of the natural love of freedom; and Purgatory, it must be remembered, is the road to Ultimate Freedom. Cato may be taken, therefore, as representative of supreme virtue short of godliness. He has accomplished everything but the purifying total surrender of his will to God. As such he serves as an apt transitional symbol, being the highest rung on the ladder of natural virtue, but the lowest on the ladder of those godly virtues to which Purgatory is the ascent. Above all, the fact that he took Marcia (see line 78, note) back to his love, makes him an especially apt symbol of God's forgiveness in allowing the strayed soul to return to him through Purgatory.

53. *A Heavenly Lady:* Beatrice.

77. *Minos:* The Judge of the Damned. The round in Hell not ruled by Minos is Limbo, the final resting place of the Virtuous Pagans. Minos (see *Inferno* V) is stationed at the entrance to the second circle of Hell. The souls in Limbo (the first circle) have never had to pass before him to be judged.

78. *Marcia:* The story of Marcia and of Cato is an extraordinary one. She was the daughter of the consul Philippus and became Cato's second wife, bearing his three children. In 56 B.C., in an un-

usual transaction approved by her father, Cato released her in order that she might marry his friend Hortensius. (Hence line 87: "that all she asked I did.") After the death of Hortensius, Cato took her back.

In *Il Convivio* IV, 28, Dante presents the newly widowed Marcia praying to be taken back in order that she may die the wife of Cato, and that it may be said of her that she was not cast forth from his love. Dante treats that return as an allegory of the return of the strayed soul to God (that it may die "married" to God, and that God's love for it be made manifest to all time). Virgil describes Marcia as still praying to Cato.

89. *the Decree:* May be taken as that law that makes an absolute separation between the damned and the saved. Cato cannot be referring here to *Mark* xii, 25 ("when they shall rise from the dead, they neither marry, nor are given in marriage") for that "decree" was not pronounced upon his ascent from Limbo.

98. *filmed by mist:* Of Hell.

100 ff. THE REED. The pliant reed clearly symbolizes humility, but other allegorical meanings suggest themselves at once. First, the Reed takes the place of the Cord that Dante took from about his waist in order to signal Geryon. The Cord had been intended to snare and defeat the Leopard with the Gaudy Pelt, a direct assault upon sin. It is now superseded by the Reed of submission to God's will. Second, the reeds are eternal and undiminishable. As such they must immediately suggest the redemption purchased by Christ's sufferings (ever-abounding grace), for the quantity of grace available to mankind through Christ's passion is, in Christian creed, also eternal and undiminishable. The importance of the fact that the reeds grow at the lowest point of the Island and that the Poets must descend to them before they can begin, has already been mentioned. Curiously, the reed is never again mentioned, though it must remain around Dante's waist. See also *Matthew* xxvii, 29.

119. *breeze shielded the dew:* The dew is a natural symbol of God's grace. The morning breeze shields it in the sense that, being cool, it retards evaporation.

Even more naturally, being bathed in the dew may be taken to signify baptism. The structure of Purgatory certainly suggests a parable of the soul's stages of sacred development: the dew, baptism; the gate of Purgatory, above, first communion; Virgil's certification of Dante as lord of himself (XXVII, 143), confirmation; and Dante's swoon and awakening (XXXI, 89), as extreme unction and the reception into the company of the blessed.

CANTO II

Ante-Purgatory: The Shore of the Island—
The Angel Boatman · Casella · Cato of Utica

It is dawn. Dante, washed, and girded by the reed, is standing by
the shore when he sees a light approaching at enormous speed
across the sea. The light grows and becomes visible as *The Angel
Boatman* who ferries the souls of the elect from their gathering
place at *The Mouth of the Tiber* to the shore of Purgatory.

The newly arrived souls debark and, taking the Poets as fa-
miliars of the place, ask directions. Virgil explains that he and
Dante are new arrivals but that they have come by the dark road
through Hell. The newly arrived souls see by his breathing that
Dante is alive and crowd about him. One of the new souls is
Casella, a musician who seems to have been a dear friend of
Dante's. Dante tries three times to clasp him to his bosom, but
each time his arms pass through empty air. Casella explains the
function of the Angel Boatman and then, at Dante's request,
strikes up a song, one of Dante's own *canzone* that Casella had set
to music. Instantly, *Cato* descends upon the group, berating them,
and they break like startled pigeons up the slope toward the
mountain.

The sun already burned at the horizon,
  while the high point of its meridian circle
  covered Jerusalem, and in opposition   3

equal Night revolved above the Ganges
  bearing the Scales that fall out of her hand
  as she grows longer with the season's changes: 6

thus, where I was, Aurora in her passage
  was losing the pale blushes from her cheeks
  which turned to orange with increasing age.   9

We were still standing by the sea's new day
  like travelers pondering the road ahead
  who send their souls on while their bones delay;   12

when low above the ocean's western rim,
  as Mars, at times, observed through the thick vapors
  that form before the dawn, burns red and slim;   15

just so—so may I hope to see it again!—
  a light appeared, moving above the sea
  faster than any flight. A moment then   18

I turned my eyes to question my sweet Guide,
  and when I looked back to that unknown body
  I found its mass and brightness magnified.   21

Then from each side of it came into view
  an unknown something-white; and from beneath it,
  bit by bit, another whiteness grew.   24

We watched till the white objects at each side
  took shape as wings, and Virgil spoke no word.
  But when he saw what wings they were, he cried: 27

"Down on your knees! It is God's angel comes!
  Down! Fold your hands! From now on you shall see
  many such ministers in the high kingdoms.   30

See how he scorns man's tools: he needs no oars
  nor any other sail than his own wings
  to carry him between such distant shores.   33

See how his pinions tower upon the air,
  pointing to Heaven: they are eternal plumes
  and do not moult like feathers or human hair."   36

Then as that bird of heaven closed the distance
  between us, he grew brighter and yet brighter
  until I could no longer bear the radiance,   39

and bowed my head. He steered straight for the shore,
  his ship so light and swift it drew no water;
  it did not seem to sail so much as soar.   42

Astern stood the great pilot of the Lord,
  so fair his blessedness seemed written on him;
  and more than a hundred souls were seated forward,   45

singing as if they raised a single voice
  in exitu Israel de Aegypto.
  Verse after verse they made the air rejoice.   48

The angel made the sign of the cross, and they
  cast themselves, at his signal, to the shore.
  Then, swiftly as he had come, he went away.   51

The throng he left seemed not to understand
  what place it was, but stood and stared about
  like men who see the first of a new land.   54

The Sun, who with an arrow in each ray
  had chased the Goat out of the height of Heaven,
  on every hand was shooting forth the day,   57

when those new souls looked up to where my Guide
  and I stood, saying to us, "If you know it,
  show us the road that climbs the mountainside."   60

Virgil replied: "You think perhaps we two
  have had some long experience of this place,
  but we are also pilgrims, come before you   63

only by very little, though by a way
  so steep, so broken, and so tortuous
  the climb ahead of us will seem like play."   66

The throng of souls, observing by my breath
  I was still in the body I was born to,
  stared in amazement and grew pale as death.   69

As a crowd, eager for news, will all but smother
  a messenger who bears the olive branch,
  and not care how they trample one another—   72

so these, each one of them a soul elect,
  pushed close to stare at me, well-nigh forgetting
  the way to go to make their beauty perfect.   75

One came forward to embrace me, and his face
  shone with such joyous love that, seeing it,
  I moved to greet him with a like embrace.   78

O solid seeming shadows! Three times there
  I clasped my hands behind him, and three times
  I drew them to my breast through empty air.   81

Amazed, I must have lost all color then,
  for he smiled tenderly and drew away,
  and I lunged forward as if to try again.   84

In a voice as gentle as a melody
  he bade me pause; and by his voice I knew him,
  and begged him stay a while and speak to me.   87

He answered: "As I loved you in the clay
  of my mortal body, so do I love you freed:
  therefore I pause. But what brings you this way?"   90

"Casella mine, I go the way I do
   in the hope I may return here," I replied.
   "But why has so much time been taken from you?"   93

And he: "I am not wronged if he whose usage
   accepts the soul at his own time and pleasure
   has many times refused to give me passage: 96

his will moves in the image and perfection
   of a Just Will; indeed, for three months now
   he has taken all who asked, without exception.   99

And so it was that in my turn I stood
   upon that shore where Tiber's stream grows salt,
   and there was gathered to my present good.   102

It is back to the Tiber's mouth he has just flown,
   for there forever is the gathering place
   of all who do not sink to Acheron."   105

"If no new law has stripped you of your skill
   or of the memory of those songs of love
   that once could calm all passion from my will,"   108

I said to him, "Oh sound a verse once more
   to soothe my soul which, with its weight of flesh
   and the long journey, sinks distressed and sore."   111

"Love that speaks its reasons in my heart,"
   he sang then, and such grace flowed on the air
   that even now I hear that music start.   114

My Guide and I and all those souls of bliss
   stood tranced in song; when suddenly we heard
   the Noble Elder cry: "What's this! What's this!   117

Negligence! Loitering! O laggard crew,
  run to the mountain and strip off the scurf
  that lets not God be manifest in you!"   120

Exactly as a flock of pigeons gleaning
  a field of stubble, pecking busily,
  forgetting all their primping and their preening,   123

will rise as one and scatter through the air,
  leaving their feast without another thought
  when they are taken by a sudden scare—   126

so that new band, all thought of pleasure gone,
  broke from the feast of music with a start
  and scattered for the mountainside like one   129

who leaps and does not look where he will land.
  Nor were my Guide and I inclined to stand.

NOTES

1–9. The bit of erudite affectation in which Dante indulges here means simply, "It was dawn." To understand the total figure, one must recall the following essentials of Dante's geography: (1) Jerusalem is antipodal to the Mount of Purgatory. Thus it is sunset at Jerusalem when it is sunrise on the mountain. (2) All the land of the earth is contained in one half of the Northern Hemisphere. That is to say, there is no land (except the Mount of Purgatory) anywhere in the Southern Hemisphere and of the total circle of the Northern Hemisphere (360°) only half (180°) is land. Jerusalem is at the exact center of this 180° arc of land. Spain, 90° to one side, is the West, and India (Ganges), 90° to the other, is the East.

Every fifteen degrees of longitude equals one hour of time. That is to say, it takes the Sun an hour to travel fifteen degrees. Thus at sunset over Jerusalem it is midnight (six hours later) over India, and noon (six hours earlier) over Spain. The journey, moreover, is conceived as taking place during the vernal equinox, when the days and nights are of the same length. Thus it is "equal Night" (line 4).

Finally, when the Sun is in Aries, midnight is in Libra (the Scales). Thus the night bears the Scales in her hand (i.e., that constellation is visible), but Libra will no longer be the sign of the night as the season changes, and thus it may be said that the Scales will fall from her hand (i.e., will no longer be visible).

47. *in exitu Israel de Aegypto:* When Israel out of Egypt came. Psalm CXIII.

50. *cast themselves, at his signal, to the shore:* Note that this is exactly what Dante says of the sinners leaving Charon's ferry in *Inferno* III, 113. In Dante there is no accident in such correspondence. Such parallels between the *Purgatorio* and the *Inferno* are essential parts of the poem's total structure.

56. *the Goat:* Capricorn.

71. *who bears the olive branch:* In Dante's time couriers bore the olive branch to indicate not only peace but good news in general.

79–84. *O solid seeming shadows:* As always, Dante treats the substance of the souls to suit his own dramatic convenience, at times giving them attributes of fleshly bodies, at others treating them as mirages.

91. *Casella:* Practically all that is known about Casella has been drawn from the text itself. He seems to have died several months before Dante began his journey, hence early in 1300 or late in 1299. There is no explanation of his delay in reaching Purgatory (the time that has been taken from him). Dante later meets several classes of sinners who must spend a certain period of waiting before they can begin their purification. Clearly it is Dante's conception that the souls bound for Purgatory do not always proceed instantly to their destination, but may be required to expiate by a delay at their gathering point by the mouth of the Tiber (line 101).

Casella was a musician and is known to have set some of Dante's *canzone* to music. The song he strikes up (line 112) is such a *canzona*.

99. *he has taken all who asked:* Boniface VIII decreed a Jubilee Year from Christmas 1299 to Christmas 1300. (*See Inferno* XVIII, 28–33

and note.) His decree extended special indulgences even to the dead. Hence the Angel's permissiveness.

Note, however, that he has taken all who wished to go, all who asked. It follows that some souls did not express such a wish, almost certainly because they did not feel themselves to be ready. As in note to I, 5, the souls of Purgatory decide for themselves when they are ready to progress from one stage to the next.

CANTO III

Ante-Purgatory: The Base of the Cliff—
The Late Repentant · Class One: The Contumacious · Manfred

The souls scatter for the mountain, and Dante draws close to Virgil as they both race ahead. The newly risen sun is at Dante's back. He runs, therefore, with his shadow stretched long and directly before him. Suddenly he becomes aware that there is only one shadow on the ground and he turns in panic, thinking Virgil is no longer at his side. Virgil reassures him, explaining that souls are so made as to cast no shadow. His remarks on the nature of souls give him occasion to define *The Limits of Reason in the Scheme of Creation.*

The poets reach *The Base of the Cliff* and are dismayed to find that it rises sheer, offering no way by which they may climb. While Virgil is pondering this new difficulty, Dante looks about and sees a band of souls approaching so slowly that they seem scarcely to move. These are the first of *The Late Repentant* souls the Poets will encounter. In life they put off the desire for grace: now, as they were laggard in life, so must they wait before they may begin their purification. The souls in this band are all souls of *The Contumacious:* they died excommunicated, but surrendered their souls to God when they were at the point of death. Their punishment is that they must wait here at the Base of the Cliff for thirty times the period of their contumacy.

One soul among them identifies himself as *Manfred* and begs Dante to bear a message to his daughter Constance in order that she may offer prayers for Manfred's soul and thereby shorten his period of waiting. Manfred explains that prayer can greatly assist the souls in Purgatory. He also explains how it is that though contumacy is punished, no act of priest or pope may keep from salvation a soul that has truly given itself to God.

Those routed souls scattered across the scene,
  their faces once again turned toward the mountain
  where Reason spurs and Justice picks us clean;   3

but I drew ever closer to my Guide:
  and how could I have run my course without him?
  who would have led me up the mountainside?   6

He seemed gnawed by remorse for his offense:
  O noble conscience without stain! how sharp
  the sting of a small fault is to your sense!   9

When he had checked that haste that urges men
  to mar the dignity of every act,
  my mind, forced in upon itself till then,   12

broke free, and eager to see all before me,
  I raised my eyes in wonder to that mountain
  that soars highest to Heaven from the sea.   15

Low at my back, the sun was a red blaze;
  its light fell on the ground before me broken
  in the form in which my body blocked its rays.   18

I gave a start of fear and whirled around
  seized by the thought that I had been abandoned,
  for I saw one shadow only on the ground.   21

And my Comfort turned full to me then to say:
  "Why are you still uncertain? Why do you doubt
  that I am here and guide you on your way?   24

Vespers have rung already on the tomb
  of the body in which I used to cast a shadow.
  It was taken to Naples from Brindisium.   27

If now I cast no shadow, should that fact
  amaze you more than the heavens which pass the
                              light
  undimmed from one to another? We react   30

within these bodies to pain and heat and cold
  according to the workings of That Will
  which does not will that all Its ways be told.   33

He is insane who dreams that he may learn
  by mortal reasoning the boundless orbit
  Three Persons in One Substance fill and turn.   36

Be satisfied with the *quia* of cause unknown,
  O humankind! for could you have seen All,
  Mary need not have suffered to bear a son.   39

You saw how some yearn endlessly in vain:
  such as would, else, have surely had their wish,
  but have, instead, its hunger as their pain.   42

I speak of Aristotle and Plato," he said.
  "—Of them and many more." And here he paused,
  and sorrowing and silent, bowed his head.   45

Meanwhile we reached the mountain's foot; and there
  we found so sheer a cliff, the nimblest legs
  would not have served, unless they walked on air.   48

The most forsaken and most broken goat-trace
  in the mountains between Lerici and Turbia
  compared to this would seem a gracious staircase.   51

My Guide exclaimed: "Now who is there to say
  in which direction we may find some slope
  up which one without wings may pick his way!"   54

While he was standing, head bowed to his shoulders,
  and pondering which direction we might take,
  I stood there looking up among the boulders,   57

and saw upon my left beside that cliff-face
  a throng that moved its feet in our direction,
  and yet seemed not to, so slow was its pace.   60

"Master," I said, "look up and you will find
  some people coming who may solve the problem,
  if you have not yet solved it in your mind."   63

He looked up then and, openly relieved,
  said: "Let us go to them, since they lag so.
  And you, dear son, believe as you have believed."   66

We were as far off yet from that slow flock
  (I mean when we had gone a thousand paces)
  as a strong slingsman could have thrown a rock,   69

when they drew in against the cliff and stood there
  like men who fear what they see coming toward
                                               them
  and, waiting for it, huddle close and stare.   72

"O well-concluded lives! O souls thus met
  already among the chosen!" Virgil said,
  "By that sweet crown of peace that shall be set   75

on each of you in time, tell us which way
  leads to some slope by which we two may climb.
  Who best knows time is most grieved by delay."   78

As sheep come through a gate—by ones, by twos,
  by threes, and all the others trail behind,
  timidly, nose to ground, and what the first does   81

the others do, and if the first one pauses,
  the others huddle up against his back,
    silly and mute, not knowing their own causes—   84

just so, I stood there watching with my Guide,
  the first row of that happy flock come on,
    their look meek and their movements dignified.   87

And when the souls that came first in that flock
  saw the light broken on the ground to my right
    so that my shadow fell upon the rock,   90

they halted and inched back as if to shy,
  and all the others who came after them
    did as the first did without knowing why.   93

"Let me confirm the thought you leave unspoken:
  it is a living body you see before you
    by which the sunlight on the ground is broken.   96

Do not be astonished: you may rest assured
  he does not seek the way to climb this wall
    without a power from Heaven."—Thus my Lord   99

addressed them, and those worthy spirits said,
  waving the backs of their hands in our direction:
    "First turn around, and then go straight ahead."   102

And one soul said to me: "Whoever you are,
  as you move on, look back and ask yourself
    if you have ever seen me over there."   105

I studied him with care, my head turned round:
  gold-blond he was, and handsomely patrician,
    although one brow was split by a sword wound.   108

When I, in all humility, confessed
  I never before had seen him, he said, "Look"
  —and showed me a great slash above his breast.   111

Then, smiling, added: "I am Manfred, grandson
  of the blessed Empress Constance, and I beg you,
  when you return there over the horizon,   114

go to my sweet daughter, noble mother
  of the honor of Sicily and of Aragon
  and speak the truth, if men speak any other.   117

My flesh had been twice hacked, and each wound
                            mortal,
  when, tearfully, I yielded up my soul
  to Him whose pardon gladly waits for all.   120

Horrible were my sins, but infinite
  is the abiding Goodness which holds out
  its open arms to all who turn to It.   123

If the pastor of Cosenza, by the rage
  of Clement sent to hunt me down, had first
  studied the book of God at this bright page,   126

my body's bones would still be in the ground
  there by the bridgehead outside Benevento,
  under the heavy guard of the stone mound.   129

Now, rattled by the wind, by the rain drenched,
  they lie outside the kingdom, by the Verde,
  where he transported them with tapers quenched.   132

No man may be so cursed by priest or pope
  but what the Eternal Love may still return
  while any thread of green lives on in hope.   135

Those who die contumacious, it is true,
  though they repent their feud with Holy Church,
  must wait outside here on the bank, as we do,   138

for thirty times as long as they refused
  to be obedient, though by good prayers
  in their behalf, that time may be reduced.   141

See, then, how great a service you may do me
  when you return, by telling my good Constance
  of my condition and of this decree   144

that still forbids our entrance to the kingdom.
  For here, from those beyond, great good may come."

NOTES

1–3. The original lines are in Dante's densest style, and every commentator has felt the need to discuss this passage at length. *once again turned:* Dante's intent here seems clear enough. On their arrival the souls had looked straight ahead at the mountain. The distraction for which Cato chastised them had led them to look away. *where Reason spurs and Justice picks us clean:* The original phrasing is *ove ragion ne fruga.* If *ragion* is taken to mean "reason" and *fruga* in one of its senses to mean "to prick on," then one meaning follows clearly enough. If, however, *ragion* is taken in context to mean Divine Justice—and many commentators have argued that it must so be taken—and if *fruga* (a very complex word) is taken in its first sense of "to probe, to search minutely, to pick clean"—then a second meaning follows. I am inclined to think that Dante always means both possibilities in such cases and I have therefore rendered both.

10–11. *that haste that urges men to mar the dignity of every act:* There can be no doubt that Dante cherished his dignity. Even in moving toward salvation he preferred a slow and stately manner. On his own premises, there is obviously a taint of pride in such a disposition. When he reaches the Cornice of the Proud, he makes it clear that

Pride is the sin that most weighs upon him. Dignity, of course, is closely related to Moderation, one of the Cardinal Virtues.

21 ff. *for I saw one shadow only on the ground:* The fact that Dante was still in his mortal body was evidenced in Hell by his breathing, by the way his weight made a boat settle in the water, by the fact that his foot dislodged a stone, and by the force with which he inadvertently kicked one of the damned. Now that he is once more in the light, his shadow becomes the principal means of identifying him as a living man, for souls cast no shadows. Dante is to use this device often in the Cantos that follow.

27. *It was taken to Naples from Brindisium:* Virgil died in Brindisium in 19 B.C. His bones were later exhumed and reinterred in Naples by order of the Emperor Augustus.

29–30. *the heavens which pass the light:* The heavens are the spheres of the Ptolemaic system. They are conceived as crystalline and as so clear that light passes from one to the other undiminished. Dante's figure, literally rendered, is: "whose rays do not block one another."

40–45. *You saw how some yearn:* Dante saw them in Limbo. As Virgil goes on to explain, he means "the masters of those who know." His clear implication is that if such monuments of human intellect could never penetrate the mystery of the All, it is folly for mankind to seek to explain the reasons for God's ways. *Of them and many more:* Part of Virgil's sorrow is due to the fact that he is one of the "many more."

50. *Lerici and Turbia:* Lerici lies on the shores of the Mediterranean near the river Magra, and Turbia stands a bit inland from the Mediterranean on the other side of Liguria. The tract of mountains between them is one of the most rugged in all Europe.

52. *Now who is there to say:* Virgil had traveled through Hell once before (see *Inferno* IX, 24, note) and knew that way, but the road of Purgatory is unknown to him.

58 ff. THE CONTUMACIOUS. The section of the Mount of Purgatory that lies below the Gate (the Ante-Purgatory) is occupied by the Late Repentant who put off their surrender to God until the end of their lives. As they made God wait, so must they now wait before they may begin their purification. These souls suffer no pain

but the burning of their own frustrated desire to mount to God. They may well be compared with the souls in Limbo, except that they are all assured that they will one day rise, whereas there is no hope in Limbo.

The Contumacious, therefore, are the first class of the Late Repentant. (Hence the slowness of their motions now. Note that such slowness, in constraining souls whose most ardent wish is to race forward to God, is a moral allegory. Purgatory, one must recall, is the way to the renunciation of sin. The soul so long curbed cannot fail to root out of itself the last laggard impulse. Such, at least, is clearly Dante's moral intention.) The present band must expiate not only personal negligence and tardiness in turning to God but disobedience to the Church from which they were excommunicated. Before they can mount to the next phase of their purification they must delay here for a period thirty times as long as the period of their disobedience.

66. *believe as you have believed:* Virgil's remark here is best taken to mean, in an extended paraphrase: "Continue as you have done [to submit yourself and your reason to the revealed fact of God without seeking to probe too deeply], for unlike these souls who put off their repentance to the moment of their deaths, you have repented early and strained every resource to win to Grace."

74. *already among the chosen:* The souls in Purgatory must suffer their purification but they are already, in effect, saved and will eventually enter Heaven.

78. *Who best knows time is most grieved by delay:* A home thrust. Who knows time better than these souls who must suffer their most grievous delay?

89–90. *to my right . . . my shadow fell upon the rock:* The sun has only recently risen. It is still, therefore, in the east. Since it threw Dante's shadow directly before him as he approached the mountain, and now throws his shadow to the right, the Poets must have moved more or less due west toward the cliff and must then have borne south.

101. *waving the backs of their hands in our direction:* To indicate the way. The gesture is Italian. We should be inclined to point.

104. *as you move on, look back:* Note that the speaker does not ask Dante to delay his journey even an instant, but only to look back while continuing on his way.

105. *over there:* In Purgatory "over there" always means "back in the world."

108. *one brow was split by a sword wound:* See also line 111: *a great slash above his breast:* Dante obviously intends the souls to be immaterial replicas of the last appearance of the mortal flesh. In future Cantos, however, he does not pursue this idea. See XXV, 34–108, note, for a discourse on the nature of aerial bodies.

112. *I am Manfred:* Manfred, King of Sicily, was the legitimized natural son of Frederick II. He was born in Sicily in 1231 and was killed at the battle of Benevento after a defeat by Charles of Anjou in 1266. (See *Inferno* XXVIII, 16, note.) He was famous as an Epicurean (see *Inferno* X, 14, note) and for his taste for physical pleasures rather than for godliness. In the everlasting internal wars of Italy, Manfred often opposed the Papal States, but was too powerful to be excommunicated while alive. He was nevertheless disobedient to Mother Church and therefore must pass thirty times the period of his disobedience outside the cliff. He has served 24 years to date. Assuming that he was contumacious for half his life ($17\frac{1}{2}$ years), his total delay would amount to 525 years, if not shortened by prayer.

112–113. *grandson of the blessed Empress Constance:* Constance was the mother of Frederick II. Since Manfred was not a legitimate son, he identifies himself by his grandmother as a delicate way of avoiding any reference to his illegitimacy.

115. *my sweet daughter:* Also named Constance. She married Peter of Aragon and bore him three sons. One died before full manhood. Of the remaining two, Frederick became King of Sicily, and Iacopo succeeded his father to the throne of Aragon.

118. *My flesh had been twice hacked:* At the battle of Benevento. After Manfred's defeat and death, Charles of Anjou ordered that every soldier in his army file past the body of the dead Manfred and place a stone upon it. Thus a great cairn was erected to the memory of a fallen warrior.

124. *the pastor of Cosenza:* Bartolommeo Pignatelli, cardinal and archbishop of Cosenza from 1254 to 1266. On orders from Pope Clement IV, he disinterred the body of Manfred and had it carried without honors (with quenched tapers) outside the kingdom of Naples, which was then a Papal State. Thus, Clement expelled from Church territory the body of the man he could not expel in life.

131. *the Verde:* Various streams may be identified as the Verde. Dante clearly enough implies that Manfred's body was carried out of the kingdom of Naples and deposited on the other side of a boundary-river.

139. *thirty times:* There seems to be no identifiable significance to Dante's choice of thirty (instead, say, of fifty, or a hundred, or any other multiple).

CANTO IV

Ante-Purgatory: The First Ledge—
The Late-Repentant · Class Two: The Indolent · Belacqua

Listening to Manfred's discourse, Dante has lost track of time.
Now, at midmorning, the Poets reach the opening in the cliff-
face and begin the laborious climb. Dante soon tires and cries
that he can go no farther, but Virgil urges him to pull himself a
little higher yet—significantly—to the *Ledge of the Indolent,* those
souls whose sin was their delay in pulling themselves up the same
hard path.

Seated on the ledge, Virgil explains that in the nature of the
mountain, the beginning of the ascent (the First Turning from
Sin to True Repentance) is always hardest. The higher one climbs
from sin to repentance, the easier it becomes to climb still higher
until, in the Perfection of Grace, the climb becomes effortless.
But to that ultimate height, as Virgil knows, Human Reason can-
not reach. It is Beatrice (Divine Love) who must guide him
there.

As Virgil finishes speaking, an ironic reply comes from behind
a boulder. The speaker is *Belacqua,* an old friend of Dante's, and
the laziest man in Florence. Because of his indolence, he put off
good works and the active desire for grace until he lay dying. In
life he made God wait. Now God makes him wait an equal pe-
riod before he may pass through the Gate into Purgatory and
begin his purification. Unless, as Belacqua adds, the prayers of the
devout intercede for him.

But now Virgil points out that the sun is already at its noon-
height and that Dante, unlike the Indolent, must not delay.

When any sense of ours records intense
  pleasure or pain, then the whole soul is drawn
  by such impressions into that one sense,   3

and seems to lose all other powers. And thus
  do I refute the error that asserts
  that one soul on another burns in us.   6

And, for this reason, when we see or hear
  whatever seizes strongly on the soul,
  time passes, and we lose it unaware.   9

For that which senses is one faculty;
  and that which keeps the soul intact, another:
  the first, as it were, bound; the second, free.   12

To this, my own experience bears witness,
  for while I listened to that soul and marveled,
  the sun had climbed—without my least awareness—   15

to fifty full degrees of its noon peak
  when, at one point along the way, that band
  cried out in chorus: "Here is what you seek."   18

Often when grapes hang full on slope and ledge
  the peasant, with one forkful of his thorns,
  seals up a wider opening in his hedge   21

than the gap we found there in that wall of stone;
  up which—leaving that band of souls behind—
  my Guide led and I followed: we two alone.   24

Go up to San Leo or go down to Noli;
  go climb Bismantova—two legs suffice:
  here nothing but swift wings will answer wholly.   27

The swift wings and the feathers, I mean to say,
  of great desire led onward by that Guide
  who was my hope and light along the way.   30

Squeezed in between two walls that almost meet
  we labor upward through the riven rock:
  a climb that calls for both our hands and feet.   33

Above the cliff's last rise we reached in time
  an open slope. "Do we go right or left?"
  I asked my Master, "or do we still climb?"   36

And he: "Take not one step to either side,
  but follow yet, and make way up the mountain
  till we meet someone who may serve as guide."   39

Higher than sight the peak soared to the sky:
  much steeper than a line drawn from mid-quadrant
  to the center, was the slope that met my eye.   42

The climb had sapped my last strength when I cried:
  "Sweet Father, turn to me: unless you pause
  I shall be left here on the mountainside!"   45

He pointed to a ledge a little ahead
  that wound around the whole face of the slope.
  "Pull yourself that much higher, my son," he said.   48

His words so spurred me that I forced myself
  to push on after him on hands and knees
  until at last my feet were on that shelf.   51

There we sat, facing eastward, to survey
  the trail we had just climbed; for oftentimes
  a backward look comforts one on the way.   54

I looked down first to the low-lying shore,
  then upward to the sun—and stopped amazed,
  for it was from the left its arrows bore.   57

Virgil was quick to note the start I gave
  when I beheld the Chariot of the Sun
  driven between me and the North Wind's cave.   60

"Were Castor and Pollux," he said, "in company
  of that bright mirror which sends forth its rays
  equally up and down, then you would see   63

the twelve-toothed cogwheel of the Zodiac
  turned till it blazed still closer to the Bears
  —unless it were to stray from its fixed track.   66

If you wish to understand why this is so,
  imagine Zion and this Mount so placed
  on earth, the one above, the other below,   69

that the two have one horizon though they lie
  in different hemispheres. Therefore, the path
  that Phaëthon could not follow in the sky   72

must necessarily, in passing here
  on the one side, pass there upon the other,
  as your own reasoning will have made clear."   75

And I then: "Master, I may truly vow
  I never grasped so well the very point
  on which my wits were most astray just now: 78

that the mid-circle of the highest Heaven,
  called the Equator, always lies between
  the sun and winter, and, for the reason given,   81

lies as far north of this place at all times
  as the Hebrews, when they held Jerusalem,
  were wont to see it toward the warmer climes.   84

But—if you please—I should be glad to know
how far we have yet to climb, for the peak soars
higher to Heaven than my eye can go."   87

And he: "Such is this Mount that when a soul
begins the lower slopes it most must labor;
then less and less the more it nears its goal.   90

Thus when we reach the point where the slopes seem
so smooth and gentle that the climb becomes
as easy as to float a skiff downstream,   93

then will this road be run, and not before
that journey's end will your repose be found.
I know this much for truth and say no more."   96

His words were hardly out when, from nearby,
we heard a voice say: "Maybe by that time
you'll find you need to sit before you fly!"   99

We turned together at the sound, and there,
close on our left, we saw a massive boulder
of which, till then, we had not been aware.   102

To it we dragged ourselves, and there we found
stretched in the shade, the way a slovenly man
lies down to rest, some people on the ground.   105

The weariest of them, judging by his pose,
sat hugging both knees while his head, abandoned,
dropped down between them halfway to his toes.   108

"Master," I said, "look at that sorry one
who seems so all-let-down. Were Sloth herself
his sister, he could not be so far gone!"   111

That heap took heed, and even turned his head
  upon his thigh—enough to look at us.
  "You climb it if you're such a flash," he said.   114

I knew him then, and all the agony
  that still burned in my lungs and raced my pulse
  did not prevent my going to him. He   117

raising his head—just barely—when I stood by,
  drawled: "So you really know now why the sun
  steers to the left of you across the sky?"   120

His short words and his shorter acts, combined,
  made me half smile as I replied: "Belacqua,
  your fate need never again trouble my mind.   123

Praise be for that. But why do you remain
  crouched here? Are you waiting for a guide, perhaps?
  Or are you up to your old tricks again?"   126

"Old friend," he said, "what good is it to climb?—
  God's Bird above the Gate would never let me
  pass through to start my trials before my time.   129

I must wait here until the heavens wheel past
  as many times as they passed me in my life,
  for I delayed the good sighs till the last.   132

Prayer could help me, if a heart God's love
  has filled with Grace should offer it. All other
  is worthless, for it is not heard above."   135

But now the Poet already led the way
  to the slope above, saying to me: "Come now:
  the sun has touched the very peak of day   138

above the sea, and night already stands
  with one black foot upon Morocco's sands."

NOTES

1–12. THE DOCTRINE OF MULTIPLE SOULS. The orig-
inal doctrine (the "error" of line 5) was set forth by Plato, who claimed
that we have three souls within us, each with its specific function: the
Vegetative Soul (roughly corresponding to what we might call the So-
matic) which is seated in the liver, the Sensitive (i.e., the Emotional)
Soul which is seated in the heart, and the Intellectual Soul which is
seated in the brain. Dante's emphatic concern over this point is easy
enough to understand. Plato was, for him, one of the fundamental
sources of the truth. Yet here, Plato was putting forth a doctrine im-
possible to reconcile with the Christian doctrine of the unity of the
soul. (If there are several souls in a man, how shall one judgment fit
them all?) Aristotle (see XXV, 52 ff.), the Church Fathers, Aquinas,
and many others also found it necessary to repudiate or to modify this
Platonic doctrine. The fact that Dante had seen himself as a follower
of Plato in the *Vita Nuova* is one more evidence that the *Purgatorio* is
intended, among other things, as a progress of the soul. Dante is cor-
recting his earlier errors and turning his mind to greater sources.

16. *to fifty full degrees of its noon peak:* Since one degree of arc
equals four minutes of time, the sun, therefore, traverses fifteen de-
grees an hour. It is, therefore, three hours and twenty minutes since
sunrise, at which time (Canto II) Dante saw the Angel Pilot bring in
his cargo of souls. On Easter in the year 1300 the sun rose a little be-
fore 6:00. It is now, therefore, a little after 9:00 A.M.

25–26. *San Leo:* An almost inaccessible town on a mountaintop
near San Marino. *Noli:* a seacoast town accessible (in Dante's time)
only from the sea or by treacherously steep steps cut into the cliffs
behind the town. *Bismantova:* a village on a mountain of the same
name about twenty miles south of Reggio Emilia. Dante selects
three places that his contemporaries would recognize as most diffi-
cult to get to, and then says in effect that the climb to them is noth-
ing as compared to the labor of climbing Purgatory.

30. *light:* The narrowness of the fissure would make it dark. Virgil's allegorical character as Human Reason is especially important in this context.

33. *a climb that calls for both our hands and feet:* Dante uses this same figure in describing the path that led up from the Bolgia of the Thieves (*Inferno* XXVI, 18): "the foot could make no way without the hand."

37 ff. *Take not one step to either side:* The original contains an ambiguity that has led many commentators to understand Virgil as saying "Take not one backward step," that being the law of the mountain. In context, however, such a rendering seems doubtful. Dante had no least thought of taking a backward step. He has asked, "Do we go right or left," and Virgil replies, logically, "no least step to either side but upward only." See also *Isaiah* xxx, 21, and *Joshua* i, 7.

41–42. *a line drawn from mid-quadrant to the center:* Of an astrolabe. Hence 45°. Note, however, that the slope is "much steeper" than 45°.

50–51. *my feet were on that shelf:* (Literally: "the shelf was under my feet.") Dante says nothing to explain why a man climbing on "hands and knees" (Italian; *carpando*) to a ledge above him would not simply crawl onto it (especially if near exhaustion) instead of first standing on it and then sitting down. He might, perhaps, have meant that he crawled onto the ledge, then sat with his knees drawn up so that the ledge was under his feet. Perhaps.

55–75. THE POSITION OF THE SUN. Dante, habituated to the phenomena of the Northern Hemisphere, is astonished to find that the sun is on his left (i.e., north) when he faces east. Virgil points out that there is nothing surprising in that, and that as the sun moves toward the summer solstice it will move even further north (toward "the Bears" of line 65, i.e., Ursa Major and Ursa Minor, the Big and the Little Dipper) into the zodiacal sign of Gemini, the Twins (i.e., Castor and Pollux). Unless, he adds with something like humor, it should depart from its fixed track.

Virgil then goes on to a more detailed statement of the case. He asks Dante to visualize the globe with the Mount of Zion and the Mount of Purgatory so placed that they are in different hemispheres but share the same celestial horizon. They are, therefore, below the Crystalline [i.e., the *Sphere of the Fixed Stars*] has two poles that are constant in relation to that heaven itself; and the ninth [the Crystalline] has two poles that are firm and fixed and immovable in every respect; and each, the ninth like all the others, has a circle which may be called the equator of its proper heaven; the which is equally distant from one pole and the other, as one may clearly understand if he revolves an apple or some other round thing."

Hence the following extended paraphrase of lines 79–84: "The mid-circle of the Crystalline Sphere, which is called the Celestial Equator, always lies between the Sun and that hemisphere in which it is winter, and, for the reason you have just given [i.e., that Purgatory and Zion are antipodal] the Celestial Equator must always lie as far to the north of this place [Purgatory] as the Hebrews [when, before the dispersion of the Jews, they looked at it from Jerusalem] were accustomed to seeing it toward the south [warmer climes]."

96. *I know this much for truth and say no more:* At that journey's end, Virgil (Human Reason) will vanish and Beatrice (Divine Love, a compound of Mercy, Light, and Contemplation) will lead Dante. Virgil has spoken as much as Reason can know to be true.

97–135. Belacqua: He was a Florentine who manufactured parts for musical instruments. Of him the Anonimo Florentino says: "He was the most indolent man who ever lived. . . . Dante was very intimate with him and used often to take him to task for his laziness." Dante's own treatment of him would certainly indicate that he is dealing with an old friend about whose indolence he has often worried.

119–120. *So you really know now . . . :* Belacqua's words are sarcastic, perhaps by way of taking revenge for Dante's description of him to Virgil, but it is the easy and fond sarcasm of a friend, and Dante accepts Belacqua's way of speaking with a half-smile.

128. *God's Bird above the Gate:* God's Angel above the Gate Dante will come to in Canto IX. Dante refers to Angels as God's Birds in a number of passages. The gate is the entrance to Purgatory proper. There is no gate between Purgatory and Heaven as there is between Earth and Hell. Those who pass the Gate of Purgatory are already effectively in Heaven, though they must first undergo their purification.

130–132. *I must wait here:* Because Belacqua indolently put off his repentance (the good sighs) until his last breath, he in effect refused God during the days of his life. Now God makes Belacqua wait, before he may begin his approach to Heaven, for as long a period as Belacqua made Him wait.

133–135. *Prayer could help me:* See VI, 30–45.

136–140. THE TIME. It is now noon at Purgatory. It must therefore be midnight in Jerusalem. Dante believed Morocco to lie exactly 90° west of Jerusalem (in the same longitude as Spain) and 90° west of midnight is six hours earlier. Hence, it is six o'clock there and night would just be beginning.

CANTO V

*Ante-Purgatory: The Second Ledge—The Late-Repentant ·
Class Three: Those Who Died by Violence Without Last Rites*

The Poets continue up the mountain and Dante's shadow once
more creates excitement among the waiting souls. These are the
souls of *Those Who Died by Violence Without Last Rites.* Since their
lives were cut off, they did not have full opportunity to repent, and
therefore they are placed a step higher than the simply Indolent.

These souls crowd about Dante, eager to have him bear news
of them back to the world and so to win prayers that will shorten
their delay. Virgil instructs Dante to listen to these souls, but
warns him not to interrupt his own climb to Grace. The Poets,
therefore, continue to press on while the souls cluster about and
follow them, each of them eager to tell his story and to beg that
Dante speak of them when he returns to the world.

I was following the footsteps of my Guide,
  having already parted from those shades,
  when someone at my back pointed and cried: 3

"Look there! see how the sun's shafts do not drive
  through to the left of that one lower down,
  and how he walks as if he were alive!"   6

I looked behind me to see who had spoken,
  and I saw them gazing up at me alone,
  at me, and at the light, that it was broken.   9

At which my Master said: "Why do you lag?
  What has so turned your mind that you look back?
  What is it to you that idle tongues will wag?   12

Follow my steps, though all such whisper of you:
  be as a tower of stone, its lofty crown
  unswayed by anything the winds may do.   15

For when a man lets his attention range
  toward every wisp, he loses true direction,
  sapping his mind's force with continual change."   18

What could I say except "I come"? I said it
  flushed with that hue that sometimes asks forgiveness
  for which it shows the asker to be fit.   21

Meanwhile across the slope a little before us
  people approached chanting the *Miserere*
  verse by verse in alternating chorus.   24

But when they noticed that I blocked the course
  of the Sun's arrows when they struck my body,
  their song changed to an "Oh! . . ." prolonged
                        and hoarse.   27

Out of that silenced choir two spirits ran
  like messengers and, reaching us, they said:
  "We beg to know—are you a living man?"   30

My Guide replied: "You may be on your way.
  And bear back word to those who sent you here
  he does indeed still walk in mortal clay.   33

If, as I think, it was his shadow drew them
  to stand and stare, they know already. Tell them
  to honor him: that may be precious to them."   36

I never saw hot vapors flashing through
  the first sweet air of night, or through the clouds
  of August sunsets, faster than those two   39

ran up to join their band, wheeled round again,
  and, with the whole band following, came toward us,
  like cavalry sent forward with a loose rein.   42

"There are hundreds in that troop that charges so,"
　　my Guide said, "and all come to beg a favor.
　　Hear them, but press on, listening as you go."　　45

"Pure spirit," they came crying, "you who thus
　　while still inside the body you were born to
　　climb to your bliss—oh pause and speak to us.　　48

Is there no one here you recognize? Not one
　　of whom you may bear tidings to the world?
　　Wait! Won't you pause? Oh please! Why do you run?　　51

We all are souls who died by violence,
　　all sinners to our final hour, in which
　　the lamp of Heaven shed its radiance　　54

into our hearts. Thus from the brink of death,
　　repenting all our sins, forgiving those
　　who sinned against us, with our final breath　　57

we offered up our souls at peace with Him
　　who saddens us with longing to behold
　　His glory on the throne of Seraphim."　　60

"Oh well-born souls," I said, "I can discover
　　no one among you that I recognize
　　however much I search your faces over;　　63

but if you wish some service of me, speak,
　　and if the office is within my power
　　I will perform it, by that peace I seek　　66

in following the footsteps of this Guide,
　　that peace that draws me on from world to world
　　to my own good." I paused, and one replied:　　69

"No soul among us doubts you will fulfill
  all you declare, without your need to swear it,
  if lack of power does not defeat your will.   72

I, then, who am no more than first to plead,
  beg that if ever you see that land that lies
  between Romagna and Naples, you speak my need   75

most graciously in Fano, that they to Heaven
  send holy prayers to intercede for me;
  so may my great offenses be forgiven.   78

I was of Fano, but the wounds that spilled
  my life's blood and my soul at once, were dealt me
  among the Antenori. I was killed   81

where I believed I had the least to fear.
  Azzo of Este, being incensed against me
  beyond all reason, had me waylaid there.   84

Had I turned toward La Mira when they set
  upon me first outside of Oriaco,
  I should be drawing breath among men yet.   87

I ran into the swamp, and reeds and mud
  tangled and trapped me. There I fell. And there
  I watched my veins let out a pool of blood."   90

Another spoke: "So may the Love Divine
  fulfill the wish that draws you up the mountain,
  for sweet compassion, lend your aid to mine.   93

I am Bonconte, once of Montefeltro.
  Because Giovanna and the rest forget me,
  I go among these souls with head bowed low."   96

And I: "What force or chance led you to stray
  so far from Campaldino that your grave
  remains to be discovered to this day?"   99

And he: "There flows below the Casentino
  a stream, the Archiana, which arises
  above the hermitage in Appennino.   102

There where its name ends in the Arno's flood
  I came, my throat pierced through, fleeing on foot
  and staining all my course with my life's blood.   105

There my sight failed. There with a final moan
  which was the name of Mary, speech went from me.
  I fell, and there my body lay alone.   108

I speak the truth. Oh speak it in my name
  to living men! God's angel took me up,
  and Hell's cried out: 'Why do you steal my game?   111

If his immortal part is your catch, brother,
  for one squeezed tear that makes me turn it loose,
  I've got another treatment for the other!'   114

You are familiar with the way immense
  watery vapors gather on the air,
  then burst as rain, as soon as they condense.   117

To ill will that seeks only ill, his mind
  added intelligence, and by the powers
  his nature gives, he stirred the mist and wind.   120

From Pratomagno to the spine, he spread
  a mist that filled the valley by day's end;
  then turned the skies above it dark as lead.   123

The saturated air changed into rain
  and down it crashed, flooding the rivulets
  with what the sodden earth could not retain;   126

the rills merged into torrents, and a flood
  swept irresistibly to the royal river.
  The Archiana, raging froth and mud,   129

found my remains in their last frozen rest
  just at its mouth, swept them into the Arno,
  and broke the cross I had formed upon my breast   132

in my last agony of pain and guilt.
  Along its banks and down its bed it rolled me,
  and then it bound and buried me in silt."   135

A third spoke when that second soul had done:
  "When you have found your way back to the world,
  and found your rest from this long road you run,   138

oh speak my name again with living breath
  to living memory. Pia am I.
  Siena gave me birth; Maremma, death.   141

As he well knows who took me as his wife
  with jeweled ring before he took my life."

NOTES

   3. *when someone at my back pointed and cried:* Dante does not explain how he could see a gesture made behind his back.

   8–9. *at me alone, at me:* Dante feels a moment of pride at attracting so much attention. He will have more to say later about Pride as his most dangerous spiritual fault.

   20. *that hue that sometimes asks forgiveness:* A typically Dantean fig-

ure. The hue, of course, is red, i.e., the blush. But one may flush red with anger as well as blush with shame. Hence, the hue only "sometimes" asks forgiveness.

22. *across:* The souls are not climbing the slope but are circling it in their long delay. *before us:* Since the poets are facing uphill, "before" must equal "above."

23. *Miserere:* The souls are singing the Fiftieth Psalm: "Have mercy upon us." Each band of souls on the mountain has its particular prayer—all, that is, but the Contumacious (who have been cut off from the offices of ritual).

24. *verse by verse in alternating chorus:* They are singing, that is to say, antiphonally, but with two choruses rather than with a single voice and a chorus as is more usual in the litany.

37–39. *hot vapors:* Dante's meteorology was built largely on a theory of the opposition of hot and wet vapors. (See *Inferno* XXIV, 142 ff., note.) Here he describes, first, falling stars (flashing through the first sweet air of night) and, second, heat lightning (flashing through the clouds of August sunsets). He attributes both phenomena to hot or "fiery" vapors.

37–42. The figure certainly goes from the instantaneous to the merely rapid with an interesting flourish of anticlimax. One may guess that Dante set out to indicate great speed, established that in the meteorological part of the figure, and then, needing time for Virgil to make the remarks that establish the following scene, slowed down the charge from the speed of lightning to the speed of horses.

52. THE LATE-REPENTANT WHO DIED BY VIOLENCE. Like the Indolent, these souls put off repentance to their last breath, but with the partially extenuating circumstance that their lives were cut short. Had they lived out their full lives, they might have repented before the end. The benefit of the doubt is at least possible. They are, therefore, a step above the merely Indolent and a step below the Negligent Princes who, powerfully occupied by worldly affairs (with the exception of Henry III of England), had a special excuse for not turning their thoughts to Heaven sooner.

69–90. *one replied:* Jacopo del Cassero. Of a leading family of Fano, a city located in the district that lay between Romagna and the kingdom of Naples, he served as chief magistrate of Bologna from 1296 to 1297 in a manner that offended the powerful Azzo VIII of Este. In 1298, Jacopo was called to Milan to serve as chief magistrate (podesta) of that city. On his way there he was set upon outside the town of Oriaco (or Oriago) and killed by Azzo's hirelings after a chase in which he foundered among the reeds and mud of a nearby swamp area. Had he turned instead toward La Mira, a Paduan city, he would have found refuge. *among the Antenori:* Among the Paduans. According to legend, Padua was founded by Antenor of Troy. *incensed . . . beyond all reason:* theologically, of course, murder is beyond all reason, but Jacopo's constant slurring references to Azzo as a traitor, and worse, would have passed as reason enough among the proud lords of that day.

94–135. *Bonconte:* Son of Guido da Montefeltro who is in Hell as an evil counselor (*Inferno* XXVII). Bonconte was a leader of the Ghibellines at the battle of Campaldino, a battle in which it has been reported that Dante took part. The Florentine Guelphs defeated the Ghibellines in his battle and Bonconte was killed (June 11, 1289). The Archiana is a nearby river that rises in the Apennines and flows into the Arno (the point at which "its name ends"). Giovanna (line 95) was his wife, and neither she nor anyone else has offered prayers to shorten his time of waiting.

The nicely functioning ambiguity of line 96 must not be missed: (1) I go among these whose heads are bowed low; (2) with head bowed low in shame for such neglect I go among these.

110–114. The incident is very similar to the one Bonconte's father describes in *Inferno* XXVII, but with opposite results. Such parallel scenes, as noted before, are very much a part of Dante's structural sense and are certainly intended to suggest moral reflection on the parallelism.

120. *his nature gives:* The demons are fallen but they still retain many of the powers given them by their angelic origins. Note that Dante implies the existence of no such power in those Angels found in the vestibule of Hell (those who took no sides in the Wars of Heaven).

121. *From Pratomagno to the spine:* The Casentino, or upper valley

of the Arno, is closed in on the east by the spine of the Apennines, and on the west by the Pratomagno range.

128. *the royal river:* The Arno.

132. *the cross I had formed upon my breast:* His arms crossed in contrition and as a symbol of surrender to God.

140. *Pia:* She has been traditionally identified as Pia de' Tolomei (Tall-oh-MAY-yee) of Siena, who married a Guelph leader and was murdered by him. The identification is doubtful, however. The text itself must say all that is certain about her. Nor can there be much doubt that Dante's principal interest in her is poetic rather than historical. After Bonconte's fulsome account of his own dramatic importance, Pia's gracious and courteous voice enters as a moving example of how effortlessly Dante can change and contrast tone. Note especially Pia's graciousness (despite her ardent desire to win the help of prayers) in asking nothing of Dante until he has returned and rested from his great journey.

CANTO VI

Ante-Purgatory: The Second Ledge — The Late-Repentant ·
Class Three: Those Who Died by Violence · Sordello

The Poets move along with the souls still crowding about them.
Dante promises all of them that he will bear word of them back
to the world, but he never pauses in his climb. Among that press
of souls, Dante specifically mentions seeing *Benincasa di Laterino,*
Guccio de' Tarlati, Federico Novello, Count Orso, and *Pierre de la*
Brosse.

Finally free of that crowd, Dante asks Virgil how it is that
prayer may sway God's will. Virgil explains in part but once more
finishes by declaring that the whole truth is beyond him and that
Dante must refer the question to Beatrice when he meets her.

The sun passes behind the mountain as they climb (midafter-
noon of Easter Sunday). The Poets press on, and there on the
shady slope they encounter the majestic spirit of Sordello who,
like Virgil, is a Mantuan. Dante watches Sordello and Virgil em-
brace in a transport of love for their common birthplace and is
moved to denounce Italy for setting brothers to war on one an-
other, to denounce the *Emperor Albert* for his failure to bring
unity and peace to Italy, and finally to utter an invective against
Florence as the type of the war-torn and corrupt state.

The loser, when a game of dice is done,
   remains behind reviewing every roll
   sadly, and sadly wiser, and alone.   3

The crowd leaves with the winner: one behind
   tugs at him, one ahead, one at his side—
   all calling their long loyalty to his mind.   6

Not stopping, he hands out a coin or two
   and those he has rewarded let him be.
   So he fights off the crowd and pushes through.   9

Such was I then, turning my face now here,
  now there, among that rout, and promising
  on every hand, till I at last fought clear.   12

There was the Aretine who came to woe
  at the murderous hand of Tacco; and the other
  who drowned while he was hunting down his foe.   15

There, hands outstretched to me as I pushed through,
  was Federico Novello; and the Pisan
  who made the good Marzucco shine so true.   18

I saw Count Orso; and the shade of one
  torn from its flesh, it said, by hate and envy,
  and not for any evil it had done—   21

Pierre de la Brosse, I mean: and of this word
  may the Lady of Brabant take heed while here,
  lest, there, she find herself in a worse herd.   24

When I had won my way free of that press
  of shades whose one prayer was that others pray,
  and so advance them toward their blessedness,   27

I said: "O my Soul's Light, it seems to me
  one of your verses most expressly states
  prayer may not alter Heaven's fixed decree: 30

yet all these souls pray only for a prayer.
  Can all their hope be vain? Or have I missed
  your true intent and read some other there?"   33

And he: "The sense of what I wrote is plain,
  if you bring all your wits to bear upon it.
  Nor is the hope of all these spirits vain.   36

The towering crag of Justice is not bent,
  nor is the rigor of its edict softened
  because the supplications of the fervent   39

and pure in heart cancel the debt of time
  decreed on all these souls who linger here,
  consumed with yearning to begin the climb.   42

The souls I wrote about were in that place
  where sin is not atoned for, and their prayers—
  they being pagan—were cut off from Grace.   45

But save all questions of such consequence
  till you meet her who will become your lamp
  between the truth and mere intelligence.   48

Do you understand me? I mean Beatrice.
  She will appear above here, at the summit
  of this same mountain, smiling in her bliss."   51

"My Lord," I said, "let us go faster now:
  I find the climb less tiring than at first,
  and see, the slope already throws a shadow."   54

"The day leads on," he said, "and we shall press
  as far as we yet may while the light holds,
  but the ascent is harder than you guess: 57

before it ends, the Sun must come around
  from its present hiding place behind the mountain
  and once more cast your shadow on the ground.   60

But see that spirit stationed all alone
  and looking down at us: he will point out
  the best road for us as we travel on."   63

We climbed on then. O Lombard, soul serene,
  how nobly and deliberately you watched us!
  how distant and majestic was your mien!   66

He did not speak to us as on we pressed
  but held us fixed in his unblinking eyes
  as if he were a lion at its rest.   69

Virgil, nonetheless, climbed to his side
  and begged him to point out the best ascent.
  The shade ignored the question and replied   72

by asking in what country we were born
  and who we were. My gentle Guide began:
  "Mantua . . ." And that shade, till then withdrawn,   75

leaped to his feet like one in sudden haste
  crying: "O Mantuan, I am Sordello
  of your own country!" And the two embraced.   78

Ah servile Italy, grief's hostelry,
  ah ship unpiloted in the storm's rage,
  no mother of provinces but of harlotry!   81

That noble spirit leaped up with a start
  at the mere sound of his own city's name,
  and took his fellow citizen to his heart: 84

while still, within you, brother wars on brother,
  and though one wall and moat surrounds them all,
  your living sons still gnaw at one another!   87

O wretched land, search all your coasts, your seas,
  the bosom of your hills—where will you find
  a single part that knows the joys of peace?   90

What does it matter that Justinian came
  to trim the bit, if no one sits the saddle?
  Without him you would have less cause for shame!   93

You priests who, if you heed what God decreed,
  should most seek after holiness and leave
  to Caesar Caesar's saddle and his steed—   96

see how the beast grows wild now none restrains
  its temper, nor corrects it with the spur,
  since you set meddling hands upon its reins!   99

O German Albert, you who turn away
  while she grows vicious, being masterless;
  you should have forked her long before today!   102

May a just judgment from the stars descend
  upon your house, a blow so weirdly clear
  that your line tremble at it to the end.   105

For you, sir, and your father, in your greed
  for the cold conquests of your northern lands,
  have let the Empire's Garden go to seed.   108

Come see the Montagues and Capulets,
  the Monaldi and Filippeschi, reckless man!
  those ruined already, these whom ruin besets.   111

Come, cruel Emperor, come and see your lords
  hunted and holed; come tend their wounds and see
  what fine security Santafior affords.   114

Come see your stricken Rome that weeps alone,
  widowed and miserable, and day and night
  laments: "O Caesar mine, why are you gone?"   117

Come see your people—everywhere the same—
  united in love; and if no pity for us
  can move you, come and blush for your good name.   120

O Supreme Jove, for mankind crucified,
  if you permit the question, I must ask it:
  are the eyes of your clear Justice turned aside?   123

Or is this the unfolding of a plan
  shaped in your fathomless counsels toward some
                          good
  beyond all reckoning of mortal man?   126

For the land is a tyrant's roost, and any clod
  who comes along playing the partisan
  passes for a Marcellus with the crowd.   129

Florence, my Florence, may you not resent
  the fact that my digression has not touched you—
  thanks to your people's sober management.   132

Others have Justice at heart but a bow strung
  by careful counsels and not quickly drawn:
  yours shoot the word forever—from the tongue.   135

Others, offered public office, shun
  the cares of service. Yours cry out unasked:
  "I will! I'll take it on! I am the one!"   138

Rejoice, I say, that your great gifts endure:
  your wealth, your peacefulness, and your good sense.
  What truth I speak, the facts will not obscure.   141

Athens and Sparta when of old they drew
  the codes of law that civilized the world,
  gave only merest hints, compared to you,   144

of man's advance. But all time shall remember
the subtlety with which the thread you spin
in mid-October breaks before November.   147

How often within living recollection
have you changed coinage, custom, law, and office,
and hacked your own limbs off and sewed them on?   150

But if your wits and memory are not dead
you yet will see yourself as that sick woman
who cannot rest, though on a feather bed,   153

but flails as if she fenced with pain and grief.
Ah, Florence, may your cure or course be brief.

NOTES

13–14. *the Aretine:* Benincasa di Laterino, a justice of the city of
Arezzo. ("Aretine" means "of Arezzo.") On the charge of highway
robbery and brigandage, he passed the death sentence on the brother
of Ghino (GHEE-no) di Tacco. Soon thereafter Benincasa was called
to Rome to a Papal Judgeship. Ghino, a fierce robber-baron, fol-
lowed him there, burst in upon him in open court, cut off his head,
and escaped safely. *the other* (Aretine): *Guccio* (GHOO-tchoe) or
Ciacco (TCHA-coe) de' Tarlati (day Tahr-LAH-tee). He drowned
in the Arno after the battle of Montaperti, or perhaps of Cam-
paldino. There is some doubt as to whether he was hunter or hunted
at the time.

17. *Federico Novello:* Little is known about him except that he
was the son of Guido Novello and that he was killed in a skirmish
with a band of Arentines.

17–18. *the Pisan . . . Marzucco:* Farinata, son of Marzucco degli
Scornigiani (Score-nih-JAH-nee) of Pisa. Farinata was killed in Pisa
and Marzucco, who had become a minor friar, went to bury his
body. In one account, he preached a funeral sermon of forgiveness
and ended by kissing the hand that had murdered his son, thus "shin-

ing so true" in Christian charity. In another account, Count Ugolino had ordered that the body be left unburied, and Marzucco went boldly before his enemy and won permission to bury his son, thus "shining so true" in courage.

19. *Count Orso:* Alessandro and Napoleone degli Alberti are two of the most infamous sinners in Hell. They lie together in the ice of Caïna among those who were treacherous against their own kin. Count Orso, son of Napoleone, was murdered by his cousin, the son of Alessandro.

19–22. *Pierre de la Brosse:* Court physician and favorite of Louis IX and later of Philip III of France. Philip had Pierre hanged in 1278. The accounts of Pierre's downfall vary. Dante clearly believes him to have been the innocent victim of the intrigues of Queen Mary of Brabant, "the Lady" he calls upon to repent while still on earth, for fear she may find herself in a worse herd (i.e., in Hell) than that in which Pierre finds himself.

29. *one of your verses:* Dante must be referring to the *Aeneid* VI, 376: Palinurus begs Aeneas to get him out of Hell, but the reply comes from the Sibyl: *Desine fata deum flecti speare precando* (Do not hope to bend the fixed decree of the Gods by prayer).

54. *the slope already throws a shadow:* The sun had declined to the west of the mountain and the Poets, on the east slope, are now in shadow. Because of the enormous height of the mountain, however, the sun would decline behind it relatively early. It is probably about 3:00 P.M. (or a bit later) on Easter Sunday.

60. *and once more cast your shadow on the ground:* Virgil is chiding Dante for having been so proud of the attention his shadow attracted, and Dante has earned the gentle reproof (which, in one sense of course, he is giving himself). When Virgil mentioned Beatrice (line 49) Dante was suddenly afire to run up the rest of the mountain to the top. (As he was ready to climb the Mount of Joy in *Inferno* I.) Virgil tells him that the climb is longer and harder than he supposes, for purification does not happen in a day. It is as if Virgil were saying: "Don't sound so suddenly zealous so soon after your proud strutting: you will still have a chance to astonish the souls here with that shadow of yours." Allegorically, if the Sun is taken as Di-

vine Illumination, it will return to make Dante see the error of Pride—as it will indeed when Dante comes upon the souls of the Proud.

77. *Sordello:* A troubadour poet of the first three-quarters of the thirteenth century. He was born in Mantua, which was also Virgil's birthplace. His life is only sketchily known, but he seems to have been a person of some political consequence. Such accounts as survive also seem to indicate his considerable accomplishments as a climber into assorted bedroom windows.

Dante has given Sordello the same relative position in Purgatory and the same majestic dignity he assigns to Farinata in Hell (*Inferno* X). There is no entirely satisfactory explanation of Dante's reasons in assigning such greatness of character to Sordello. Aside from his love poems, Sordello did write several impassioned political pieces, and Dante probably honors him for their integrity and sincerity. Great political integrity would make Sordello an especially apt guide to the souls of the Negligent Princes, the next group above, and in lines 91–137 of Canto VII, Sordello repeats exactly the sort of charges he made against the rulers of his day in *Complaint (Planh)* on the death of Baron Blacas, whom he represented as the figure of high chivalry dying from the world.

These correspondences may serve to explain his selection as guide to what follows, but why is he drawn so majestically? High indignation such as Sordello had shown in his *Complaint* seems always to have had a special attraction for Dante, who had his own gift for indignation. It would, moreover, honor Virgil to honor his noble fellow Mantuan. I am tempted to guess, however, that it was Dante's structural sense that ruled. Sordello is one of three majestic figures that occur at roughly equivalent points of the three kingdoms: Farinata in Hell, Sordello in Purgatory, and Cacciaguida (Dante's own ancestor) in Paradise. Since all three are political figures, it follows, too, that it is for Sordello's politics rather than for his poetry or for his amours that Dante has so ennobled him. Note too, as evidence of Dante's own character, the traits of slow dignity and hauteur for which Dante admires Sordello (*cf.* III: 10–11, and note).

91. *Justinian:* The Emperor Justinian. His reorganization and

codification of Roman law trimmed the bit and adjusted the bridle of the horse (the Empire), making a unified Italy possible, but his work has gone for nothing.

94–99. *You priests . . . set meddling hands upon its reins:* Dante has already (*Inferno* XIX, 109–111, and see note) asserted that the corruption of the Church began when it acquired wealth and power. He now charges the priests with having helped create the bloody chaos of Italian politics by meddling in temporal affairs. Thus by disregarding the Biblical injunction to render unto Caesar what is Caesar's and unto God what is God's, they have brought corruption upon the Church and destruction upon the State.

100. *German Albert:* Albert of Austria, born 1248, Emperor 1298, assassinated 1308. He was, therefore, Emperor at the purported time of Dante's journey.

At that time Italy was a part of the Holy Roman Empire though torn by internal strife between the Ghibellines (nominally the party of the Emperor though the party lines were blurred by local urgencies) and the Guelphs (nominally for independence and more often for anarchy). Many of the warring lords were, moreover, lieges of the Emperor. Dante's lament for Italy is always for her bloody internal wars, which he attributed, logically enough, to the lack of a central authority. The Emperor had that authority and could easily have brought unification and peace to Italy. But Albert and his father Rudolph (see VII, 91–96, and note) concerned themselves with affairs to the north and neither ever so much as visited Italy. Because of their negligence, Italy had all but slipped out of the Empire and the many Italian robber-barons warred on unceasingly at the very time that the northern kingdoms of the Empire were enjoying a long era of peace.

Dante goes on to specify the charges against Albert and his father more fully. They have allowed the Ghibelline lords to fall into ruinous feuds which could have been stopped by a word from the Emperor since the feuding parties were all lieges of the Emperor. Dante cites two such feuding Ghibelline pairs. The Montagues and the Capulets are the same Veronese family made familiar by *Romeo and Juliet.* The Monaldi and the Filippeschi were of Orvieto. All should have served as pillars of Empire in Italy, and all ruined themselves in their feuds.

The Emperor has, moreover, allowed robber barons to destroy the peace of the land. Dante's reference to the district of Santafiora in the Sienese Maremma is ironic: Santafiora was a robber's roost that afforded no security whatever.

The Emperor has, further, allowed Rome, the seat and glory of his Empire, to fall into decay by withholding his authority (the strong hand of Caesar).

By such neglect (lines 118–120) he has destroyed his own people ("united in love" is a bitter irony) and his own good name.

121. *Supreme Jove:* The usage must seem strange to modern ears, but there can be no doubt that Dante is referring here to God. In Dante's view the pagan names Zeus and Jove referred always to the Christian God as (dimly) perceived by the ancients who lacked Christ's clarifying word.

129. *Marcellus:* Marcellus opposed Caesar and was forgiven by him. Dante may, therefore, mean that anyone who calls himself a local partisan may safely oppose Caesar-Emperor and win support by doing so.

130–155. INVECTIVE AGAINST FLORENCE. (Cf. *Inferno* XXVI, 1–12.) Having bewailed the anarchy of Italy under Imperial neglect, Dante now turns to another of his invectives against his own city as the type of the bloodily self-divided and corrupt state. His praises are, of course, ironic and every semblance of a good quality ascribed to Florence should be understood to imply the opposite.

133. *Others have Justice at heart . . . :* Sense: Others have justice sincerely at heart and are ready to defend the right by arms, but they deliberate carefully, as wise men should, and are slow to draw the bow. You, Florence, have the word "justice" forever on your tongue and are forever ready to fire, but it is only the word you shoot, and from the tongue only, the deed never fulfilling the word.

136–137. *Others, offered public office, shun the cares of service:* They refuse out of conscientious misgivings because they take duty seriously, or perhaps because they are lazy, but your greedy politicians, Florence, are forever exclaiming their pious readiness to sacrifice themselves, even before they are asked—but they have no other aim than to raid the till.

140.   *your wealth, your peacefulness, and your good sense:* The last two have already expired from Florence, and Dante seems to imply that the first will not last long as things are going.

145–146.   *But all time shall remember the subtlety:* A mocking comparison between the stability of Athenian and Spartan law, one of the foundations of Western civilization, and the "more advanced" Florentine way of doing things in which nothing—not coinage, nor custom, nor law, nor office, nor pledged word—lives out the month.

152.   *that sick woman:* Though she lies in luxury (on a feather bed) she can find no relief from what is wrong with her but flails about as if she were fencing with her pain and grief, seeking to overcome it by outmaneuvering it. The last line (154) is not in the original. It is my own addition, forced upon me by the need to rhyme.

CANTO VII

Ante-Purgatory: The Second Ledge—The Late-Repentant

The Flowering Valley—Class Four: The Negligent Rulers

Sordello, discovering Virgil's identity, pays homage to him and offers to guide the Poets as far as Peter's Gate. It is nearly sunset, however, and Sordello explains that by *The Law of the Ascent* no one may go upward after sundown. He suggests that they spend the night in the nearby *Flowering Valley* in which the souls of *The Negligent Rulers* wait to begin their purification. The three together climb in the failing light to the edge of the valley. In it, they observe, among others: *Rudolph of Hapsburg, Ottocar of Bohemia, Philip the Bold of France, Henry of Navarre, Pedro III of Aragon, Charles I of Anjou, Henry III of England,* and *William VII, Marquis of Monferrato.*

All of the rulers, except Henry of England, were in one way or another connected with the Holy Roman Empire. Thus they were specially sanctified by the Divine Right of Kings and again sanctified for their place in the temporal hierarchy of Christ's Empire. Dante signalizes this elevation by the beauty of the valley in which he places them, a flower-strewn green hollow of unearthly beauty and fragrance. The valley is certainly a counterpart of the Citadel of the Virtuous Pagans in Limbo, but it outshines that lower splendor by as much as Divine Love outshines Human Reason.

Three or four times in brotherhood the two
   embraced and re-embraced, and then Sordello
   drew back and said: "Countryman, who are *you*?"   3

"Before those spirits worthy to be blessed
   had yet been given leave to climb this mountain,
   Octavian had laid my bones to rest.   6

I am Virgil, and I am lost to Heaven
   for no sin, but because I lacked the faith."
   In these words was my Master's answer given.   9

Just as a man who suddenly confronts
   something too marvelous either to believe
   or disbelieve, and so does both at once—   12

so did Sordello. Then his great head lowered,
   and, turning, he once more embraced my Master,
   but round the knees, as a menial does his lord.   15

"Eternal Glory of the Latin race,
   through whom our tongue made all its greatness clear!
   Of my own land the deathless pride and praise!   18

What grace or merit lets me see you plain?"
   he said. "And oh, if I am worthy, tell me
   if you come here from Hell, and from what pain."   21

"Through every valley of the painful kingdom
   I passed," my Lord replied. "A power from Heaven
   marked me this road, and in that power I come.   24

Not what I did but what I left undone,
   who learned too late, denies my right to share
   your hope of seeing the Eternal Sun.   27

There is a place below where sorrow lies
   in untormented gloom. Its lamentations
   are not the shrieks of pain, but hopeless sighs.   30

There do I dwell with souls of babes whom death
   bit off in their first innocence, before
   baptism washed them of their taint of earth.   33

There do I dwell with those who were not dressed
   in the Three Sacred Virtues but, unstained,
   recognized and practiced all the rest.   36

But if you know and are allowed to say,
  show us how we may reach the true beginning
  of Purgatory by the shortest way."   39

"We are not fixed in one place," he replied,
  "but roam at will up and around this slope
  far as the Gate, and I will be your guide.   42

But the day is fading fast, and in no case
  may one ascend at night: we will do well
  to give some thought to a good resting place.   45

Some souls are camped apart here on the right.
  If you permit, I will conduct you to them:
  I think you will find pleasure in the sight."   48

"What is it you say?" my Guide asked. "If one sought
  to climb at night, would others block his way?
  Or would he simply find that he could not?"   51

"Once the sun sets," that noble soul replied,
  "you would not cross this line"—and ran his finger
  across the ground between him and my Guide.   54

"Nor is there anything to block the ascent
  except the shades of night: they of themselves
  suffice to sap the will of the most fervent.   57

One might, indeed, go down during the night
  and wander the whole slope, were he inclined to,
  while the horizon locks the day from sight."   60

I heard my Lord's voice, touched with wonder, say:
  "lead us to the place of which you spoke
  where we may win some pleasure from delay."   63

We had not traveled very far from there
  before I saw a hollow in the slope
  such as one often finds in mountains here.   66

"There," said that spirit, "where the mountain makes
  a lap among its folds: that is the place
  where we may wait until the new day breaks."   69

The dell's rim sank away from left to right.
  A winding path, half-level and half-steep,
  led us to where the rim stood at mid-height.   72

Indigo, phosphorescent wood self-lit,
  gold, fine silver, white-lead, cochineal,
  fresh emerald the moment it is split—   75

all colors would seem lusterless as shade
  if placed beside the flowers and grassy banks
  that made a shining of that little glade.   78

Nor has glad Nature only colored there,
  but of a thousand sweet scents made a single
  earthless, nameless fragrance of the air.   81

Salve Regina!—from that green the hymn
  was raised to Heaven by a choir of souls
  hidden from outer view by the glade's rim.   84

"Sirs," said that Mantuan, "do not request
  that I conduct you there while any light
  remains before the Sun sinks to its nest.   87

You can observe them from this rise and follow
  their actions better, singly and en masse,
  than if you moved among them in the hollow.   90

He who sits highest with the look of one
  ashamed to move his lips when others praise,
  in life left undone what he should have done.   93

He was the Emperor Rudolph whose high state
  could once have stayed the death of Italy.
  Now, though another try, 't will be too late.   96

That one who comforts him ruled formerly
  the land where rise the waters that flow down
  the Moldau to the Elbe to the sea.   99

He was Ottocar, and more respected and feared
  while still in diapers than his dissipated
  son Wenceslaus is now with a full beard.   102

That Snubnose there who talks with head
                        close-pressed
  to the kindly looking one, died while in flight,
  dishonoring the Lily on his crest.   105

Observe the way he beats his breast and cries.
  And how the other one has made his palm
  a bed to rest his cheek on while he sighs.   108

They are father and father-in-law of The Plague
                        of France.
  They know his dissolute and vicious ways,
  and hence their grief among these holy chants.   111

The heavy-sinewed one beside that spirit
  with the manly nose, singing in harmony,
  bore in his life the seal of every merit.   114

And if that younger one who sits in place
  behind him, had remained king after him,
  true merit would have passed from vase to vase.   117

As it has not, alas, in their successors.
  Frederick and James possess the kingdoms now.
  Their father's better heritage none possesses.   120

Rare is the tree that lifts to every limb
  the sap of merit—He who gives, so wills
  that men may learn to beg their best from Him.   123

And what I say goes for that bignosed one
  no less than for the other who sings with him.
  On his account Provence and Puglia mourn.   126

By as much as Margaret and Beatrice
  must yield when Constance speaks her husband's
                                              worth,
  that much less than the tree the seedling is.   129

See Henry of England seated there alone,
  the monarch of the simple life: his branches
  came to good issue in a noble son.   132

The other lone one seated on the ground
  below the rest and looking up to them
  was the Marquis William Longsword, he who found 135

such grief in Allesandria, for whose pride
  both Monferrato and Canavese cried."

NOTES

General Note: THE NEGLIGENT RULERS. The Negligent
Rulers are the fourth and final class of the Late-Repentant. All of
the Late-Repentant made God wait by putting off their surrender
to His will until the end. Accordingly God now makes them wait
before they may begin their ascent to Him through the purifying
pains of Purgatory-proper. The Negligent Rulers, however, had

special cause to be preoccupied by worldly affairs. Their responsibility for their subjects was not only a duty but a duty in some measure imposed upon them by God's Will since kings were believed to be divinely selected. Just as those who died by violence are elevated a step above the merely indolent, so the Negligent Rulers are elevated above their negligent subjects because their special duties made it difficult for them to think about the welfare of their own souls.

4–6. THE FIRST SALVATION. Before Christ's redemption, the souls of the virtuous went to Limbo. In *Inferno* IV, Dante refers to Christ's apocryphal descent into Limbo in 33 A.D. The incident is known as The Harrowing of Hell, and in it Christ was said to have taken with him to Heaven the first souls to win salvation. (Adam and Eve were among those so elevated.) From the time of the Fall until 33 A.D., therefore, Purgatory existed but was not in use. Virgil died in 19 A.D. under the Emperor Octavian.

19. *What grace or merit:* I.e., what special grace granted me by Heaven, or what merit of my own I know not of?

33. *taint of earth:* Original sin. Unbaptized infants have not yet been taken to Christ and have not, accordingly, been cleaned of their part in Adam's guilt. They must, therefore, share the fate of the virtuous pagans (*Inferno* IV) whom they resemble in being sinless but lacking Christ's sacrament. Infant damnation is one of the most vexed and least attractive tenets of dogmatic Christianity.

35–36. *The Three Sacred Virtues:* Faith, Hope, and Charity. These are the "revealed" or "theological" virtues. *the rest:* The Four Cardinal Virtues. They are Justice, Prudence, Temperance, and Fortitude. (See I, 23, and 31 ff., notes.)

40–60. THE LAW OF THE ASCENT. No allegory, by its nature, is containable within a paraphrase. The center of the allegory here is clearly in the fact that the Sun symbolizes Divine Illumination. Note that Dante underlines this idea by referring to God in line 27 above as "the Eternal Sun." Thus the primary meanings of the allegory may be clearly enough stated: first, that one cannot achieve true repentance and purification except in the sight of God (light of the Sun); second, that one has no difficulty in backsliding (going down the mountain) once he is out of God's sight (darkness); and third, that once out of sight of God/Sun one simply cannot find within himself the will to climb. See also note to lines 85–87, below.

Once in Heaven, it should be noted, there is no night: one is constantly in the presence and light of God, the Sun. Here is another of those harmonies of concept that mark Dante's structural power: in Heaven there is no darkness; in Hell there is no light (except the dimness of Human Reason unaided); in Purgatory—the Kingdom between—there is both light and darkness.

70–72. THE SHAPE OF THE VALLEY. The point is much disputed. I conceive the valley to lie in a U-shaped fold with the mouth of the U facing East and the sides inclining upward into the mass of the Mountain. The incline would seem to be regular. Hence, when the Poets come to the point at which the rim stands at mid-height, they are halfway up what I understand to be the southern side of the U, a position from which they can best observe the whole valley, being as it were at the fifty-yard line.

82. *Salve Regina!:* The beginning of the Compline Hymn in the Roman Catholic Breviary. It is an especially apt choice as the hymn of these souls: "Hail Queen, mother of Mercy . . . to thee we sigh . . . in this valley of tears."

85–87. *"Sirs," said that Mantuan:* This is the first time Sordello's form of address includes both the poets. Dante has not yet even been presented to him. *do not request that I conduct you there while any light remains:* See note on The Law of the Ascent. Sordello here carries it a step further: one may descend into the valley after dark (as they will in the next Canto), but no downward step may be taken while any of the Sun's light remains. Characteristically, the detail is sound both as allegory and as narrative, for the valley is in fact best observed from the rim.

91–95. *the Emperor Rudolph:* Rudolph of Hapsburg, 1218–1291, crowned Emperor, 1273. He is the Father of "German Albert" (VI, 100, note) and with him shared the blame for failing to unify Italy. Dante's dream of a unified Italy was not realized until the mid-nineteenth century.

96. *Now, though another try, 't will be too late:* The other is Henry

VII of Luxemburg, Emperor from 1308 to 1313. Henry, as Emperor, tried to accomplish, under circumstances that had by then made it impossible, what Rudolph and Albert had neglected to do under circumstances that assured success.

This line contains another of Dante's political "prophecies," the accuracy of which (see *Inferno* VI, 61, note) was made possible by the fact that he was writing *as if* in 1300 but actually *as of* ten to fifteen years later. The exact dates of the composition of the *Commedia* cannot be fixed, though likely dates would be from 1308 to 1321. Clearly *Purgatory* must have been written after Henry had attempted to unify Italy and had failed, hence, after 1310.

97. *That one who comforts him:* Ottocar II, King of Bohemia (the land whose waters drain into the Moldau, to the Elbe, to the sea) from 1253 to 1278. In life he was Rudolph's enemy and a tyrant whose acts might well have reserved for him a bath in Phlegethon (*Inferno* XII) with the Violent against their Neighbors. Dante may have known him only as a valiant warrior. His object in placing him here seems to be to show the reconciliation of enemies after true repentance and forgiveness.

102. *Wenceslaus:* Wenceslaus IV (the Good), born in 1270, succeeded his father as King of Bohemia in 1278. He was elected King of Poland in 1300, and died 1305. Despite a promising beginning as king, Wenceslaus was forced to cede many territories for which his warrior father would have fought to the death. Wenceslaus preferred piety to warfare, habitually hearing several masses daily. With his spirits thus restored, he seems to have found the strength for scouting various bedrooms, for he had begotten numerous illegitimate children by the time he was twenty-five. Hence Dante's charge that he was dissipated.

103. *That Snubnose:* Philip III of France (the Bold, also The Snubnose), 1245–1285, succeeded his father, Louis IX, in 1270. He did not die while actually in flight from the field of battle, but at Perpignan, to which he had retired after the French navy had been annihilated by Pedro III of Aragon.

104. *the kindly looking one:* Henry (the Fat) of Navarre, reigned 1270–1274. He died reportedly "suffocated by the fat of his own

body." In life he was quite other than kindly, and might have made excellent Hell-bait, but Dante obviously credits him with having breathed a true repentance from somewhere among the folds of his "suffocating fat."

109. *The Plague of France:* Philip IV (the Fair) of France, born 1268, crowned 1285, died 1314. Second son of Philip III, he married Juana, daughter of Henry of Navarre. It is his misrule and his vicious life that unite (line 103: their heads "close pressed") his father and father-in-law.

Philip IV was for Dante the archetype of the evil ruler, in much the same way that Boniface VIII (whom Philip humiliated and drove to an early death) was the archetype of the evil Pope. Internally, Philip ruined whole provinces by his extortions and currency frauds. He systematically jailed Italian merchants (for ransom) on false charges, cruelly robbed the Jews, and suppressed the Knights Templars in order to confiscate their properties. Externally, he played a disastrous hand in Italian politics. Soon after he had eliminated Boniface VIII, he succeeded in placing one of his puppet cardinals on the Papal Throne as Clement V. Under Clement V the Papal Seat was transferred to Avignon. (*Inferno* XIX, refers to Clement's intrigue with Philip and makes clear that a place in Hell is awaiting Clement.) In XX and XXXII, below, Dante inveighs against Philip, and again in *Paradiso* XIX.

112–113. *The heavy-sinewed one . . . that spirit with the manly nose:* Another pair of former enemies reconciled. The first is Pedro III of Aragon, 1236–1285, King of Aragon, 1276, and (after the bloody Sicilian Vespers of 1282 in which all the French were massacred) King of Sicily. He married Manfred's "good Constance" (III, 143). Dante's phrasing in these lines obviously suggests that the first spirit is virile, whereas the second is virile only in the nose.

That second spirit, Pedro's equal only in the nose, is Charles I of Anjou, 1220–1285, crowned King of Sicily and Puglia (Apulia) in 1265. It was Charles who destroyed Manfred at Benevento in 1265 and who was overthrown in the Sicilian Vespers. Dante inveighs against his misrule in XX and again in *Paradiso* VIII, 73 ff. Once again Dante's intent in presenting the soul of such a man in Purgatory must have been to show that no amount of wickedness will damn a man if he achieves true repentance.

115. *that younger one:* Alfonso III (the Magnificent), 1271–1291, crowned King of Aragon, 1286. He left no heirs and his rule passed to his degenerate younger brothers, the throne of Aragon to James, and that of Sicily to Frederick, both of whom were ruling in 1300, hence the "now" of line 119. Thus the meaning of lines 119–120 is that the younger sons have the material heritage of their father, Pedro, but that no one (now that Alfonso is dead) possesses his better heritage (i.e., his merit).

124–129. A difficult passage. Dante refers again to Charles and Pedro, still developing the theme of the degeneracy of sons. The theme applies not only to Pedro in the degeneracy of James and of Frederick, but to Charles as well. Dante's meaning is that the son, Charles the Lame, is as inferior to his father, Charles I, as Charles I is to Pedro. Hence their kingdoms mourn. But Dante carries the figure through a very complicated comparison, which may be read: "The seedling [Charles II] is inferior to the tree [Charles I] by as much as Constance [widow of Pedro III] may praise her husband above the husband of Margaret and Beatrice [they were the two wives of Charles I]."

130. *Henry of England:* Henry III, 1216–1278. A pious but pallid king. His son, Edward I, however (who was ruling in 1300), crowned a glorious reign with an enduring reform of English law. Hence Henry's "branches came to a good issue in a noble son."

Henry is seated alone in part, perhaps, because he had no connection with the Holy Roman Empire, but much more importantly because he is unique in this company. Henry attended so many masses daily that he never got around to governing his kingdom. His sin, therefore, could not have been neglect of God, but rather neglect of his divinely imposed duties to rule his kingdom well. His presence in this company adds an interesting dimension to Dante's concept, for Henry's sin is the reverse of the general pattern here. Dante's Aristotelian mind could not cherish any excess: the Good is the Golden Mean, to wander from the mean in either direction is equally culpable.

133–137. *The Marquis William:* William VII (Longsword), Marquis of Monferrato, 1245–1292. A lesser prince than the others, hence he sits below and looks up to them. As Imperial Vicar to Italy he headed a coalition of Ghibelline towns. In 1290 the Republic of Asti formented a rebellion in Alessandria, a town held by William. William, attempting to put down the rebellion, was captured, locked in an iron cage, and exposed to public ridicule. He died in the cage, and even in death his body was shockingly abused by the Alessandrians. William's son moved against Alessandria to avenge his father, but the Alessandrians defeated him and invaded Monferrato and Canavese, the two districts of William's fief. Their invasion left the citizens with ample reasons for tears.

CANTO VIII

Ante-Purgatory: The Flowering Valley—The Negligent Rulers

Nightfall, easter sunday ·
The guardian angels · The serpent

As the light fades, Dante, Virgil, and Sordello stand on the bank and watch the souls below gather and sing the *Compline Hymn,* asking for protection in the night. In response to the hymn *Two Green Angels* descend from Heaven and take their posts, one on each side of the valley. Full darkness now settles, and the Poets may make their *Descent into the Valley.*

Dante immediately finds a soul he knows, *Judge Nino de' Visconti,* and has a long conversation with him in which both bemoan the infidelity of widows who remarry.

When Judge Nino has finished speaking, Dante looks at the South Pole and sees that *Three Stars* (the Three Theological Virtues) have replaced *The Four Stars* (The Four Cardinal Virtues) he had seen at dawn.

As he is discussing them with Virgil *The Serpent* appears and is immediately routed by the Angels, who return to their posts. Dante then has a conversation with *Conrad Malaspina,* whom Judge Nino had summoned when he found out Dante was a living man. Dante owes a debt of gratitude to the Malaspina House for its hospitality to him in his exile, and he takes this opportunity to praise the house and to have Conrad prophesy that Dante shall live to know more about it.

It was the hour that turns the memories
   of sailing men their first day out, to home,
   and friends they sailed from on that morning's breeze;   3

that thrills the traveler newly on his way
   with love and yearning when he hears afar
   the bell that seems to mourn the dying day—   6

when I began, for lack of any sound,
  to count my hearing vain: and watched a spirit
  who signaled for attention all around.   9

Raising his hands, he joined his palms in prayer
  and turned his rapt eyes east, as if to say:
  "I have no thought except that Thou art there." 12

"Te lucis ante" swelled from him so sweetly,
  with such devotion and so pure a tone,
  my senses lost the sense of self completely.   15

Then all the others with a golden peal
  joined in the hymn and sang it to the end,
  their eyes devoutly raised to Heaven's wheel.   18

Reader, if you seek truth, sharpen your eyes,
  for here the veil of allegory thins
  and may be pierced by any man who tries.   21

I saw that host of kings, its supplication
  sung to a close, stand still and pale and humble,
  eyes raised to Heaven as if in expectation.   24

I saw two angels issue and descend
  from Heaven's height, bearing two flaming swords
  without a point, snapped off to a stub end.   27

Green as a leaf is at its first unfurling,
  their robes; and green the wings that beat and blew
  the flowing folds back, fluttering and whirling. 30

One landed just above me, and one flew
  to the other bank. Thus, in the silent valley,
  the people were contained between the two.   33

I could see clearly that their hair was gold,
　but my eyes drew back bedazzled from their faces,
　defeated by more light than they could hold.　　36

"They are from Mary's bosom," Sordello said,
　"and come to guard the valley from the Serpent
　that in a moment now will show its head."　　39

And I, not knowing where it would appear,
　turned so I stood behind those trusted shoulders
　and pressed against them icy-cold with fear.　　42

Once more Sordello spoke: "Now let us go
　to where the great souls are, and speak to them.
　The sight of you will please them much, I know."　　45

It was, I think, but three steps to the base
　of the little bank; and there I saw a shade
　who stared at me as if he knew my face.　　48

The air was closing on its darkling hour,
　yet not so fast but what it let me see,
　at that close range, what it had veiled before.　　51

I took a step toward him; he, one toward me—
　Noble Judge Nin! how it rejoiced my soul
　to see you safe for all eternity!　　54

No welcome was left unsaid on either side.
　Then he inquired: "How long since did you come
　to the mountain's foot over that widest tide?"　　57

"Oh," I replied, "I came by the pits of woe—
　this morning. I am still in my first life,
　though I gain the other on the road I go."　　60

He and Sordello, when they heard me thus
  answer the question, suddenly drew back
  as if surprised by something marvelous.   63

One turned to Virgil and one turned aside
  to a shade who sat nearby. "Conrad! Get up!
  See what the grace of God has willed!" he cried.   66

And then to me: "By all the thankful praise
  you owe to Him who hides His primal cause
  so deep that none may ever know His ways—   69

when you have once more crossed the enormous tide,
  tell my Giovanna to cry out my name
  there where the innocent are gratified.   72

I do not think her mother cares for me
  since she put off the weeds and the white veil
  that she will once more long for presently.   75

She shows all men how long love's fire will burn
  within a woman's heart when sight and touch
  do not rekindle it at every turn.   78

Nor will the Milanese viper she must bear
  upon her tomb do her such honor in it
  as would Gallura's cock emblazoned there."   81

So spoke he; and his features bore the seal
  of that considered anger a good man
  reaches in reason and may rightly feel.   84

I looked up at the Heavens next, and eyed
  that center point at which the stars are slowest,
  as a wheel is next the axle. And my Guide: 87

"My son, what is it that you stare at so?"
  And I: "At those three stars there in whose light
  the polar regions here are all aglow."   90

And he to me: "Below the rim of space
  now ride the four bright stars you saw this morning,
  and these three have arisen in their place."   93

Sordello started as my Guide said this;
  and clutching him, he pointed arm and finger,
  crying: "Our Adversary! There he is!"   96

Straight through the valley's unprotected side
  a serpent came, perhaps the very one
  that gave the bitter food for which Eve cried.   99

Through the sweet grass and flowers the long snake
                                      drew,
  turning its head around from time to time
  to lick itself as preening beasts will do.   102

I did not see and cannot tell you here
  how the celestial falcons took to flight;
  but I did see that both were in the air.   105

Hearing their green wings beating through the night,
  the serpent fled. The angels wheeled and climbed
  back to their posts again in equal flight.   108

The shade the Judge had summoned with his cry
  had not moved from his side; through all that fray
  he stared at me without blinking an eye.   111

"So may the lamp that leads to what you seek
  find oil enough," he said, "in your own will
  to light your way to the enameled peak;   114

if you can say for certain how things stand
  in Val di Magra or those parts, please do,
  for I was once a great lord in that land.   117

Conrad Malaspina I was—the grandson
  and not the Elder. Here I purify
  the love I bore for those who were my own."   120

"Oh," I replied, "I never have been near
  the lands you held; but is there in all Europe
  a hamlet ignorant of the name you bear?   123

The glories of your noble house proclaim
  its lords abroad, proclaim the lands that bear them;
  and he who does not know them knows their fame. 126

I swear to you—so may my present course
  lead me on high—your honored house has never
  put by its strict sword and its easy purse.   129

Usage and nature have so formed your race
  that, though the Guilty Head pervert all else,
  it still shuns ill to walk the path of grace."   132

And he: "Go now, for the Sun shall not complete
  its seventh rest in that great bed the Ram
  bestrides and covers with its four spread feet,   135

before this testimony you have given
  shall be nailed to the center of your head
  with stouter nails, and more securely driven,   138

than ever hearsay was. And this shall be
  certain as fate is in its fixed decree."

NOTES

7–9. The original passage is hard to interpret. I think it is best taken as another of Dante's extraordinary accounts of how his senses work. (*Cf. Inferno* XX, 10, and XXXI, 14–15, and notes thereto.) Dante's descriptions of how his senses work seem ever to call forth his pedantry. His basic idea here seems to be most nearly related to that with which he opens Canto IV—that the soul, under intense stimulus, is absorbed into one sense at a time. Up to this point he has been absorbed in listening to the spirits sing *Salve Regina!* and to Sordello's account of the spirits. Now both have fallen still, and Dante gives what amounts to a sort of physiological report of his re-actions, stating that bit by bit he emerges from his absorption in the sense of hearing, now useless for lack of anything to hear, and re-settles his attention in his sense of sight. (*Cf.* also lines 13–15, below.)

13. *Te lucis ante:* The beginning of the Compline Hymn, *Te lucis ante terminum* ("To Thee before the light is done"). The hymn is a prayer for protection against the evils that walk the dark. Like all of Dante's hymn choices, it is fitted to the situation, the vision that fol-lows being precisely in answer to the hymn's plea.

15. *my senses lost the sense of self completely:* (Lit.: "It made me from myself pass from all awareness.") Here, too, I think the key to the proper interpretation lies in the opening lines of Canto IV.

26–27. THE BROKEN SWORDS. Symbols, well used, can sel-dom be narrowed to a single meaning that excludes other possibili-ties. The swords may symbolize God's Justice, and the broken points that it is tempered with Mercy. They may equally symbolize that the Angel Guardians are for defense only and not for offense. There is also a possible reference to the legend that the guardian angels broke their swords when Christ entered Paradise, thereby symbolizing that they would no longer exclude with the whole sword, *i.e.,* com-pletely.

34–36. In line 36, Dante clearly meant one of his characteristic comments on the behavior of *all* of our senses. A more literal ren-dering of this tercet would be:

> I could distinctly see their golden hair,
>> but my eyes drew back defeated from their faces,
>> like a sense perceiving more than it can bear.

I have preferred the less literal rendering because it seems to manage a better effect as English poetry.

46. *three steps:* I am inclined to think Dante intended only to show that the bank was not very high, but three is an important number and any of its symbolic possibilities could be argued here.

51. *before:* Then Dante was standing on the bank.

53. *Judge Nin:* Nino de' Visconti da Pisa, nephew of Count Ugolino (see *Inferno* XXXIII) was Justiciary of Gallura in Sardinia, then a Pisan possession. It was he who ordered the hanging of Friar Gomita (see *Inferno* XXII, 82, note). He should be thought of as more nearly a viceroy for his uncle than as a judge in the modern sense. Dante knew him intimately. Lines 53–54 should be taken not as an implication that Dante knew of any great sin for which Nino should have been damned, but rather as a simple rejoicing that a man so deeply involved in worldly affairs had yet managed not to lose his soul to worldliness. Nino died in 1296.

68–69. *Cf.* III, 34–39.

70. *enormous tide:* Figuratively, the enormous tide between life and death. Literally, the sea between the mouth of the Tiber and the shores of Purgatory, the longest sea-route on earth as Dante conceived it.

71. *my Giovanna:* his daughter.

72–81. JUDGE NINO'S REPROACH OF HIS WIFE BEATRICE. Nino Visconti's widow was Beatrice, daughter of Opizzo da Este (*Inferno* XII, 111). She put off the weeds and white veil (the mourning costume of Dante's time) first in being betrothed to Alberto Scotti, Lord of Piacenza, and then in jilting him to marry Galeazzo Visconti of Milan, all under the pressure of her family's insistence and for political motives. Nino makes no allowance for the pressures that must have been brought to bear upon Beatrice, and Dante (see below) endorses his sentiments with the same lack of reservation.

Nino proceeds to prophesy (it had already happened between

1300 and the time of the writing) that Beatrice will one day wish she had remained a widow, for the jilted Scotti took his revenge by ruining Visconti, and Beatrice had to share his poverty. Nino carries his reproach to eternity in saying that even her burial will be less honorable than it would have been had she remained true. (It was the custom for the tombs of ladies to be marked with their husbands' coats of arms.) The Milanese is Galeazzo Visconti, whose arms contained a viper eating a child. That viper on her tomb, says Nino, will do her less honor than would the cock of Gallura from Nino's arms. A piece of family pride: the arms of Gallura were more ancient than those of the Visconti of Milan and Nino looks upon Galeazzo as an upstart.

In 1328 Beatrice's son (she was then a widow for the second time) was made Lord of Milan and her fortunes thereafter (she died in 1334) rode high once again—a turn of events Dante could not have prophesied at the time of the writing, and which, in fact, he did not live to see.

73. *her mother:* Nino's wife. But note that he refers to her not as "my wife" but as "her mother."

83. *considered anger:* Cf. *Inferno* VIII, 43, and note.

85–87. *I looked up . . . next:* Students regularly take this line to mean that Dante is avoiding Nino's eyes. It is simply one of Dante's fast transitions. Nino's remarks are closed, Dante has emphatically approved them, and with no time wasted, he passes on to the next thing of interest—the South Pole, whose stars he has never before seen except for a glimpse at dawn.

90. *the polar regions here:* "Here," equals "on this side of the Equator." The stars are important symbols and will recur. At dawn, on the shore (at the beginning of the Ante-Purgatory) Dante had seen Four Stars representing the Four Cardinal Virtues. Now, just before beginning the True Purgatory, he sees three evening stars which may be taken as the Three Theological Virtues. In Canto XXIX, just before the appearance of Beatrice in the Earthly Paradise, Dante sees all seven together in the form of Heavenly Nymphs.

106. *hearing their green wings:* How even the Serpent can register with his hearing the color of the wings remains an unanswered ques-

tion. This sort of figure is one of Dante's mannerisms. *Cf.* his first description of Virgil in *Inferno* I, where Virgil is described as appearing (visual) hoarse (auditory) with long silence. Some critics have labeled both these passages as master ambiguities. Perhaps so.

107–108. *climbed back to their posts again:* Dante does not specify whether to the bank (their watch posts) or to Heaven (their original posts). I think he meant watch posts, for the souls' prayer (which the Angels answer) is for night-long protection. In Purgatory, only the souls below the Gate (Ante-Purgatory) are subject to temptation, and that, it would seem, of only the most perfunctory sort. In any case it is certain that they will not yield to temptation, for they are saved. The Serpent, therefore, is best taken as a formal masque-like allegory, like the Heavenly Pageant Dante will encounter at the top of the mountain.

109–111. *The shade the Judge had summoned with his cry:* Conrad. See line 65. *stared at me without blinking an eye:* Another Dantean peculiarity. If Dante was staring at the Angels and the Serpent, he could not know this detail.

112–113. *the lamp:* The light of Divine Grace must be merited (i.e., find oil within the soul). The summit of Purgatory (the Earthly Paradise) is an "enameled" plateau. Dante uses the same word to describe the Citadel of Limbo (*Inferno* IV, 115). Sense: "So may you find within your soul all the merit you need to win to the summit. . . ."

118. *Conrad Malaspina:* Very little is known about this Conrad except that he was the son of Frederick I, Marchese di Villafranca, and the grandson of Conrad I. The house of Malaspina, on the other hand, was honorably known, though scarcely as well as Dante declares below. In his praise of the Malaspina family, Dante is paying a debt of gratitude for the honor and hospitality with which it received him after his exile from Florence.

119–120. *Here I purify . . . :* Various interpretations of these lines have been offered. I think Conrad means that for love of friends and kin he remained so occupied in wordly affairs that he neglected God. Now in Purgatory he purifies and offers to God the love that formerly led him to be negligent.

129. *strict sword . . . easy purse:* valor . . . liberality.

131. *the Guilty Head:* Certainly the primary meaning is the Devil. The corrupt Papacy and the negligent Emperor may be secondary meanings.

133–134. *the Sun shall not complete its seventh rest:* The sun will not have completed its seventh transit of Aries (the Ram), *i.e.,* the seven years will not pass, before Dante will know from his own experience the truth of what he has here uttered as hearsay (of the virtue and liberality of the Malaspina family). *the great bed the Ram bestrides:* That portion of the zodiac which falls under the sign of Aries. Aries is often depicted with his four feet spread wide.

CANTO IX

The Gate of Purgatory—The Angel Guardian

Dawn is approaching. Dante has a dream of *A Golden Eagle* that
descends from the height of Heaven and carries him up to the
Sphere of Fire. He wakes to find he has been transported in his
sleep, that it was *Lucia* who bore him, laying him down beside an
enormous wall, through an opening in which he and Virgil may
approach *The Gate of Purgatory.*

Having explained these matters, Virgil leads Dante to the Gate
and its *Angel Guardian.* The Angel is seated on the topmost of
Three Steps that symbolize the three parts of a perfect *Act of Con-
fession.* Dante prostrates himself at the feet of the Angel, who cuts
Seven P's in Dante's forehead with the point of a blazing sword.
He then allows the Poets to enter. As the Gates open with a sound
of thunder, the mountain resounds with a great *Hymn of Praise.*

Now pale upon the balcony of the East
   ancient Tithonus' concubine appeared,
   but lately from her lover's arms released.   3

Across her brow, their radiance like a veil,
   a scroll of gems was set, worked in the shape
   of the cold beast whose sting is in his tail.   6

And now already, where we were, the night
   had taken two steps upward, while the third
   thrust down its wings in the first stroke of flight;   9

when I, by Adam's weight of flesh defeated,
   was overcome by sleep, and sank to rest
   across the grass on which we five were seated.   12

At that new hour when the first light grows
   and the little swallow starts her mournful cry,
   perhaps in memory of her former woes;   15

and when the mind, escaped from its submission
  to flesh and to the chains of waking thought,
  becomes almost prophetic in its vision;   18

in a dream I saw a soaring eagle hold
  the shining height of heaven, poised to strike,
  yet motionless on widespread wings of gold.   21

He seemed to hover where old history
  records that Ganymede rose from his friends,
  borne off to the supreme consistory.   24

I thought to myself: "Perhaps his habit is
  to strike at this one spot; perhaps he scorns
  to take his prey from any place but this."   27

Then from his easy wheel in Heaven's spire,
  terrible as a lightning bolt, he struck
  and snatched me up high as the Sphere of Fire.   30

It seemed that we were swept in a great blaze,
  and the imaginary fire so scorched me
  my sleep broke and I wakened in a daze.   33

Achilles must have roused exactly thus—
  glancing about with unadjusted eyes,
  now here, now there, not knowing where he was—   36

when Thetis stole him sleeping, still a boy,
  and fled with him from Chiron's care to Scyros,
  whence the Greeks later lured him off to Troy.   39

I sat up with a start; and as sleep fled
  out of my face, I turned the deathly white
  of one whose blood is turned to ice by dread.   42

There at my side my comfort sat—alone.
  The sun stood two hours high, and more. I sat
  facing the sea. The flowering glen was gone.   45

"Don't be afraid," he said. "From here our course
  leads us to joy, you may be sure. Now, therefore,
  hold nothing back, but strive with all your force.   48

You are now at Purgatory. See the great
  encircling rampart there ahead. And see
  that opening—it contains the Golden Gate.   51

A while back, in the dawn before the day,
  while still your soul was locked in sleep inside you,
  across the flowers that made the valley gay,   54

a Lady came. 'I am Lucia,' she said.
  'Let me take up this sleeping man and bear him
  that he may wake to see his hope ahead.'   57

Sordello and the others stayed. She bent
  and took you up. And as the light grew full,
  she led, I followed, up the sweet ascent.   60

Here she put you down. Then with a sweep
  of her sweet eyes she marked that open entrance.
  Then she was gone; and with her went your sleep."   63

As one who finds his doubt dispelled, sheds fear
  and feels it change into new confidence
  as bit by bit he sees the truth shine clear—   66

so did I change; and seeing my face brim
  with happiness, my Guide set off at once
  to climb the slope, and I moved after him.   69

Reader, you know to what exalted height
  I raised my theme. Small wonder if I now
  summon still greater art to what I write.   72

As we drew near the height, we reached a place
  from which—inside what I had first believed
  to be an open breach in the rock face—   75

I saw a great gate fixed in place above
  three steps, each its own color; and a guard
  who did not say a word and did not move.   78

Slow bit by bit, raising my lids with care,
  I made him out seated on the top step,
  his face more radiant than my eyes could bear.   81

He held a drawn sword, and the eye of day
  beat such a fire back from it, that each time
  I tried to look, I had to look away.   84

I heard him call: "What is your business here?
  Answer from where you stand. Where is your Guide?
  Take care you do not find your coming dear."   87

"A little while ago," my Teacher said,
  "A Heavenly Lady, well versed in these matters,
  told us 'Go there. That is the Gate ahead.' "   90

"And may she still assist you, once inside,
  to your soul's good! Come forward to our three
                                             steps,"
  the courteous keeper of the gate replied.   93

We came to the first step: white marble gleaming
  so polished and so smooth that in its mirror
  I saw my true reflection past all seeming.   96

The second was stained darker than blue-black
   and of a rough-grained and a fire-flaked stone,
   its length and breadth crisscrossed by many a crack.   99

The third and topmost was of porphyry,
   or so it seemed, but of a red as flaming
   as blood that spurts out of an artery.   102

The Angel of the Lord had both feet on
   this final step and sat upon the sill
   which seemed made of some adamantine stone.   105

With great good will my Master guided me
   up the three steps and whispered in my ear:
   "Now beg him humbly that he turn the key."   108

Devoutly prostrate at his holy feet,
   I begged in mercy's name to be let in,
   but first three times upon my breast I beat.   111

Seven *P*'s, the seven scars of sin,
   his sword point cut into my brow. He said:
   "Scrub off these wounds when you have passed
                                    within."   114

Color of ashes, of parched earth one sees
   deep in an excavation, were his vestments,
   and from beneath them he drew out two keys.   117

One was of gold, one silver. He applied
   the white one to the gate first, then the yellow,
   and did with them what left me satisfied.   120

"Whenever either of these keys is put
   improperly in the lock and fails to turn it,"
   the Angel said to us, "the door stays shut.   123

One is more precious. The other is so wrought
   as to require the greater skill and genius,
   for it is that one which unties the knot.   126

They are from Peter, and he bade me be
   more eager to let in than to keep out
   whoever cast himself prostrate before me."   129

Then opening the sacred portals wide:
   "Enter. But first be warned: do not look back
   or you will find yourself once more outside."   132

The Tarpeian rock-face, in that fatal hour
   that robbed it of Metellus, and then the treasure,
   did not give off so loud and harsh a roar   135

as did the pivots of the holy gate—
   which were of resonant and hard-forged metal—
   when they turned under their enormous weight.   138

At the first thunderous roll I turned half-round,
   for it seemed to me I heard a chorus singing
   Te deum laudamus mixed with that sweet sound.   141

I stood there and the strains that reached my ears
   left on my soul exactly that impression
   a man receives who goes to church and hears   144

the choir and organ ringing out their chords
   and now does, now does not, make out the words.

NOTES

1–9. There is no wholly satisfactory explanation of this complex
opening description. Dante seems to be saying that the third hour of

darkness is beginning (hence, if sunset occurred at 6:00 it is now a bit after 8:00 P.M.) and that the aurora of the rising moon is appearing above the horizon.

He describes the moon as the concubine of Tithonus. Tithonus, however, married the daughter of the sun, Aurora (dawn), and it was she who begged Jove to give her husband immortality while forgetting to ask perpetual youth for him. Thus Tithonus lived but grew older and older beside his ageless bride. (In one legend he was later changed into a grasshopper.) Despite his advanced years, however, he seems here to be philandering with the moon as his concubine. Dante describes the moon as rising from Tithonus' bed and standing on the balcony of the East (the horizon) with the constellation Scorpio gemmed on her forehead, that "cold [blooded] beast whose sting is in his tail" being the scorpion.

Having given Tithonus a double life, Dante now adds a mixed metaphor in which the "steps" of the night have "wings." Two of the steps (hours) have flown, and the third has just completed the first downstroke of its wings (i.e., has just begun its flight).

15. *former woes:* Tereus, the husband of Procne, raped her sister Philomela, and cut out her tongue so that she could not accuse him. Philomela managed to communicate the truth to Procne by means of her weaving. The two sisters thereupon took revenge by killing Itys, son of Procne and Tereus, and serving up his flesh to his father. Tereus, learning the truth, was about to kill the sisters when all were turned into birds. Ovid (*Metamorphoses* VI, 424 ff.) has Tereus changed into a hoopoe, and probably (though the text leaves some doubt) Procne into a swallow and Philomela into a nightingale. Dante clearly takes the swallow to be Philomela.

18. *prophetic in its vision:* (Cf. *Inferno* XXVI, 7.) It was an ancient belief that the dreams that came toward dawn were prophetic.

19–33. DANTE'S DREAM. Each of Dante's three nights on the Mount of Purgatory ends with a dream that comes just before dawn. The present dream is relatively simple in its symbolism, and as we learn shortly after Dante's awakening, it parallels his ascent of the mountain in the arms of Lucia. The dream is told, however, with such complexities of allusion that every reference must be carefully weighed.

To summarize the symbolism in the simplest terms, the Golden Eagle may best be rendered in its attributes. It comes from highest Heaven (from God), its feathers are pure gold (Love? God's splendor?), its wings are outspread (the open arms of Divine Love?), and it appears poised to descend in an instant (as is Divine Grace). The Eagle snatches Dante up to the Sphere of Fire (the presence of God? the beginning of Purgatorial purification? both?), and both are so consumed by the fire that Dante, in his unpurified state, cannot bear it.

On another level, of course, the Eagle is Lucia (Divine Light), who has descended from Heaven, and who bears the sleeping Dante from the Flowering Valley to the beginning of the true Purgatory. Note that Lucia is an anagram for *acuila,* "eagle."

On a third level, the dream simultaneously connects with the earlier reference to Ganymede, also snatched up by the eagle of God, but the two experiences are contrasted as much as they are compared. Ganymede was carried up by Jove's eagle, Dante by Lucia. Ganymede was out hunting in the company of his worldly associates; Dante was laboring for grace, had renounced worldliness, and was in the company of great souls who were themselves awaiting purification. Ganymede was carried to Olympus; Dante to the beginning of a purification which, though he was still too unworthy to endure it, would in time make him a perfect servant of the true God. Thus, his experience is in the same pattern as Ganymede's, but surpasses it as Faith surpasses Human Reason, and as Beatrice surpasses Virgil.

23. *Ganymede:* Son of Tros, the mythical founder of Troy, was reputedly the most beautiful of mortals, so beautiful that Jove sent an eagle (or perhaps went himself in the form of an eagle) to snatch up the boy and bring him to Heaven, where he became cupbearer to the gods. The fact that Dante himself is about to begin the ascent of Purgatory proper (and hence to Heaven) inevitably suggests an allegory of the soul in the history of Ganymede. God calls to Himself what is most beautiful in man.

The fact that Dante always thought of the Trojans as an especially chosen people is also relevant (*cf. Inferno* II, 13–30 and note). Ganymede was the son of the founder of Troy; Troy, in Dante's Virgilian view, founded Rome. And through the Church of Rome men's souls were enabled to mount to Heaven.

24. *consistory:* Here, the council of the gods on Olympus. Dante uses the same term to describe Paradise (*Paradiso* XXIX, 67).

30. *Sphere of Fire:* The four elemental substances are earth, water, fire, and air. In Dante's cosmography, the Sphere of Fire was located above the Sphere of Air and just under the Sphere of the Moon. Hence the eagle bore him to the top of the atmosphere. The Sphere of Fire, however, may also be taken as another symbol for God.

34–39. ACHILLES' WAKING. It had been prophesied that Achilles would be killed at Troy. Upon the outbreak of the Trojan War, his mother, Thetis, stole him while he was sleeping, from the care of the centaur Chiron who was his tutor (see *Inferno* XII, 71 ff.) and fled with him to Scyros, where she hid him disguised as a girl. He was found there and lured away by Ulysses and Diomede, who burn for that sin (among others) in Malebolge (see *Inferno* XXVI, 56–63, and note). Thus Achilles, like Dante, was borne off in his sleep and awoke to find himself in a strange place.

51. *that opening:* The Gate, as the Poets will find, is closed and guarded. Dante (here and in line 62, below) can only mean "the opening in which the gate was set" and not "an open entrance." At this distance, they do not see the Gate itself but only the gap in the otherwise solid wall.

55. *Lucia* (Loo–TCHEE–ya): Symbolizes Divine Light, Divine Grace. (See *Inferno* II, 97, and note.).

77. *three steps:* (See also lines 94–102, below.) The entrance into Purgatory involves the ritual of the Roman Catholic confessional with the Angel serving as the confessor. The three steps are the three acts of the perfect confession: candid confession (mirroring the whole man), mournful contrition, and burning gratitude for God's mercy. The Angel Guardian, as the priestly confessor, does not move or speak as the Poets approach, because he can admit to purification only those who ask for admission.

86. *Where is your Guide?* It must follow from the Angel's question that souls ready to enter Purgatory are led up the mountain by

another Angel. Dante and Virgil are arriving in an irregular way, as they did to the shore below, where they were asked essentially the same question by Cato. Note, too, that Virgil answers for the Poets, as he did to Cato. The allegory may be that right thinking answers for a man, at least to start with, though the actual entrance into the state of Grace requires an act of Faith and of Submission.

90. *told us:* Lucia spoke only with her eyes, and what Virgil is quoting is her look. What he is quoting is, in essence, correct, but it does seem he could have been a bit more accurate in his first actual conversation with an Angel.

94–96. *the first step:* Contrition of the heart. White for purity, shining for hope, and flawless for perfection. It is not only the mirror of the soul, but it is that mirror in which the soul sees itself as it truly is and not in its outward seeming.

97–99. *the second:* Contrition of the mouth, i.e., confession. The color of a bruise for the shame that envelopes the soul as it confesses, rough-grained and fire-flaked for the pain the confessant must endure, and cracked for the imperfection (sin) the soul confesses.

100–102. *the third:* Satisfaction by works. Red for the ardor that leads to good works. Porphyry is, of course, a purple stone, but Dante does not say the stone was porphyry; only that it resembled it, though red in color.

"Artery" here is, of course, an anachronism, the circulation of the blood having yet to be discovered in Dante's time. Dante uses the word *vena* (vein), but it seems to me the anachronism will be less confusing to a modern reader than would be the idea of bright red and spurting venous blood.

103–105. The Angel, as noted, represents the confessor, and, more exactly, the Church Confessant. Thus the Church is founded on adamant and rests its feet on Good Works.

112. *Seven* P's: P is for the Latin *peccatum.* Thus there is one P for each of the Seven Deadly Sins for which the sinners suffer on the seven ledges above: Pride, Envy, Wrath, Acedia (Sloth), Avarice (Hoarding and Prodigality), Gluttony, and Lust.

Dante has just completed the act of confession and the Angel confessor marks him to indicate that even in a shriven soul there remain traces of the seven sins which can be removed only by suffering.

115–117. *Color of ashes, of parched earth:* The colors of humility which befit the office of the confessor. *two keys:* (*Cf.* the Papal Seal, which is a crown above two crossed keys, and also *Inferno* XXVII, 99–102.) The keys symbolize the power of the confessor (the Church, and hence the Pope) to grant or withhold absolution. In the present context they may further be interpreted as the two parts of the confessor's office of admission: the gold key may be taken to represent his ordained authority, the silver key as the learning and reflection with which he must weigh the guilt before assigning penance and offering absolution.

126. *unties the knot:* Another mixed metaphor. The soul-searched judgment of the confessor (the silver key) decides who may and who may not receive absolution, and in resolving that problem the door is opened, provided that the gold key of ordained authority has already been turned.

133–138. *The Tarpeian rock-face:* The public treasury of Rome was kept in the great scarp of Tarpeia on the Campidoglio. The tribune Metellus was its custodian when Caesar, returned to Rome after crossing the Rubicon, moved to seize the treasury. Metellus opposed him but was driven away and the great gates were opened. Lucan (*Pharsalia* III, 154–156 and 165–168) describes the scene and the roar that echoed from the rock face as the gates were forced open.

139–141. The thunder of the opening of the Gates notifies the souls within that a new soul has entered, and they burst into the hymn "We Praise Thee, O God." (Contrast these first sounds of Purgatory with the first sounds of Hell—*Inferno* III, 22–24.) Despite the thunderous roar right next to him, Dante seems to hear with his "allegorical ear" what certainly could not have registered upon his physical ear.

This seeming incongruity has long troubled me. I owe Professor MacAllister a glad thanks for what is certainly the essential clarification. The whole *Purgatorio,* he points out, is built upon the structure of a Mass. The Mass moreover is happening not on the mountain but in church with Dante devoutly following its well-known steps. I have not yet had time to digest Professor MacAllister's suggestion, but it strikes me immediately as a true insight and promises another illuminating way of reading the *Purgatorio*.

CANTO X

The Needle's Eye

The First Cornice—The Proud

THE WHIP OF PRIDE

The gate closes behind them and the Poets begin the ascent to
The First Cornice through a tortuous passage that Dante describes
as a *Needle's Eye.* They reach the Cornice about 9:00 or 10:00 of
Monday morning.

At first the Cornice seems deserted. Dante's eye is caught by
a series of three marvelously wrought bas-reliefs in the marble of
the inner cliff face. Three panels depict three scenes that serve as
The Whip of Pride, exemplifying to each sinner as he enters how
far greater souls have put by far greater reasons for pride in order
to pursue the grace of humility.

As Dante stands in admiration before the carvings, Virgil calls
his attention to a band of souls approaching from the left, and
Dante turns for his first sight of the souls of *The Proud,* who crawl
agonizingly round and round the Cornice under the crushing
weight of enormous slabs of rock. Their punishment is so simple
and so terrible that Dante can scarcely bear to describe it. He
cries out in anguish to the proud of this world to take heed of
the nature of their sin and of its unbearable punishment.

When we had crossed the threshold of that gate
  so seldom used because man's perverse love
  so often makes the crooked path seem straight,   3

I knew by the sound that it had closed again;
  and had I looked back, to what water ever
  could I have gone to wash away that stain?   6

We climbed the rock along a narrow crack
  through which a zigzag pathway pitched and slid
  just as a wave swells full and then falls back.   9

"This calls for careful judgment," said my guide.
  "Avoid the places where the rock swells up
  and weave among the troughs from side to side."   12

Our steps became so difficult and few,
  the waning moon had reached its western bed
  and sunk to rest before we could work through   15

that needle's eye. But when we had won clear
  to an open space above, at which the mountain
  steps back to form a ledge, we halted there;   18

I tired, and both of us confused for lack
  of any sign or guide. The ledge was level,
  and lonelier even than a desert track.   21

From brink to cliff-face measured three men's height,
  and the Cornice did not vary in its width
  as far as I could see to left or right.   24

Our feet had not yet moved a step up there,
  when I made out that all the inner cliff
  which rose without a foothold anywhere   27

was white and flawless marble and adorned
  with sculptured scenes beside which Polyclitus',
  and even Nature's, best works would be scorned.   30

The Angel who came down from God to man
  with the decree of peace the centuries wept for,
  which opened Heaven, ending the long ban,   33

stood carved before us with such force and love,
  with such a living grace in his whole pose,
  the image seemed about to speak and move.   36

One could have sworn an *Ave!* sounded clear,
  for she who turned the key that opened to us
  the Perfect Love, was also figured there;   39

and all her flowing gesture seemed to say—
  impressed there as distinctly as a seal
  impresses wax—*Ecce ancilla Dei.*   42

"Do not give all your thoughts to this one part,"
  my gentle Master said. (I was then standing
  on that side of him where man has his heart.)   45

I turned my eyes a little to the right
  (the side on which he stood who had thus urged me)
  and there, at Mary's back, carved in that white   48

and flawless wall, I saw another scene,
  and I crossed in front of Virgil and drew near it
  the better to make out what it might mean.   51

Emerging from the marble were portrayed
  the cart, the oxen, and the Ark from which
  the sacrilegious learned to be afraid.   54

Seven choirs moved there before it, bringing
  confusion to my senses; with my hearing
  I thought "No," with my sight, "Yes, they are singing." 57

In the same way, the smokes the censers poured
  were shown so faithfully that eyes and nose
  disputed yes and no in happy discord.   60

And there before the Holy Vessel, dancing
  with girt-up robes, the humble Psalmist moved,
  less than a king, and more, in his wild prancing.   63

Facing him, portrayed with a vexed frown
  of mingled sadness and contempt, Michal
  stood at a palace window looking down.   66

I moved a little further to the right,
  the better to observe another panel
  that shone at Michal's back, dazzling and white.   69

Here was portrayed from glorious history
  that Roman Prince whose passion to do justice
  moved Gregory to his great victory.   72

I speak of Trajan, blessed Emperor.
  And at his bridle was portrayed a widow
  in tears wept from the long grief of the poor.   75

Filling the space on both sides and behind
  were mounted knights on whose great golden
                                        banners
  the eagles seemed to flutter in the wind.   78

The widow knelt and by consummate art
  appeared to say: "My Lord, avenge my son
  for he is slain and I am sick at heart."   81

And he to answer: "Justice shall be done;
  wait only my return." And she: "My Lord"—
  speaking from the great grief that urged her on—   84

"If you do not?" And he: "Who wears my crown
  will right your wrong." And she: "Can the good deed
  another does grace him who shuns his own?"   87

And he, then: "Be assured. For it is clear
  this duty is to do before I go.
  Justice halts me, pity binds me here."   90

The Maker who can never see or know
  anything new, produced that "visible speaking":
  new to us, because not found below.   93

As I stood relishing the art and thought
  of those high images—dear in themselves,
  and dearer yet as works His hand had wrought—   96

the poet said: "Look there: they seem to crawl
  but those are people coming on our left:
  they can tell us where to climb the wall."   99

My eyes, always intent to look ahead
  to some new thing, finding delight in learning,
  lost little time in doing as he said.   102

Reader, I would not have you be afraid,
  nor turn from your intention to repent
  through hearing how God wills the debt be paid.   105

Do not think of the torments: think, I say,
  of what comes after them: think that at worst
  they cannot last beyond the Judgment Day.   108

"Master," I said, "those do not seem to me
  people approaching us; nor do I know—
  they so confuse my sight—what they may be."   111

And he to me: "Their painful circumstance
  doubles them to the very earth: my own eyes
  debated what they saw there at first glance.   114

Look hard and you will see the people pressed
  under the moving boulders there. Already
  you can make out how each one beats his breast."   117

O you proud Christians, wretched souls and small,
  who by the dim lights of your twisted minds
  believe you prosper even as you fall—   120

can you not see that we are worms, each one
  born to become the Angelic butterfly
  that flies defenseless to the Judgment Throne?   123

What have your souls to boast of and be proud?
  You are no more than insects, incomplete
  as any grub until it burst the shroud.   126

Sometimes at roof or ceiling-beam one sees
  a human figure set there as a corbel,
  carved with its chest crushed in by its own knees, 129

so cramped that what one sees imagined there
  makes his bones ache in fact—just such a sense
  grew on me as I watched those souls with care.   132

True, those who crawled along that painful track
  were more or less distorted, each one bent
  according to the burden on his back;   135

yet even the most patient, wracked and sore,
  seemed to be groaning: "I can bear no more!"

NOTES

2. *perverse love:* All human actions, in Dante's view, are motivated
by love: right love produces good actions and perverse love produces
bad. Virgil discusses this concept in detail in XVII, 103 ff.

7–12. THE NEEDLE'S EYE. "It is easier for a camel to pass
through the eye of a needle than for a rich man to enter into the
kingdom of God." (*Matthew* xix, 24, and *Mark* xx, 25. See also *Luke*

xvii, 25.) I understand Dante to mean here that there shall be no passage to purification without the ardor of the spirit that strips a man of worldliness. Once again, as in the first climb at the very foot of the mountain, the beginning is the most difficult part of the ascent.

14. *waning moon:* The moon had been full on the night before Good Friday (*Inferno* XX, 127). It is now four and a half days later. In two and a half more days it will be a half moon.

15. *sunk to rest:* The moon rose sometime after 8:00 P.M., perhaps closer to 9:00, as described at the beginning of Canto X. It would set about twelve hours later. But Dante says it has *already* set. It is, therefore, sometime after 8:00 A.M. But to assume that it has just set, would make it only two hours after sunrise, and would mark the hour of Dante's awakening outside the Gate. The passage, moreover, was a slow one. Something between 9:00 and 10:00 A.M. would, therefore, seem to be a reasonable time for Dante's emergence on the first ledge. See XII, 80–81, note.

22–24. The turns of Dante's style and the natural tendency of Italian to use more syllables than does English in stating a similar thought, sometimes make it desirable to render six lines of Dante into three of English. I have so rendered it here. A literal translation of the original would read: "From its edge where it borders the void, to the foot of the high bank which rises again, would measure three times a human body; and as far as my eyes could extend their flight either to the left or to the right side, this Cornice seemed to me to be that [wide]."

26 ff. THE WHIP AND THE REIN. At the entrance to each Cornice, Dante presents high examples of the virtue opposite the sin punished on that Cornice. Their purpose is clearly to whip the souls on to emulation. The form in which these examples are presented varies from Cornice to Cornice, but the examples are usually three, and the first of them is always taken from the life of the Virgin.

At the end of the passage of each Cornice, also in various forms, Dante presents examples of the terrible price one must pay for succumbing to each particular sin. The opening exhortations designed to drive the souls on to emulation may be called the Whip of each sin; the closing examples, or admonitions, may be called the Rein, serving to check the impulse toward that sin. See XIII, 39–40.

29. *Polyclitus:* Greek sculptor of the late fifth century B.C., contemporary with Phidias. His name seems to have been the word for artistic perfection during the late Middle Ages and early Renaissance, probably because he is often mentioned by Aristotle.

31–90. THE WHIP OF PRIDE. It consists of three bas-relief panels carved on the inner cliff-face, each panel portraying a scene of great humility, humility being, of course, the virtue opposite pride.

The first panel (lines 31–42) depicts the Annunciation. The angel Gabriel appears to Mary, bringing the word of her great election, and Mary, untouched by pride, answers in her great hour, *Ecce ancilla Dei,* "Behold the handmaiden of God." (*Luke* i, 38.) *the key:* Christ.

The second panel (lines 49–66) depicts King David putting aside all the offices of majesty to dance in humility and total abandonment before the Lord (see *II Samuel* vi, 14) on bringing the Ark to Jerusalem from the house of the Gittite, Obed-edom. Dante has confused, or deliberately blended, two scenes into one. The first journey of the Ark began with an ox-drawn cart and it was then that Uzzah (an example of overweening pride) was struck dead for laying unsanctified hands upon the Ark, a sacrilegious act. (See *II Samuel* vi, 6–7.) David laid up the Ark in the house of the Gittite and returned for it three months later, on which occasion it was carried to Jerusalem by the Levites. It was on the second journey that David put by his majesty to dance before the Lord. Michal, daughter of King Saul, and David's first wife, looked on scornfully and was punished for her arrogance by sterility: "therefore Michal the daughter of Saul had no child unto the day of her death." (*II Samuel* vi, 23.)

The third panel (lines 70–90) depicts the Emperor Trajan halting his royal cavalry en route to battle and dismounting in order to secure justice for a poor woman. Dante places Trajan in *Paradiso* XX, his soul according to legend having been summoned back to earth and baptized by St. Gregory.

100 ff. THE PUNISHMENT OF THE PROUD. The simple and terrible penance of these souls is that each must crawl round and round the Cornice bearing enormous slabs of rock that press him down, each according to the degree of his sin. The higher a soul tried to raise itself in its pride, the more it is crushed to earth. For pride is a weight of worldliness and bears down the spirit, and therefore it is crushed under the rock of the earth. It is, moreover, the primal sin and the father of all other sins, for the proud man seeks to set himself up as God, and therefore his soul, here, is crushed agonizingly into the very dust until it has suffered itself clean and may rise free of the weight it has placed upon itself.

CANTO XI

The First Cornice—The Proud

As the souls of the Proud creep near, the Poets hear them recite a long and humble prayer based on the Paternoster. When the prayer is ended, Virgil asks one of the souls, hidden from view under its enormous burden, the way to the ascent. The sinner, who identifies himself as *Omberto Aldobrandesco,* instructs the Poets to follow along in the direction the souls are crawling. He recites his history in brief, and it becomes clear that Dante means him to exemplify *Pride of Birth.* The conversation between Dante and Omberto is overheard by *Oderisi d'Agobbio,* who turns in pain and speaks to Dante, explaining his sin of *Pride of Talent,* the avidity of the artist for pre-eminence. Oderisi also points out the soul that struggles along just ahead of him as *Provenzano Salvani,* once war lord of Siena, who is being punished for *Pride of Temporal Power,* though he has been advanced toward his purification in recognition of a single *Act of Great Humility* performed in order to save the life of a friend.

Oderisi concludes with a *Dark Prophecy of Dante's Exile* from Florence.

Our Father in Heaven, not by Heaven bounded
but there indwelling for the greater love
Thou bear'st Thy first works in the realm first-founded,   3

hallowed be Thy name, hallowed Thy Power
by every creature as its nature grants it
to praise Thy quickening breath in its brief hour.   6

Let come to us the sweet peace of Thy reign,
for if it come not we cannot ourselves
attain to it however much we strain.   9

And as Thine Angels kneeling at the throne
  offer their wills to Thee, singing Hosannah,
  so teach all men to offer up their own.   12

Give us this day Thy manna, Lord we pray,
  for if he have it not, though man most strive
  through these harsh wastes, his speed is his delay.   15

As we forgive our trespassers the ill
  we have endured, do Thou forgive, not weighing
  our merits, but the mercy of Thy will.   18

Our strength is as a reed bent to the ground:
  do not Thou test us with the Adversary,
  but deliver us from him who sets us round.   21

This last petition, Lord, with grateful mind,
  we pray not for ourselves who have no need,
  but for the souls of those we left behind.   24

—So praying godspeed for themselves and us,
  those souls were crawling by under such burdens
  as we at times may dream of. Laden thus,   27

unequally tormented, weary, bent,
  they circled the First Cornice round and round,
  purging away the world's foul sediment.   30

If they forever speak our good above,
  what can be done for their good here below
  by those whose will is rooted in God's love?   33

Surely, we should help those souls grow clear
  of time's deep stain, that each at last may issue
  spotless and weightless to his starry sphere.   36

"Ah, so may Justice and pity soon remove
   the load you bear, that you may spread your wings
   and rise rejoicing to the Perfect Love—   39

help us to reach the stairs the shortest way,
   and should there be more than one passage, show us
   the one least difficult to climb, I pray;   42

for my companion, who is burdened still
   with Adam's flesh, grows weak in the ascent,
   though to climb ever higher is all his will."   45

I heard some words in answer to my Lord's,
   but could not tell which of those souls had spoken,
   nor from beneath which stone. These were the words: 48

"Your way is to the right, along with ours.
   If you will come with us, you will discover
   a pass within a living person's powers.   51

And were I not prevented by the stone
   that masters my stiff neck and makes me keep
   my head bowed to the dust as I move on,   54

I would look up, hoping to recognize
   this living and still nameless man with you,
   and pray to find compassion in his eyes.   57

I was Italian. A Tuscan of great fame—
   Guglielmo Aldobrandesco—was my father.
   I do not know if you have heard the name.   60

My ancient lineage and the hardihood
   my forebears showed in war, went to my head.
   With no thought that we all share the one blood   63

of Mother Eve, I scorned all others so
  I died for it; as all Siena knows,
  and every child in Campagnatico.   66

I am Omberto, and my haughty ways
  were not my ruin alone, but brought my house
  and all my followers to evil days.   69

Here until God be pleased to raise my head
  I bear this weight. Because I did not do so
  among the living, I must among the dead."   72

I had bowed low, better to know his state,
  when one among them—not he who was speaking—
  twisted around beneath his crushing weight,   75

saw me, knew me, and cried out. And so
  he kept his eyes upon me with great effort
  as I moved with those souls, my head bowed low.   78

"Aren't you Od'risi?" I said. "He who was known
  as the honor of Agobbio, and of that art
  Parisians call *illumination*?"   81

"Brother," he said, "what pages truly shine
  are Franco Bolognese's. The real honor
  is all his now, and only partly mine.   84

While I was living, I know very well,
  I never would have granted him first place,
  so great was my heart's yearning to excel.   87

Here pride is paid for. Nor would I have been
  among these souls, had I not turned to God
  while I still had in me the power to sin.   90

O gifted men, vainglorious for first place,
  how short a time the laurel crown stays green
  unless the age that follows lacks all grace!   93

Once Cimabue thought to hold the field
  in painting, and now Giotto has the cry
  so that the other's fame, grown dim, must yield.   96

So from one Guido has another shorn
  poetic glory, and perhaps the man
  who will un-nest both is already born.   99

A breath of wind is all there is to fame
  here upon earth: it blows this way and that,
  and when it changes quarter it changes name.   102

Though loosed from flesh in old age, will you have
  in, say, a thousand years, more reputation
  than if you went from child's play to the grave?   105

What, to eternity, is a thousand years?
  Not so much as the blinking of an eye
  to the turning of the slowest of the spheres.   108

All Tuscany once sounded with the fame
  of this one who goes hobbling on before me;
  now, one hears scarce a whisper of his name,   111

even in Siena, where he was in power
  when he destroyed the rage of Florence (then,
  as much a shrew as she is now a whore).   114

The fame of man is like the green of grass:
  it comes, it goes; and He by whom it springs
  bright from earth's plenty makes it fade and pass."   117

And I to him: "These truths bend my soul low
  from swollen pride to sweet humility.
  But who is he of whom you spoke just now?"   120

"That's Provenzan Salvani, and the stone
  is on him," he replied, "for his presumption
  in making all Siena his alone.   123

So he goes on and has gone since his death,
  without a pause. Such coin must one pay here
  for being too presumptuous on earth."   126

And I: "But if the souls that do not mend
  their sinful ways until the brink of life,
  must wait below before they can ascend   129

(unless the prayers of those whom God holds dear
  come to their aid) the period of their lives—
  how was he given license to be here?"   132

"At the peak of his life's glory," said the ghost,
  "in the Campo of Siena, willingly,
  and putting by all pride, he took his post;   135

and there, to free his dear friend from the pains
  he suffered in the dungeons of King Charles,
  stood firm, although he trembled in his veins.   138

I say no more; and though you well may feel
  I speak in riddles, it will not be long
  before your neighbors' actions will reveal   141

all you need know to fathom what I say.
  —It was this good work spared him his delay."

NOTES

1–24. THE PRAYER OF THE PROUD. The sinners on each cornice of Purgatory recite a prayer appropriate to their particular penance. The prayer spoken by the souls under the stones is, of course, an extended form of the Lord's Prayer, and Dante's choice of it must be understood by its relevance to the sin of Pride.

The Lord's Prayer is so basic to Christian practice, and so much the possession of every Christian child, that its very nature as a primer of the creed must explain its first relevance here. If Pride is seen as a blind and arrogant assertion of secondary things (self, power, family name, talent, etc.), it follows that such a wrong emphasis on what is secondary can only be arrived at by ignoring what is primary. It is in these terms, I believe, that Dante's intent can be best grasped. The proud must begin over again as children, learning the first expression of the first principles of faith. It is exactly relevant that the first child's prayer is also the most central to Christian belief. Note, moreover, that every petition of the prayer is for the grace of humility and subservience to God's will, and that the last petition is for the good of others.

1–3. *Our Father . . . not by Heaven bounded:* God lives in Heaven by choice, not in confinement. He is drawn to Heaven by the greater love (greater than His love for man) he bears his first works (the Angels) in His first realm (Heaven).

6. *Thy quickening breath:* The breath of life.

21. *but deliver us from him:* In the original form, the Lord's Prayer reads "Deliver us from the Evil One."

22–24. *This last petition:* The last petition is for deliverance from the Evil One. It is obviously not needed by the souls in Purgatory proper, since they are no longer subject to temptation, but is offered up (a happy instance of concern for others) for the souls of those left behind on earth, and perhaps also in Ante-Purgatory.

25. *us:* Refers not to the Poets but to all mankind.

28. *unequally tormented:* As Dante has already indicated (X, 134–135) the burdens of the sinners varied according to the degree of their sin.

30. *the world's foul sediment:* The traces of pride and worldliness surviving in each soul.

33. *by those . . . God's love:* No other prayer helps. *Cf.* Belacqua, IV, 130–135.

43. *for my companion, who is burdened still:* Virgil's famous tact hardly shines brilliantly in begging these souls, bowed as they are under their enormous loads, to help Dante so heavily burdened with his own flesh.

47. *could not tell which of those souls had spoken:* It must be remembered that Dante and Virgil are standing above the souls, who are bent to the ground under slabs of stone that must, in some cases at least, completely hide them from sight.

53. *stiff neck:* A recurring biblical figure for pride and obstinacy. *Cf. Acts* vii, 51: "Ye stiffnecked and uncircumcised in heart and ears." (An interesting piece of language.) See also *Exodus* xxxii, 9, and xxxiii, 3, 5.

58–72. THE ALDOBRANDESCHI. Guglielmo Aldobrandesco (Gool-YELL-mo Ahl-doe-brahnd-ESS-coe) was a powerful Ghibelline of the Sienese Maremma, and Count of Santafiora, the district Dante has already cited as a lawless robber-barony. Little is known of Omberto, and such accounts as there are contradict one another, though all agree that he was excessively proud of his lineage. The Aldobrandeschi were in constant conflict with Siena. In 1259, according to varying accounts, the Sienese either besieged the Aldobrandeschi castle in Campagnatico (Cahm-pahn-YAH-tee-coe), killing Omberto in battle, or their agents crept in and strangled Omberto in bed. Since Dante refers to it (line 66) as an event known to every child, he was probably following the account in which Omberto, though with very few men at his disposal, scorned his enemies, refused to surrender, killed many Sienese, and even made a mad charge into the thick of the enemy's forces, where he was killed after giving a bloody account of himself. Omberto's words seem to indicate that his main motive in this action was utter contempt for those who opposed him. Thus (lines 64–65) his scorn was so great that he died for it.

Omberto's death broke the power of the Aldobrandeschi, their rule passing to the Sienese. Thus (lines 67–69) his pride destroyed not only Omberto but all of his line and its adherents.

60. *I do not know if you have heard the name:* One of those Dantean touches that must not be missed. As Omberto goes on to say, he was, while alive, overweeningly proud of his father's fame. The proud mention of him may, thus, be taken as a relapse into his besetting sin. He immediately covers it with a deliberate act of modesty, as if to say, "You probably never heard of him." The fact is that everyone in Italy would have known of Guglielmo Aldobrandesco.

73. *I had bowed low, better to know his state:* I think Dante intends an ambiguity here. He had bowed low physically better to hear Omberto, and he had bowed low in the spirit of humility better to experience the state of those who purify themselves of pride by making themselves humble. Line 78 reinforces this second meaning.

79. *Od'risi:* Oderisi d'Agobbio. Agobbio or Gubbio is a small city in Umbria, and was known to the Romans as Eugubium. Oderisi was a famous illuminator of manuscripts and a miniaturist. He is reputed to have illuminated many Vatican manuscripts on Papal commission. He probably died in Rome in 1299, though the record is not certain.

As Omberto typifies pride of lineage, Oderisi typifies the pride of the artist avid for reputation. Dante's praise of him may be a test to see how a Proud-one so recently dead (within the year) would respond.

83. *Franco Bolognese* (Bo-lo-NYEA-zeh): Oderisi's student. He was alive in 1300 (hence the "now" of line 84). A few mentions of his name and some disputed traces of his work still exist, but the words Dante puts into Oderisi's mouth will have to explain themselves, there being no other record.

Note especially that Dante cites little-known artists working in what is generally considered to be a minor art. He could, of course, have demonstrated artistic pride in artists of much greater stature, but his point is certainly the more strongly made when he presents great pride swelling in little men.

86–87. *I never would have granted him first place:* Oderisi may mean that in his lifetime he so desired to excel that he would have labored for greater mastery and so have wrested first place from his student. In context, however, the far more likely meaning is that he was then too proud to admit what he now, in his new-found humility, well knows.

88–90. *Nor would I have been among these souls:* Oderisi would still have been in Ante-Purgatory enduring his delay had he waited for a deathbed repentence. *while I still had in me the power to sin:* While I was yet alive.

91–93. The difficulty of Dante's condensed way of speaking is here compounded by his easy way with mixed metaphors. Sense: "O talented men [of arts, crafts, government, and every human attainment], what a vanity it is to seek to be known as foremost in your field! How short a while the laurel crown stays green, unless the age that succeeds you is graceless [*i.e.,* lacks the talent to produce rivals who will excel you]."

94. *Cimabue:* Giovanni dei Cimabui (Joe-VAH-nee day Tcheem-ah-BOO-ee), 1240?–1308. He was esteemed by his Florentine contemporaries as the master painter. His particular innovation was in liberating painting from strict Byzantine domination in favor of a more natural style. If he is no longer hailed as a supreme master, succeeding ages have generally been aware of his genius.

95. *Giotto* (DJAW-toe): A shepherd boy who became Cimabue's pupil and who went on to excel his teacher, becoming the true father of the Renaissance tradition of painting from nature. He was probably a friend of Dante's. The most familiar portrait of Dante is one commonly, but uncertainly, attributed to Giotto.

97–99. THE TWO GUIDOS. The first is Guido (GWEE-doe) Cavalcanti (1250?–1300), a fellow poet whom Dante saluted in the *Vita Nuova* as "he whom I call first among my friends." (See also *Inferno* X, 52 ff. for a different feeling toward him.) The other Guido, whose poetic glory was shorn by Cavalcanti, is generally taken to be Guido Guinizelli (Gwee-nee-TZELL-ee) of Bologna (died approx. 1275–1276).

Dante may mean himself by "the man who will un-nest them both," or he may be making a general statement. Good arguments can support either interpretation. If it is argued that Dante, his head bowed in humility and observing the terrible penance of the proud, would not be praising himself, it can as forcibly be shown that Dante has already (*Inferno* X, 52 ff.) asserted his poetical supremacy to Guido, ascribing it modestly to the fact that Guido did not give his whole devotion to the high models Dante took for his own.

108. *the turning of the slowest of the spheres:* The Ptolemaic cosmography attributed to the Sphere of the Fixed Stars a west-to-east rotation of 1 degree per 100 years, hence 36,000 years for one revolution. (See *Il Convivio* II, 6, lines 140–143.)

110. *this one:* Provenzano Salvani, the Ghibelline chief of Siena at the battle of Montaperti (see *Inferno* X, 85–87, 91–93, and note to 32–51). After the defeat of the Florentine forces, he led the cry for the destruction of Florence. In 1269 the Florentines defeated the Sienese at Colle di Val d'Elsa, and Salvani, taken prisoner, was beheaded on the field of battle.

116. *He:* God is constantly identified with the Sun in Dante. Here the identification is especially apt.

127–132. *But . . . how was he given license to be here?:* Salvani died, as noted, in 1269. He has, therefore, been dead thirty-one years. Dante assumes that he put off repentance till the end. Normally, therefore, he would have had to wait in Ante-Purgatory for a period equal to his lifetime, and though his exact age at death is not known, his normal delay would still have years to run. Dante asks the cause of this exception and Oderisi tells of an incident of great self-abasement that won special grace for Salvani. See below.

133–138. The incident here referred to is variously told, but the gist of it remains the same in all accounts. A friend of Salvani's was captured, probably by Charles of Anjou at Tagliacozza, and held for a great ransom to be paid within a month, failing which the friend would be executed. Salvani, despite his great pride, posted himself in the Piazza del Campo in Siena and begged alms to raise his friend's ransom. Whether beggars do especially well in Siena, or whether Salvani's action was the sort of thing we now call a "promotional campaign," the sum was made up and the friend freed.

Note how the law is still, as in Hell, an eye for an eye and a tooth for a tooth, but now in reverse: as ye merited, so shall ye be rewarded—with the additional boons that may be procured by the prayers of the pure in heart.

139–142. *I say no more:* Still another of the dark prophecies of impending exile Dante hears throughout his journey. (His "neighbors" are, of course, the Florentines. Their "actions" will be to exile him, thus forcing him to beg as did Salvani. Then only will he understand what it means to tremble in his veins.) Dante left Florence in 1301 and a decree of banishment was read against him in 1302. He never returned.

It is especially appropriate that Dante should be reminded of his banishment to beggary at just this point. Dante, as he makes clear later, was especially concerned about Pride as his own besetting sin. The reminder of his banishment serves aptly to humble him.

CANTO XII

The First Cornice—The Proud

THE REIN OF PRIDE · THE ANGEL OF HUMILITY

Virgil instructs Dante to arise from where he has been walking
bent beside Oderisi and to move on. Dante follows obediently,
and soon Virgil points out to him *The Rein of Pride* carved in thir-
teen scenes into the stone beneath their feet. The scenes portray
dreadful examples of the destruction that follows upon great
pride.

The Poets pass on and find *The Angel of Humility* approaching
to welcome them. The Angel strikes Dante's forehead with his
wings and, though Dante does not discover it till later, *The First
P* instantly disappears without a trace, symbolizing the purifica-
tion from the sin of Pride. The Poets pass on, up a narrow *Ascent
to the Second Cornice,* but though the way is narrow, Dante finds
it much easier than the first, since steps have been cut into it, and
since he is lighter by the weight of the first *P.* As they climb they
hear the first beatitude, *Beati pauperes spiritu,* ring out behind
them, sung by the Angel of Humility.

As oxen go in yoke—step matched, head bowed—
  I moved along beside that laden soul
  as long as the sweet pedagogue allowed.   3

But when he said: "Leave him his weary trail:
  here each must speed his boat as best he can
  urging it onward with both oars and sail"—   6

I drew myself again to the position
  required for walking: thus my body rose,
  but my thoughts were still bent double in contrition. 9

I was following my Guide, and we had put
   those laden souls behind us far enough
   to make it clear that we were light of foot,   12

when he said, without turning back his head:
   "Look down. You will find solace on the way
   in studying what pavement your feet tread."   15

In order that some memory survive
   of those who die, their slabs are often carved
   to show us how they looked while yet alive.   18

And often at the sight a thought will stir
   the passer-by to weep for what has been—
   though only the compassionate feel that spur.   21

Just so, but with a far more lifelike grace—
   they being divinely wrought—stone figures covered
   the track that jutted from the mountain's face.   24

Mark there, on one side, him who had been given
   a nobler form than any other creature.
   He plunged like lightning from the peak of Heaven.   27

Mark, on the other, lying on the earth,
   stricken by the celestial thunderbolt,
   Briareus, heavy with the chill of death.   30

Mark there, still armed, ranged at their father's side,
   Thymbraeus, Mars, and Pallas looking down
   at the Giants' severed limbs stewn far and wide.   33

Mark Nimrod at the foot of his great tower,
   bemused, confounded, staring at his people
   who shared at Shinar his mad dream of power.   36

Ah, Niobe! with what eyes wrung with pain
  I saw your likeness sculptured on that road
  between your seven and seven children slain!   39

Ah, Saul! how still you seemed to me, run through
  with your own sword, dead upon Mount Gilboa,
  which never after that felt rain nor dew.   42

Ah mad Arachne! so I saw you there—
  already half turned spider—on the shreds
  of what you wove to be your own despair.   45

Ah Rehoboam! your image in that place
  no longer menaces; a chariot bears it
  in panic flight, though no one gives it chase.   48

Now see Alcmaeon, there on the hard pavement,
  standing above her mother when she learned
  the full cost of the fatal ornament.   51

Now see there how his own sons fell upon
  Sennacherib at prayer within the temple,
  and how they left him dead when they were done.   54

Now see Tomyris bloody with her kill
  after the ruin she wrought, saying to Cyrus:
  "Your thirst was all for blood. Now drink your fill."   57

Now see how the Assyrians broke and ran
  from Israel after Holofernes' murder;
  and showed the slaughtered remnants of the man.   60

Mark Troy there in its ashes overthrown.
  Ah, Ilion! how lowly and how lost!
  Now see your hollow shell upon that stone!   63

What brush could paint, or etching-stylus draw
  such lineaments and shadings? At such skill
  the subtlest genius would have stared in awe.   66

The dead seemed dead, the living alive. A witness
  to the event itself saw it no better
  than I did, looking down there at its likeness.   69

Now swell with pride and cut your reckless swath
  with head held high, you sons of Eve, and never
  bow down to see the evil in your path!   72

We had, I found, gone round more of the mount,
  and the sun had run more of its daily course,
  than my bound soul had taken into account;   75

when Virgil, ever watchful, ever leading,
  commanded: "Lift your head. This is no time
  to be shut up in your own thoughts, unheeding.   78

Look there and see an Angel on his way
  to welcome us; and see—the sixth handmaiden
  returns now from her service to the day.   81

That he may gladly send us up the mountain,
  let reverence grace your gestures and your look.
  Remember, this day will not dawn again."   84

I was well used to his warnings to abjure
  all that delayed me from my good: on that point
  nothing he said to me could be obscure.   87

Toward us, dressed in white, and with a face
  serenely tremulous as the Morning Star,
  the glorious being came, radiant with Grace.   90

First his arms and then his wings spread wide.
  "Come," he said, "the stars are near, and now
  the way is easy up the mountainside.   93

Few, all too few, come answering to this call.
  O sons of man, born to ascend on high,
  how can so slight a wind-puff make you fall?"   96

Straight to where the rock was cut he led.
  There he struck my forehead with his wings,
  then promised us safe journeying ahead.   99

When a man has climbed the first slope toward the
                                              crown
  on which is built the church that overhangs
  at the Rubaconte, the well-managed town,   102

the abrupt ascent is softened on his right
  by steps cut in the rock in other days,
  before the stave and ledger had grown light—   105

just so the bank here, plunging like a slide
  from the Round above, has been made easier,
  though towering cliffs squeeze us from either side.   108

We set out on the climb, and on the way
  Beati pauperes spiritu rang out,
  more sweetly sung than any words could say.   111

Ah, what a difference between these trails
  and those of Hell: here every entrance fills
  with joyous song, and there with savage wails!   114

We were going up the holy steps, and though
  the climb was steep, I seemed to feel much lighter
  than I had felt on level ground below.   117

"Master," I said, tell me what heaviness
    has been removed from me that I can climb
    yet seem to feel almost no weariness."   120

He answered: "When the *P*'s that still remain,
    though fading, on your brow, are wiped away
    as the first was, without a trace of stain—   123

then will your feet be filled with good desire:
    not only will they feel no more fatigue
    but all their joy will be in mounting higher."   126

A man with some strange thing lodged on his hat
    will stroll, not knowing, till the stares of others
    set him to wonder what they're staring at: 129

whereat his hand seeks out and verifies
    what he suspected, thus performing for him
    the office he could not serve with his eyes—   132

just so, I put my right hand to my brow,
    fingers outspread, and found six letters only
    of those that had been carved there down below   135

by the Angel with the keys to every grace;
    at which a smile shone on my Master's face.

NOTES

3. *the sweet pedagogue:* Virgil.

5–6. *boat . . . oars and sail:* Virgil may simply be saying something
equivalent to "every man must do his utmost." More likely, however,
each item mentioned had some allegorical significance in Dante's
mind. Thus *boat* might equal "the will to grace"; *oars*, "the individ-
ual's own efforts"; and *sail,* "assistance from the prayers of others."

12. *light of foot:* Dante intends eagerness, of course. But one must remember that weight is always equated to sin. (See *Inferno* XXXII, 73, note.) Every step toward purification makes the soul lighter.

17. *slabs:* Dante specifically means a kind of gravestone rare in the United States but common in Europe and usually found in churches where the dead are sometimes buried under the pavement, their gravestones being set flush with the pavement and forming part of it.

25–63. THE REIN OF PRIDE. The Whip of Pride consisted of examples of great humility designed to whip the soul on to emulation. Now as the Poets leave the First Cornice, their souls made humble, they find set before them as a final lesson, examples of great Pride and of the downfall to which it brings men. Their thoughts are reined in and brought under God's control by a final reminder of what disasters they have escaped.

The present rein is elaborately conceived and consists of thirteen bas-reliefs cut into the pavement over which the souls pass. Dante's description of the first four panels begins with "I saw," of the next four, with "Oh!" and of the next four, with "It showed." In Italian these phrases are: *Vedea . . . O! . . . Mostrava.* Acrostically (*V* being equal to *U* in Latin), this combination reads *UOM,* i.e., "Man." The tercet describing the thirteenth panel repeats the three phrases in order at the beginning of each of the three lines. The pattern in the original reads, therefore: *UUUU, OOOO, MMMM, UOM.*

This elaborate structure is clearly intended to show not only that Pride is the first and heaviest of man's sins, but that it is so characteristic of him that PRIDE and MAN are practically synonymous.

25. *him:* Satan.

30. *Briareus:* One of the Titans (Giants) who now guard the central well of Hell. (See *Inferno* XXXI, 97–99, and note.) He stormed Olympus and tried to unseat Jupiter (as Satan tried to unseat God) but was felled by a thunderbolt.

31–33. *their father:* Jupiter. *Thymbraeus:* Apollo, so called after his temple at Thymbra. *Pallas:* Minerva. The scene portrays another repulse of the Titans in their effort to storm heaven, this time at Phlegra in Thessaly.

34–36. *Nimrod:* (See *Inferno,* XXXI, 77, note.) The first king of Babylon and builder of the Tower of Babel at Shinar. ". . . the Lord scattered them abroad from thence upon the face of all the earth; and they left off to build the city. Therefore is the name of it called Babel; because the Lord did there confound the language of all the earth." (*Genesis* xi, 8–9.)

37–39. *Niobe:* Had seven sons and seven daughters. In her pride, she mocked Latona, concubine of Jupiter, for having only one son (Apollo) and one daughter (Diana). Thereupon, Apollo took his bow and killed all the sons; Diana, hers and killed all the daughters. Dante follows Ovid's version of this happy little legend on the solaces of religion (*Metamorphoses* VI, 146–312).

40. *Saul:* The proud first king of Israel. Defeated by the Philistines on Mount Gilboa, he fell on his own sword to avoid capture (*I Samuel* xxxi, 4–5). David, mourning the death of Saul, cursed Mount Gilboa: "Ye mountains of Gilboa, let there be no dew, neither let there be rain upon you, nor fields of offerings." (*II Samuel* i, 21.)

43. *Arachne:* Her story runs much like that of the Pierides (I, 11, note). So proud was Arachne of her weaving that she boasted that it was superior to Minerva's. Minerva in disguise challenged her to a contest. Arachne presumed to disparage the gods in her tapestry and was changed into a spider by Minerva, who had portrayed the glory of the gods.

46–48. *Rehoboam:* The arrogant king of Israel who would not lighten the taxes of the ten tribes. He sent Adoram to collect the taxes, and when Adoram was stoned to death, Rehoboam fled in panic from Jerusalem, though no one pursued him (see *I Kings* xii, 1–18).

49–51. *Alcmaeon:* Son of Amphiareus, the Soothsayer (*Inferno* XX, 34, note). Through his arts, Amphiareus foresaw that he would die at Thebes, and to avoid having to go there he hid in a place known only to Eriphyle, his wife. Eriphyle accepted a gold necklace as a bribe for revealing his hiding place, whereupon Amphiareus instructed his son, Alcmaeon, to avenge him. The panel, therefore, would represent Alcmaeon killing his mother, her downfall being the result of vanity, which is, of course, a form of pride. The ornament (certainly a further moral) was, moreover, predestined to be

CANTO XIII

The Second Cornice—The Envious

THE WHIP OF ENVY

The Poets reach *The Second Cornice* and find the blue-black rock unadorned by carvings. There are no souls in sight to guide them and Virgil, therefore, turns toward the Sun as his Guide, *Bearing Right* around the Cornice.

As they walk on, Dante hears voices crying out examples of great love of others *(Caritas),* the virtue opposed to Envy. These voices are *The Whip of Envy.*

A short way beyond, Dante comes upon the souls of *The Envious* and describes *Their Punishment.* The Cornice on which they sit is the color of a bruise, for every other man's good fortune bruised the souls of the Envious. They offended with their eyes, envying all the good they saw of others, and therefore their eyes are wired shut. So blinded, they sit supporting one another, as they never did in life, and all of them lean for support against the blue-black cliff (God's Decree). They are dressed in haircloth, the further to subdue their souls, and they intone endlessly *The Litany of the Saints.*

Among them Dante encounters *Sapìa of Siena* and has her relate her story. When she questions him in turn, Dante confesses his fear of *His Own Besetting Sin,* which is Pride.

We climbed the stairs and stood, now, on the track
  where, for a second time, the mount that heals
  all who ascend it, had been terraced back.   3

The terrace circles the entire ascent
  in much the same way as the one below,
  save that the arc it cuts is sooner bent.   6

There were no spirits and no carvings there.
  Bare was the cliff-face, bare the level path.
  The rock of both was livid, dark and bare.   9

"Were we to wait till someone came this way
  who might direct us," Virgil said to me,
  "I fear that would involve a long delay."   12

Then he looked up and stared straight at the sun;
  and then, using his right side as a pivot,
  he swung his left around; then he moved on.   15

"O Blessed Lamp, we face the road ahead
  placing our faith in you: lead us the way
  that we should go in this new place," he said.   18

"You are the warmth of the world, you are its light;
  if other cause do not urge otherwise,
  your rays alone should serve to lead us right."   21

We moved on with a will, and in a while
  we had already gone so far up there
  as would be reckoned, here on earth, a mile;   24

when we began to hear in the air above
  invisible spirits who flew toward us speaking
  sweet invitations to the feast of love.   27

The first voice that flew past rang to the sky
  "Vinum non habent." And from far behind us
  we heard it fade repeating the same cry.   30

Even before we heard it cry its last
  far round the slope, another voice rang out:
  "I am Orestes!"—and it, too, sped past.   33

"Sweet Father," I began, "what are these cries?"—
  and even as I asked, I heard a third
  bodiless voice say: "Love your enemies."   36

And my good Master then: "This circle purges
  the guilt of Envious spirits, and for these
  who failed in Love, Love is the lash that scourges.   39

The Rein must cry the opposite of Love:
  you will hear it, I expect, before you reach
  the pass of absolution that leads above.   42

But now look carefully across the air
  ahead of us, and you will see some people
  seated against the inner cliff up there."   45

I opened my eyes wider: further on
  I saw a group of spirits dressed in cloaks
  exactly the same color as the stone.   48

As we drew nearer I heard prayers and plaints.
  "O Mary, pray for us," I heard them cry;
  and to Michael, and to Peter, and all Saints.   51

I cannot think there walks the earth today
  a man so hard that he would not be moved
  by what I saw next on that ashen way.   54

For when I drew near and could see the whole
  penance imposed upon those praying people,
  my eyes milked a great anguish from my soul.   57

Their cloaks were made of haircloth, coarse and stiff.
  Each soul supported another with his shoulder,
  and all learned for support against the cliff.   60

The impoverished blind who sit all in a row
  during Indulgences to beg their bread
  lean with their heads together exactly so,　　　　63

the better to win the pity they beseech,
  not only with their cries, but with their look
  of fainting grief, which pleads as loud as speech.　　66

Just as the sun does not reach to their sight,
  so to those shades of which I spoke just now
  God's rays refuse to offer their delight;　　　　69

for each soul has its eyelids pierced and sewn
  with iron wires, as men sew new-caught falcons,
  sealing their eyes to make them settle down.　　72

Somehow it seemed to me a shameful act
  to stare at others and remain unseen.
  I turned to Virgil. He, with perfect tact,　　　75

knew what the mute was laboring to say
  and did not wait my question. "Speak," he said,
  "but count your words and see they do not stray."　78

Virgil was walking by me down the ledge
  on the side from which—because no parapet
  circled the cliff—one might plunge off the edge.　81

On the other side those spirits kept their places
  absorbed in prayer, while through the ghastly stitches
  tears forced their way and flowed down from
                        their faces.　84

I turned to them and said: "O souls afire
  with hope of seeing Heaven's Light, and thus
  already certain of your heart's desire—　　　87

so may High Grace soon wash away the scum
  that clogs your consciousness, that memory's stream
  may flow without a stain in joys to come—   90

tell me if there is any Latin soul
  among you here: I dearly wish to know,
  and telling me may help him to his goal."   93

—"We are all citizens of one sublime
  and final city, brother; you mean to ask
  who lived in Italy in his pilgrim-time."   96

These are the words I heard a spirit say
  from somewhere further on. I moved up, therefore,
  in order to direct my voice that way.   99

I saw one shade who seemed to have in mind
  what I had said.—How could I tell? She sat
  chin raised, the waiting gesture of the blind.   102

"O soul self-humbled for the climb to Grace,"
  I said, "if it was you who spoke, I beg you,
  make yourself known either by name or place."   105

"I was Sienese," she answered. "On this shelf
  I weep away my world-guilt with these others
  in prayers to Him that he vouchsafe Himself.   108

Sapìa was I, though sapient I was not;
  I found more joy in the bad luck of others
  than in the good that fell to my own lot.   111

If this confession rings false to your ears,
  hear my tale out; then see if I was mad.
  —In the descending arc of my own years,   114

the blood of my own land was being spilled
  in battle outside Colle's walls, and I
  prayed God to do what He already willed.   117

So were they turned—their forces overthrown—
  to the bitter paths of flight; and as I watched
  I felt such joy as I had never known;   120

such that I raised my face, flushed with false power,
  and screamed to God: 'Now I no longer fear you'—
  like a blackbird when the sun comes out an hour.   123

Not till my final hour had all but set
  did I turn back to God, longing for peace.
  Penance would not yet have reduced my debt   126

had not Pier Pettinaio in saintly love
  grieved for my soul and offered holy prayers
  that interceded for me there above.   129

But who are you that you come here to seek
  such news of us; and have your eyes unsewn,
  as I believe; and breathe yet when you speak?"   132

"My eyes," I said, "will yet be taken from me
  upon this ledge, but not for very long:
  little they sinned through being turned in envy.   135

My soul is gripped by a far greater fear
  of the torment here below, for even now
  I seem to feel the burden those souls bear."   138

And she: "Then who has led you to this Round,
  if you think to go below again?" And I:
  "He who is with me and who makes no sound.   141

And I still live: if you would have me move
   my mortal feet down there in your behalf,
   ask what you will, O soul blessed by God's love."   144

"Oh," she replied, "this is a thing so rare
   it surely means that God has loved you greatly;
   from time to time, then, help me with a prayer.   147

I beg by all you most desire to win
   that if you walk again on Tuscan soil
   you will restore my name among my kin.   150

You will find them in that foolish mob whose dream
   is Talamone now, and who will lose there
   more than they did once in their silly scheme   153

to find the lost Diana. Though on that coast
   it is the admirals who will lose the most."

NOTES

6. *the arc it cuts is sooner bent:* As the mountain tapers, the circumference of each succeeding circle shrinks; its arc, therefore, is "sooner bent."

9. *livid:* I have found this word to be so frequently misunderstood that it seems well to remind readers that Latin *livious* means "ashen blue-black, the color of a bruise." The color is symbolic of Envy, the fortune of all others bruising the souls of the Envious. There are no carvings on this ledge, only the first ledge is so carved, and carvings would in any case be lost on these blind shades.

13–15. Having contemplated the Divine Light for a while, Virgil executes a sort of military right-face, swinging his left side around on the pivot of his right heel, and then moves toward the sun. He has learned the rule of the Mountain, which is, to follow the Light of God. In the first twenty-seven Cantos of the *Purgatorio* (up to the time Virgil disappears), there are two pilgrims. In the *Inferno,* only Dante was the pilgrim. There, Virgil was an experienced guide. Dante's rather strange way of describing Virgil's action is almost certainly meant to indicate how utterly Virgil gives himself to the Sun's (God's) guidance.

It is shortly after noon (see XII, 80–81); the Sun is a little beyond the mid-point from east to west, and, of course, to the north of the Poets. They have, therefore, entered the second Cornice at a point just a bit north of east.

19–21. VIRGIL'S ADDRESS TO THE SUN. Virgil seems to be confusing the allegorical and the literal function of the Sun in this apostrophe. How could the Sun as Divine Illumination fail to lead men right? Virgil can only mean, "Since no other guide is available to us, let us walk toward the [literal] Sun." Yet his words seem clearly to take the Sun in more than its literal significance.

25 ff. THE WHIP OF ENVY. Since the Envious have their eyes wired shut, it is appropriate that the Whip of Envy be oral rather than visual. The Whip, accordingly, consists of three disembodied voices that cry out the key lines from scenes that exemplify great Charity (i.e., *Caritas,* the love of others). Thus "sweet invitations to the feast of love" (line 27) may be read in two senses. The feast may be in contemplating these high examples, and it may as readily be taken to mean the feast of Divine Love these sinners will share in the sight of God when they have been purified.

29. *Vinum non habent:* "They have no wine." These words were spoken by Mary at the Wedding Feast in Cana of Galilee (*John* ii, 1–10). Mary, instead of envying those about her, thought only of their happiness, and noting that there was not enough wine, she turned to Jesus and spoke her loving dismay. Thereupon Jesus turned the water into wine, his first miracle. Note that it was in response to an act of *Caritas* that the first miracle took place.

Structurally, it may be well to note again, that the first incident in each Whip is drawn from the life of Mary.

33. *I am Orestes:* The second lesson in love of others clearly reflects *John* xv, 13: "Greater love hath no man than this, that a man lay down his life for his friends."

Orestes and Pylades were famous for the depth of their friendship. Cicero (*De Amicitia* VII, 24) relates the incident in which, Orestes having been condemned to death, Pylades pretended to be Orestes in order to die in his friend's place. Orestes then came forward asserting his own identity, and thereupon both friends argued "I am Orestes," each trying to save the other.

36. *Love your enemies:* These words were spoken by Jesus in the Sermon on the Mount (*cf.* the Mount of Purgatory). "Love your enemies, bless them that curse you, Mount (*cf.* the Mount of Purgatory). "Love your enemies, bless them that curse you, do good to them that hate you, and pray for them which despitefully use you, and persecute you." (*Matthew* v, 44.) Dante specifies that the first two voices were loud, but in their special dignity the words of Christ are not rung out; they are "said."

So the third lesson in love: not only to love others, and to love friends, but to love those who offer injury. When the Envious have suffered their souls to this understanding, they will be free to ascend to the next ledge.

37–42. It must be remembered that Virgil is not speaking here from experience. His earlier journey (see *Inferno* IX, 19–24) was only as far as Judaïca. Virgil, in his capacity as Human Reason, is deducing what probably lies ahead by analogy to what has gone before, and from his understanding of the nature of Envy.

46. *I opened my eyes wider:* Another example of Dante's characteristically strange way of describing how his senses work.

50. *I heard them cry:* They are chanting the Litany of the Saints, hence invoking those who were most free of Envy. Note, moreover, that they are chanting "pray for *us*" rather than "pray for *me*," as they might have prayed on earth in their Envy.

57. *my eyes milked a great anguish from my soul:* The line literally rendered would be: "Through my eyes: I was milked of heavy grief," a strange and daring figure.

58. *haircloth:* A coarse, heavy fabric made of goat hair. Even today peasants wear haircloth capes in heavy weather, but in the Middle Ages, and beyond, haircloth was worn against the skin as a penance, and to discipline the flesh. Such hair shirts were not only intolerably

itchy; they actually rubbed the flesh open, causing running sores. In an age, moreover, that was very slightly given to soap and water, such hair shirts offered an attractive habitat to all sorts of bodily vermin that were certain to increase the odor of sanctity, even to the point of the gangrenous. I am told, and have no wish to verify, that hair shirts are still worn today by some penitential and unventilated souls.

59–60. *each soul supported another:* As they had failed to do in life. *and all leaned for support against the cliff:* The cliff is probably best taken as God's Decree: their punishment, which is also their purification, sustains them.

61–66. The figure here is based on the behavior of blind beggars at church doors, and particularly at the doors of those churches which offer special Indulgences (Pardons for Sin) during certain feast days. English readers, long devoted to the illustrations of Doré, will do well to visualize Dante's scenes in terms of Dante's own details rather than in terms of Doré's romantic misconceptions.

71–72. *sew new-caught falcons:* Since diurnal birds sit still in the dark, the eyelids of newly caught falcons were sewn shut by their trainers to make them sit still, partly, as I understand it, to keep them from battering themselves against the cage, and partly to break them for their later training. In hunting, the birds were normally carried hooded to the point of release.

76. *the mute:* Dante himself.

81. *one might plunge off the edge:* Allegorically, therefore, Dante places Human Reason between him and a fall.

86. *Heaven's Light:* God.

88–90. Dante is alluding here to the River Lethe, the same stream along whose banks he climbed from Hell. At the top of Purgatory, the finally purified souls are washed in Lethe, and it removes from them the very memory of sin. Thus Dante is uttering a wish for the more rapid advancement of these souls, a sentiment all of them would take in good part.

93. *and telling me may help him to his goal:* Dante is making use here of one of those narrator's devices in which the reader will understand the remark made, more fully than will the characters to whom it is addressed. We know that Dante is alive and that he may

therefore win prayers for these souls on earth. The souls addressed, however, know only that an unknown voice is making a vague but attractive offer.

94 ff. SAPIA OF SIENA. Dante speaks briefly and to the point, as Virgil instructed him, but Sapìa responds with a long and rambling narrative, to understand which one must recall the story of Provenzano Salvani (Canto XI). Sapìa was Salvani's paternal aunt. As the wife of another nobleman, she resented Salvani's rise to great power. When Salvani attacked the Florentines at Colle in 1269, she stationed herself at a palace window to watch the battle, and when she saw Salvani defeated and beheaded on the field, she is reported to have cried: "Now God, do what you will with me, and do me any harm you can, for after this I shall live happily and die content."

The dates of her birth and death are unknown, but she seems to have been about sixty at the time of the Battle of Colle, and Dante makes clear that she died before Pier Pettinaio, whose death occurred in 1289.

94–95. *one sublime and final city:* Heaven, The New Jerusalem.

96. *his pilgrim-time:* His time on earth. As any concordance to the Bible will show, "pilgrim" for "wayfarer through life" and "pilgrimage" for "man's time on earth" are common Biblical usages.

103. *self-humbled for the climb to Grace:* A poor compromise rendering of *che per salir ti dome* (literally: "who master yourself in order to ascend"). The idea not to be missed here touches upon *the* essence of Purgatory: that the souls purify themselves. Just as Hell is the state of things the damned truly desire (see *Inferno* III, 123, note), so the souls in Purgatory *will* their purifying pains upon themselves, and nothing but their own will keeps them from ascending, for they themselves decide when they are worthy to move up.

105. *either by name or place:* I.e., "Let me know who you are or from what city you came."

109. *Sapìa was I, though sapient I was not:* The pun is based, of course, upon the fact that the name "Sapìa" is derived from Latin *sapiens*.

114. *the descending arc of my own years:* The figure seems to envision life as a semicircle. Since Dante has already made clear (*Inferno*

I, 1) that thirty-five is the midpoint, the arc would rise on one side of thirty-five and descend on the other. Since Sapìa was actually about sixty at the time she refers to, the figure may be taken to mean simply "my declining years."

117. *prayed God to do what He already willed:* Sapìa's prayer that the Sienese be defeated was granted, and at the time she took the defeat as the answer to her prayer. Now, however, she sees that her prayer was answered by accident: she had simply happened to pray for what God had already willed should happen.

123. *like a blackbird:* The occasional warm, sunny days that occur in Italy in January and February are called in Tuscany and Lombardy "the days of the blackbird." The European blackbird is reputed by Italians to dread cold. When the winter sun shines brightly, however, it immediately perks up and acts as if it owned the world. But as soon as the cold returns, it huddles shivering and miserable.

126. *Penance would not yet have reduced my debt:* As one of the Negligent who put off repentance till her final hour, Sapìa would still be waiting below but for the prayers of Pier Pettinaio. Her presently accomplished penance, therefore, would not yet have begun to reduce her debt of pain.

127. *Pier Pettinaio* (Peh-tin-EYE-oh): Literally, Peter Comb-seller. He came to Siena as a boy from the country, became a Sienese citizen, and grew into a local legend of piety, later being honored by an annual feast day such as is normally reserved for saints. He operated a small shop in which he sold combs, hence his name. The legend of his piety is general among Sienese writers, but the incidents they cite from his life seem at least as daft as they are saintly. He was, however, much given to public prayer and to elaborate ideas of honesty, and as Dante might say, either tendency would be more than enough to distinguish him from the rest of the Sienese.

131–132. *and have your eyes unsewn:* Sapìa could certainly tell from Dante's words that he was not one of the Envious, but his very freedom in walking around would have been enough to tell her he was not blind. *and breathe yet when you speak:* The blind are well known for the sharpness of their hearing; even a slight aspiration on Dante's part would reveal him to Sapìa. How the spirits managed to talk without breathing is a matter Dante would, of course, refer to God's Will.

Throughout this Cornice, Dante's description of the behavior of the blind is marvelously acute: the way they turn their heads, the way they talk (in the next Canto) about a man who is standing in front of them as if he were not there, the way they put their heads together to speak to one another—all bear evidence to Dante's powers of observation.

142–143. *if you would have me move:* If you would like me to bestir myself to solicit prayers for you when I return to Earth.

150. *restore my name:* In her final years Sapìa performed a number of good works for Siena, but there are several reports that she was generally condemned as a traitor.

151–155. A complicated passage of local reference certainly put into Sapìa's mouth by Dante as a Florentine jibe at the Sienese ("that foolish mob"). Dante (who fears the Ledge of Pride just below him) may have to carry his stone a bit further for his addiction to such touches, but his poem is certainly the livelier for them.

Talamone is a point on Italy's west coast about eighty miles almost due south of Siena. The Sienese, lacking a port, and wanting to compete with Genoa, bought the site in 1303 and invested heavily in building and dredging operations. The scheme, not nearly as unreasonable as Dante would have it seem, failed because of malarial conditions and because the hoped-for port silted in almost as fast as it could be dredged.

The Diana was another project intermittently undertaken by the Sienese over a long period. Siena was water-poor, but the magnificent flow at certain wells suggested to the Sienese the presence of an underground river which they christened the Diana, and which they dug for at great expense. All efforts had failed up to Dante's time and the failures were used as a standing joke against the Sienese as overambitious crackpots trying to make themselves better than they were. The Sienese, however (and largely out of hard necessity), continued their expensive digging and did, sometime later, locate a substantial underground flow. There is still a Well of Diana in a convent in Siena.

A third difficulty in this passage is in the meaning of "admirals."
Some of the old commentators report "admiral" was the term for
what we should call "contractor" or "engineer in charge of con-
struction." (*Cf.* British-English "navvy," derived from "navigator.")
Or it may be that Dante meant that "port-admirals" (i.e., "port-
masters" or "harbor-masters") supervised the work. If these are
proper interpretations, then the "admirals" would "lose the most"
because they would die of malaria. If, however, Dante means "admi-
rals" as "ships' captains," they would lose the most if they tried to use
the port, or if they waited until the Sienese finished it. Dante may, of
course, have intended all three possibilities at once.

The Second Cornice—The Envious

THE REIN OF ENVY

Dante's conversation with Sapìa of Siena is overheard by two
spirits who sit side by side against the inner cliff-face. They are
Guido del Duca and *Rinieri da Calboli*.

Dante enters into conversation with them, and Guido de-
nounces the inhabitants of the cities of the Valley of the Arno. He
then prophesies the slaughter that Rinieri's grandson, *Fulcieri,*
shall visit upon Florence. And he prophesies also that Fulcieri's
actions will have a bearing on Dante's approaching exile from
Florence. Guido concludes with a lament for the past glories of
Romagna as compared to its present degeneracy.

Leaving the two spirits in tears, Dante and Virgil move on,
and they have hardly left when Dante is struck with terror by two
bodiless voices that break upon them like thunder. The voices are
The Rein of Envy. The first is *The Voice of Cain* lamenting that he
is forever cut off from mankind. The second is *The Voice of Aglau-
ros,* who was changed to stone as a consequence of her envy of
her sister.

Virgil concludes the Canto with a denunciation of mankind's
stubborn refusal to heed the glory of the Heavens and to prepare
for eternal Grace.

"Who do you think that is? He roams our hill
  before death gives him wings, and he's left free
  to shut his eyes or open them at will."   3

"I don't know, but I know he's not alone.
  Ask him—you're nearer—but put in a way
  that won't offend him. Take a careful tone."   6

Thus, on my right, and leaning head to head,
  two of those spirits were discussing me.
  Then they turned up their faces, and one said: 9

"O soul that though locked fast within the flesh
  still makes its way toward Heaven's blessedness,
  in charity, give comfort to our wish: 12

tell us your name and city, for your climb
  fills us with awe at such a gift of grace
  as never has been seen up to this time."   15

And I: "In Falterona lies the source
  of a brook that grows and winds through Tuscany
  till a hundred miles will not contain its course.   18

From its banks I bring this flesh. As for my name—
  to tell you who I am would serve no purpose:
  I have as yet won very little fame."   21

And the first spirit: "If I rightly weigh
  your words upon the balance of my mind,
  it is the Arno you intend to say."   24

And the other to him: "Why is he so careful
  to avoid the river's name? He speaks as men do
  when they refer to things too foul or fearful."   27

To which the shade he had addressed replied:
  "That I don't know; but it would be a mercy
  if even the name of such a valley died.   30

From its source high in the great range that outsoars
  almost all others (from whose chain Pelorus
  was cut away), to the point where it restores   33

in endless soft surrender what the sun
  draws from the deep to fall again as rain,
  that every rill and river may flow on,   36

men run from virtue as if from a foe
  or poisonous snake. Either the land is cursed,
  or long corrupted custom drives them so.   39

And curse or custom so transform all men
  who live there in that miserable valley,
  one would believe they fed in Circe's pen.   42

It sets its first weak course among sour swine,
  indecent beasts more fit to grub and grunt
  for acorns than to sit to bread and wine.   45

It finds next, as it flows down and fills out,
  a pack of curs, their snarl worse than their bite;
  and in contempt it turns aside its snout.   48

Down, down it flows, and as the dogs grow fewer
  the wolves grow thicker on the widening banks
  of that accursed and God-forsaken sewer.   51

It drops through darkened gorges, then, to find
  the foxes in their lairs, so full of fraud
  they fear no trap set by a mortal mind.   54

Nor will I, though this man hear what I say,
  hold back the prophecy revealed to me;
  for well may he recall it on his way.   57

I see your grandson riding to the chase.
  He hunts the wolves that prowl by the fierce river.
  He has become the terror of that place.   60

He sells their living flesh, then—shame on shame—
　the old beast slaughters them himself, for sport.
　Many will die, and with them, his good name.　　63

He comes from that sad wood covered with gore,
　and leaves it in such ruin, a thousand years
　will not serve to restock its groves once more."　　66

Just as a man to whom bad chance announces
　a dreadful ill, distorts his face in grief,
　no matter from what quarter the hurt pounces—　　69

just so that shade, who had half turned his head
　better to listen, showed his shock and pain
　when he had registered what the other said.　　72

So moved by one's words and the other's face,
　I longed to know their names, I asked them, therefore,
　phrasing my plea with prayers to win their grace;　　75

at which the spokesman of the two replied:
　"You beg me of my good grace that I grant you
　what I have asked of you and been denied;　　78

but God has willed His favor to shine forth
　so greatly in you, I cannot be meager:
　Guido del Duca was my name on earth.　　81

The fires of envy raged so in my blood
　that I turned livid if I chanced to see
　another man rejoice in his own good.　　84

This seed I sowed; this sad straw I reap here.
　O humankind, why do you set your hearts
　on what it is forbidden you to share?　　87

This is Rinier, the honor and the pride
  of the house of the Calboli, of which no one
  inherited his merit when he died.   90

Nor in that war-torn land whose boundary-lines
  the sea and the Reno draw to the east and west;
  and, north and south, the Po and the Apennines,   93

is his the only house that seems to be
  bred bare of those accomplishments and merits
  which are the good and truth of chivalry.   96

For the land has lost the good of hoe and plow,
  and poisonous thorns so choke it that long years
  of cultivation would scarce clear it now.   99

Where is Mainardi? Have you lost the seed
  of Lizio? Traversaro? di Carpigna?
  O Romagnoles changed to a bastard breed!   102

When will a Fabbro evermore take root
  in all Bologna? or in Faenza, a Fosco?—
  who was his little plant's most noble shoot.   105

O Tuscan, can I speak without a tear
  of Ugolino d'Azzo and Guido da Prata,
  who shared our time on earth? and with them there   108

Federico di Tignoso and his train?
  the house of the Traversari and the Anastagi,
  both heirless now? or, dry-eyed, think again   111

of knights and ladies, of the court and field
  that bonded us in love and courtesy
  where now all hearts are savagely self-sealed?   114

O Brettinoro, why do you delay?
  Your lords and many more have fled your guilt;
  and why, like them, will you not melt away?   117

Bagnacaval does well to have no heirs;
  and Castrocaro badly, and Conio worse
  in bothering to breed such Counts as theirs.   120

The Pagani will do well enough, all told,
  when once their fiend is gone, but not so well
  their name will ever again shine as pure gold.   123

O Ugolin de' Fantolini, your name
  remains secure, since you have none to bear it
  and, in degeneracy, bring it to shame.   126

But leave me Tuscan, I am more inclined
  to spell my grief in tears now than in words;
  for speaking thus has wrung my heart and mind."   129

We knew those dear souls heard us go away.
  Their silence, therefore, served as our assurance
  that, leaving them, we had not gone astray.   132

We had scarce left those spirits to their prayer,
  when suddenly a voice that ripped like lightning
  struck at us with a cry that split the air: 135

"All men are my destroyers!" It rolled past
  as thunder rolls away into the sky
  if the cloud bursts to rain in the first blast.   138

Our ears were scarcely settled from that burst
  when lo, the second broke, with such a crash
  it seemed the following thunder of the first: 141

"I am Aglauros who was turned to stone!"
  Whereat, to cower in Virgil's arms, I took
  a step to my right instead of going on.   144

The air had fallen still on every hand
  when Virgil said: "That was the iron bit
  that ought to hold men hard to God's command.   147

But still you gulp the Hellbait hook and all
  and the Old Adversary reels you in.
  Small good to you is either curb or call.   150

The Heavens cry to you, and all around
  your stubborn souls, wheel their eternal glory,
  and yet you keep your eyes fixed on the ground. 153

And for each turning from the joys of Love
  the All-Discerning flails you from above."

NOTES

16. *Falterona:* One of the major peaks of the Tuscan Apennines. It is northeast of Florence and both the Arno and the Tiber spring from its sides.

18. *a hundred miles:* "Hundred" is used here as a large round number; the Arno with all its windings has a course of at least a hundred and fifty miles.

22–24. *If I rightly weigh:* The first spirit is Guido (see below). He does most of the talking here and hereafter. Dante has answered in words that run like a riddle, and Guido, knowing that Falterona gives rise to both the Arno and the Tiber, has to weigh out his own conclusion. He would have decided that Dante meant the Arno because the Tiber is so much longer that "a hundred miles" would be out of all reason for its length.

31–36. The gist of these lines may be stated as: "From the Arno's source to the point at which it enters the sea." *the great range:* The Apennines. *Pelorus:* A mountain in Sicily, part of the Apennine system, but cut off from the rest of the chain by the Straits of Messina.

42. *they fed in Circe's pen:* Circe changed men into beasts of various kinds. Guido goes on to specify four species of beasts into which the Arno transforms the people along its course: the swine of the Casentine, the curs of Arezzo, the wolves of Florence, and the foxes of Pisa.

Dante's riddle-like answer to a simple question, though it appears to be mere ornamentation at first, serves to introduce the whole discussion of the degeneracy of the city-states of the Arno Valley.

43. *its first weak course:* In the Upper Casentine the Arno is not yet swollen by any tributaries.

46–48. *a pack of curs:* The Arentines. *turns aside its snout:* The Arno flows from the Upper Casentine straight toward Arezzo but at a point a few miles north of the town its wings east without entering the town proper. Note how Dante's phrasing gives the river itself bestial characteristics, beast scorning beast.

53–57. For the sense of this difficult passage one must remember that Guido (not yet identified) is speaking to Rinieri (not yet identified) and not to Dante. Guido is about to reveal a prophecy concerning the evil actions of Rinieri's grandson, and further concerning Dante's banishment from Florence. The prophecy will grieve Rinieri, but it will be well for Dante to hear it and ponder it. The sense then: "Though it grieve you to hear me say this, especially in front of others, I still must say it, and it will in fact be well for this man to think about it as he moves on." Note that Guido obviously knows who Dante is, though Dante has refused to identify himself by name.

These lines imply strongly, and lines 67 ff. confirm, that Rinieri does not share Guido's prophetic powers, at least at this point. I know of nothing in Dante that will explain why one soul in a given category should be more prophetic than another, but it can certainly be assumed that the prophetic vision comes in flashes now to one soul, now to another.

58–66. *your grandson:* Rinieri's grandson (Dante calls him *nipote,* which may mean either "nephew" or "grandson") was Fulcieri da Calboli (Ful-CHYEH-ree dah KAHL-boe-lee), who in 1302 became podesta (chief magistrate) of Florence.

In Dante's time many of the city-states of Italy were so torn by internal strife that they could not hope to agree on one of their own citizens as podesta. The practice grew, therefore, of electing a (presumably neutral) outsider to administer impartial justice for a given term. Fulcieri (either bribed by the Black Guelphs, or put into office in the first place as part of their plot) arrested and put to painful death many leaders of the White Guelphs (Dante's party) as well as some of the few remaining and powerless Ghibellines. The leaders disposed of, he proceeded murderously against the Whites in general. The "wolves" he hunts (line 59) are, of course, the White Florentines; the "sad wood" (line 64) is, of course, Florence. "The old beast" is Fulcieri, who, after selling them alive, piles shame on shame by killing them himself for sport.

69. *no matter from what quarter the hurt pounces:* I have no satisfactory explanation of this line. Dante seems to stress the unexpectedness of the news. "Pounces" in the original is *l'assanni* (i.e., "seizes him by the teeth"). But what the source of the bad news has to do with the man's reaction to it, in this case at least, remains unexplained, though one may, of course, conjecture at will.

81. *Guido del Duca:* Little is known about him. He was a Ghibelline of Brettinoro, a member of the prominent Onesti family of Ravenna. He served in various judicial posts in Romagna from 1195 on, and is known to have been alive in 1229.

85. *This seed:* Envy. *this sad straw:* His present pains. "Be not deceived; God is not mocked: for whatsoever a man soweth, that shall he also reap" (*Galatians* vi, 7).

87. *on what it is forbidden you to share:* These words puzzle Dante and remain in his mind. In the next Canto he asks Virgil what they mean. For Virgil's reply see XV, 46–57, and 64–81. See also note on Dante's Doctrine of Wealth (p. 164), and *Inferno* VII, 68, note on Dame Fortune.

88. *Rinier:* Rinieri dei Paolucci da Calboli di Forlì. (Rih-NYEH-ree DAY-ee Pah-oh-LOO-tchee da KAHL-boe-lee dee

For-LEE.) A Guelph leader, podesta of Faenza in 1247, and later of other cities. In 1292 he was re-elected podesta of Faenza, but he and his supporters were expelled by the Ghibellines in 1294. In 1296 Rinieri seized Faenza while the Ghibellines were away paying a social call on Bologna. Those courtesies concluded, they returned in force, and Rinieri was killed in the homecoming festivities.

91–96. To avoid a tangle of scholarly references and disputes I have simplified the text here and taken six lines to render three of Dante's, into what I hope is a reasonably clear exposition. The wartorn land is Romagna. The Reno is a river that bounds Romagna on the west. The sea on the east is the Adriatic.

100–102. All the persons mentioned here were leaders of Romagna during the last decades of the twelfth century and into the first three quarters of the thirteenth. All are cited as examples of knightly grace, bravery, largesse, and sound counsel. *Romagnoles:* People of Romagna (Roe-MAH-nyah). Dante's phrasing unmistakably suggests here the opening lines of Ariosto's *Orlando Furioso.*

103–105. Dante is carrying out the agricultural metaphor begun in lines 97–99. *Fabbro:* Fabbro de' Lambertazzi, leader of all Romagna's Ghibellines, died in 1259. *Fosco:* Bernardin di Fosco, son of a small landholder (hence his family tree was "a little plant"), rose to high estate through great merit and served as podesta of Pisa in 1248 and of Siena in 1249. Both men are cited for the same virtues exemplified by Mainardi and the others listed in lines 100–114.

The first part of Guido's denunciation of Romagna cites the glories of its past. All those mentioned here by Duca were prominent leaders of Romagna, and all were alive during some part of Guido's lifetime. He laments their passing as the passing of chavalric virtue.

110. *the house of the Traversari:* Guido has cited Pier Traversaro among the best lords of the land. Here he extends his praise to the whole house, along with his lament that it is an expiring line. *the Anastagi:* (Ah-nah-STAH-djee) of Ravenna. Another great house left without heirs.

115–117. *Brettinoro:* (Now Bertinoro.) A small town between Forlì and Cesena, it was Guido's birthplace. Some of the details of this passage may be variously interpreted, but the general sense is clear enough: "Since the best of your people have fled you to escape the contagion of your guilt, why don't you just do away with yourself?" *Your lords:* Your ruling house. *and many more:* and many more of your citizens.

118–120. The towns here mentioned are small fortified towns of Romagna. In Guido's view, their ruling houses have bred down to degenerate stock. In 1300 the Malvacini di Bagnacavallo (Mahl-vah-TCHEE-nee dee Bah-nya-kah-VAH-loe) had no male heirs and the line was doomed to extinction.

121–123. The Pagani ruled over various holdings in Romagna, Faenza and Imola among them. The "fiend" of the Pagani was Count Maginardo (see *Inferno* XXVII, 47–49, and note). Maginardo died in 1302, and after him his sons ruled well, but never well enough to remove the stain left on the family name by Maginardo's misrule.

124. *Ugolin de' Fantolini:* Of Faenza. A lord of great good reputation. He died in 1278 leaving two sons and two daughters, but both sons had died without issue by 1286.

130–132. *We knew those dear souls heard us . . . . :* A good example of Dante's characteristic sparseness and precision. The souls, well disposed toward the Poets, could hear in which direction they walked away. Had the Poets turned the wrong way (left), the souls would have spoken up. Since nothing was said, the Poets knew they were headed the right way—and each pair knew that the other knew.

134–141. Dante's theory of electric storms (see *Inferno* XXIV, 145–149, and note at end of that Canto) is likely to confuse modern readers. His basic theory is that fiery vapors (lightning) try to shatter watery vapors (clouds), bringing them down as rain. (So line 138, *if the cloud bursts . . .*)

136–144. THE REIN OF ENVY. Like the Whip, the Rein consists of bodiless voices racing through the air.

The first voice is that of Cain crying to God at his punishment: "Everyone that findeth me shall slay me." (*Genesis* iv, 14.) Thus the first crash resounds with the cry of the first man punished for envy.

The second voice is of Aglauros, daughter of Cecrops, King of Athens. Her sisters were Herse and Pandrace. Mercury fell in love with the beautiful Herse and bribed Aglauros to arrange for him an assignation with her sister. Aglauros took the bribe, but in envy that her sister should lie with a god, she turned Mercury away when he arrived for his appointment. Mercury, enraged, turned her to stone.

Thus the doom brought on by envy cries in the voice of brother sinning against brother and sister sinning against sister.

146–150. VIRGIL'S REPLY. As mixed metaphors go, this one ranks high even for Dante. "You [mankind] ought to be bridled [like a horse] but instead you swallow the hook [like a fish] and are not saved by either curb [bridle] or call [the original word is *richiamo,* signifying the whistle used to call a falcon back from the hunt]."

CANTO XV

The Second Cornice—The Envious
The Ascent—The Angel of Caritas
The Third Cornice—The Wrathful

THE WHIP OF WRATH

It is 3:00 P.M. and the Poets are walking straight into the sun
when an even greater radiance blinds Dante and he finds himself
in the presence of *The Angel of Caritas* who passes the Poets on to
the ledge above. As they ascend, they hear the Angel sing *The
Fifth Beatitude.*

As soon as the Poets enter *The Third Cornice,* Dante is en-
tranced by *Three Visions* which constitute *The Whip of Wrath,* ex-
tolling the virtue of *Meekness* toward kin, toward friends, and
toward enemies.

These events consume three hours. It is, therefore, 6:00 P.M. of
The Second Day in Purgatory when the Poets, moving forward, ob-
serve an enormous *Cloud of Smoke* ahead of them.

Of that bright Sphere that, like a child at play,
  skips endlessly, as much as lies between
  the third hour's end and the first light of day   3

remained yet of the Sun's course toward the night.
  Thus, it was Vespers there upon the mountain
  and midnight here in Italy, where I write.   6

The Sun's late rays struck us full in the face,
  for in our circling course around the mountain
  we now were heading toward his resting place.   9

Suddenly, then, I felt my brow weighed down
  by a much greater splendor than the first.
  I was left dazzled by some cause unknown   12

and raised my hands and joined them in the air
  above my brows, making a sunshade of them
  which, so to speak, blunted the piercing glare.   15

When a ray strikes glass or water, its reflection
  leaps upward from the surface once again
  at the same angle but opposite direction   18

from which it strikes, and in an equal space
  spreads equally from a plumb-line to mid-point,
  as trial and theory show to be the case.   21

Just so, it seemed to me, reflected light
  struck me from up ahead, so dazzlingly
  I had to shut my eyes to spare my sight.   24

"Dear Father, what is that great blaze ahead
  from which I cannot shade my eyes enough,
  and which is still approaching us?" I said.   27

"Do not be astonished," answered my sweet Friend
  "if those of the Heavenly Family still blind you.
  He has been sent to bid us to ascend.   30

Soon now, such sights will not aggrieve your sense
  but fill you with a joy as great as any
  Nature has fitted you to experience."   33

We stand before the Blessed Angel now.
  With joyous voice he cries: "Enter. The stair
  is far less steep than were the two below."   36

We had gone past him and were climbing on
  when *Blessed are the merciful* hymned out
  behind us, and *Rejoice you who have won.*   39

My Guide and I were going up the stair—
    we two alone—and I, thinking to profit
    from his wise words as we were climbing there,   42

questioned him thus: "What deep intent lay hidden
    in what the spirit from Romagna said?
    He spoke of 'sharing' and said it was 'forbidden.' "   45

And he: "He knows the sad cost of his own
    besetting sin: small wonder he reviles it
    in hope that you may have less to atone.   48

It is because you focus on the prize
    of wordly goods, which every sharing lessens
    that Envy pumps the bellows for your sighs.   51

But if, in true love for the Highest Sphere,
    your longing were turned upward, then your hearts
    would never be consumed by such a fear;   54

for the more there are there, who say 'ours'—not
                                        'mine'—
    by that much is each richer, and the brighter
    within that cloister burns the Love Divine."   57

"I am left hungrier being thus fed,
    and my mind is more in doubt being thus answered,
    than if I had not asked at all," I said.   60

"How can each one of many who divide
    a single good have more of it, so shared,
    than if a few had kept it?" He replied: 63

"Because within the habit of mankind
    you set your whole intent on earthly things,
    the true light falls as darkness on your mind.   66

The infinite and inexpressible Grace
  which is in Heaven, gives itself to Love
  as a sunbeam gives itself to a bright surface.   69

As much light as it finds there, it bestows;
  thus, as the blaze of Love is spread more widely,
  the greater the Eternal Glory grows.   72

As mirror reflects mirror, so, above,
  the more there are who join their souls, the more
  Love learns perfection, and the more they love.   75

And if this answer does not yet appease
  your hunger, you will soon see Beatrice,
  and this, and every wish, shall find surcease.   78

Only strive hard that soon no trace may show
  of the five scars which true contrition heals—
  as the first two have faded from your brow."   81

I was about to say, "I am satisfied,"
  when suddenly we came to the next Round,
  and my eyes' avidity left me tongue-tied.   84

Here suddenly, in an ecstatic trance,
  I find myself caught up into a vision.
  I see a crowded temple, and in the entrance   87

a lady by herself, her eyes aglow
  with the sweet grace of a mother, saying gently:
  "My son, my son, why do you treat us so?   90

Your father and I were seeking you in tears."
  So saying, she falls silent, and as quickly
  as it first came, the vision disappears.   93

Another lady now appears, her cheeks
  bathed in those waters that are born of grief
  when grief is born of anger. Now she speaks: 96

"O Pisistratus, if you are true Lord
  of the city for whose name the Gods debated,
  and whence all learning shone forth afterward,   99

avenge yourself on the presumptuous one
  who dared embrace our daughter." And her master,
  sweetly forbearing, in a placid tone,   102

and smiling gently at her, answers thus:
  "What shall we do to those that wish us harm
  if we take vengeance upon those that love us?"   105

Then there appears a wild and murderous spill
  of people hate-incensed, stoning a boy,
  and roaring to each other's wrath: "Kill! Kill!"   108

I see the boy sink to the ground, his death
  already heavy on him, but his eyes,
  like gates of Heaven, open through such wrath;   111

and even in his last extremity
  he prays God to forgive his murderers,
  turning to Him the look that unlocks pity.   114

When finally my soul could see and feel
  things which were true outside it, I understood
  my not-false errors had been dreams, though real.   117

My Guide, who watched me as I moved along
  like one just wakened and still sleep-stunned, said:
  "You barely seem to keep your feet—what's wrong?   120

You've stumbled on now for a good half-league
　with eyes half-shut and legs too-wide, like one
　groggy with wine or dropping with fatigue."　　　123

"O my sweet Father, if you wish to know,
　listen, and I shall tell you what I saw,"
　I answered, "when my legs were stricken so."　　　126

"Were you to wear a hundred masks," he said,
　"to hide your face, it would lie open to me
　so that your slightest thought might yet be read.　　129

These visions warn your soul on no account
　still to refuse the water of that peace
　which flows to man from the Eternal Fount.　　　132

I did not ask 'what's wrong' as a man might
　who sees with eyes alone, and when the body
　is lying senseless has no other sight;　　　135

but rather to put strength into your stride:
　for so must laggards be spurred on to use
　their reawakening senses as a guide."　　　138

Through the last vesper-hour we traveled on,
　looking ahead as far as eye could see
　against the level rays of the late sun.　　　141

And there ahead of us against the light
　we saw come billowing in our direction
　by slow degrees, a smoke as black as night.　　　144

Nor was there refuge from it anywhere.
　It took our sight from us, and the pure air.

NOTES

1–6. *that bright Sphere that . . . skips endlessly:* Despite the fact that Dante says "Sphere" rather than "great circle" or "zone," the reference here is best taken to be to the Zodiac, which dips above and below the horizon and may, therefore, be said to "skip endlessly." Dante uses the word *scherza,* which may signify any kind of play. *as much as lies between:* Three full hours (from the end of the third hour of the day, i.e., 9:00 A.M., back to the dawn, i.e., 6:00 A.M.). Since one hour equals 15°, "as much as" must equal 45°. If the sun has 45° remaining of its daily course, it is three hours short of sunset, hence 3:00 P.M. *it was Vespers there . . . and midnight here:* Purgatory is antipodal to Jerusalem. If it is 3:00 P.M. in Purgatory, it is 3:00 A.M. in Jerusalem. But by Dante's reckoning, Italy is taken as lying exactly 45° west of Jerusalem. As above, 45° converts to three hours, and since Italy is to the west (hence in an earlier time zone), it must be midnight there.

16–21. *a ray. . . . its reflection:* In the old didactic tradition, Dante is describing the reflection of a beam of light.

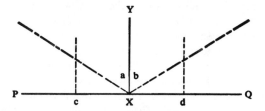

Angle *a* equals angle *b. YX* is a "plumb-line to mid-point." If from any two points on line *PQ* equally distant from *X* (*c* and *d,* for example) perpendiculars are raised to intersect that ray of light and its reflection, they will intersect an amount of reflection equal to the amount of ray.

Allegorically, this process of reflection may best be taken for the perfection of outgoing love, which the Angel—as the true opposite of the Envious—represents.

34. *the Blessed Angel:* Since the Angel of each Cornice represents the virtue opposite the sin there punished, this would be the Angel of *Caritas,* i.e., of Love of Others.

38–39. *Blessed are the merciful:* The fifth beatitude. See *Matthew* v, 7. It is probably the Angel who sings this beatitude and the spirits of the Envious who reply: *Rejoice you who have won.* The words are chosen from no particular text, but their sentiment is that which concludes the beatitudes, a rejoicing in the triumph over sin. See *Matthew* v, 12.

48. *you:* You living men. Mankind in general.

51. *that Envy pumps the bellows for your sighs:* A Dantean figure. Envy seems to change the breast into a bellows which does nothing but pump out sighs of envious desire.

52–57. *the Highest Sphere:* The Empyrean. *such a fear:* that someone else will get the material good one cherishes. *that cloister:* Heaven.

DANTE'S DOCTRINE OF WEALTH. Virgil is propounding a favorite Dantean doctrine. Since there is a limit to material wealth, everything that one man possesses lessens what others may possess. Those, therefore, who are avid for the goods of the world must live in fear that it will be taken by others, and therefore Envy drives them to lament everyone else's material gains. The treasure of Heaven, however, grows greater in being shared.

67. *The infinite and inexpressible Grace:* God's love. It shines forth to the souls of those who love Him as a sunbeam shines upon a bright surface, dazzling it full of light without in any way diminishing the source but rather, by giving, increasing the total of light.

76–77. *appease your hunger:* The phrasing here responds to the phrasing of line 58: "I am left hungrier being thus fed."

84. *my eyes' avidity left me tongue-tied:* The avidity of my eyes [to observe new sights] left me [so busy staring at all about me that I was] tongue-tied. *Cf.,* the opening lines of Canto IV, and Dante's discussion of how one sense may so absorb the soul that all others fail.

85–114. THE WHIP OF WRATH. Consists of three visions that seize upon the souls on their way to enter the cloud of smoke.

The first (lines 85–93) is, as always, from the life of Mary. It is based on *Luke* ii, 41–52. When the Nazarenes started back from Jerusalem after Passover, Jesus did not leave with them, but stayed behind without informing either Joseph or Mary. They, thinking he must be in some other part of the caravan, had traveled a whole day before they learned the truth. They turned back to search for him and spent three days combing Jerusalem before they found him in the Temple disputing with the learned men. Mary, despite the anxieties and exertions to which Jesus had put her, remonstrates without wrath.

The second (lines 94–105) is of an incident from the life of Pisistratus, Tyrant of Athens from 560–527 B.C., the usurper who ruled so wisely and gently that the Athenians forgave his usurpation. A young man who loved the daughter of Pisistratus and wished to marry her, but who had not won the parents' consent, embraced her in public in a moment of high spirits. The wife of Pisitratus, seething with wrath, demands a bloody vengeance for what she takes to be an act of dishonor, but Pisistratus turns away wrath with a soft answer. (Valerius Maximus, *Facta et Dicta* VI, i.)

The third (lines 106–114) is of the martyrdom of St. Stephen. (*Acts* vii, 58.) Dante is in error in making Stephen a boy at the time of his death.

Thus the Whip once more presents three degrees of the virtue opposed to the sin being punished, and thus the Wrathful are whipped on by high examples of Meekness toward kin, toward friends, and toward enemies.

98. *for whose name the Gods debated:* The legend is that Neptune and Athena both wished the new city to bear their names. Ovid (*Metamorphoses* VI, 70–82) describes the resultant contest, which Athena won.

131. *still to refuse:* Dante has already recognized that his own besetting sin is Pride, and Pride is clearly related to Wrath. He seems to have had so strong a sense of his own rightness that any indignity or error could arouse his anger. Boccaccio says that everyone in Romagna was sure Dante would throw stones even at women and children if he heard them insult his principles. His mistreatment by the Florentines, moreover, must have left him with some substantial

hunger for revenge. Thus these examples of high meekness have special point for him, and Virgil (his own reason) tells him so.

132. *the Eternal Fount: Jeremiah* ii, 13, and xvii, 13, refers to God as "the fountain of living waters."

133–138. *lying senseless:* Virgil means "so caught up in a trance that the soul is beyond the reach of the senses." In extension, he is saying: "I do not ask in a material way, seeing things only with the physical senses, but rather in terms of your newly awakened spiritual understanding of your faults, and to urge you to act upon that new understanding."

In a second sense, of course, Dante is analyzing himself. If he is to move higher up the mountain he must put by all his Wrath, all his sense of outraged righteousness, all his desire for vindication and vengeance. But he knows it will not be easy for him truly to forgive his enemies, for he knows how deeply Wrath is rooted in his nature. It requires, therefore, a special urging to act truly upon the three visions he has seen. (Contrast, for example, how lightly Dante was able to dismiss Envy as a personal concern of his soul.)

139–141. It is nearing 6:00 P.M., the last hour of Vespers. Note that about three hours ago (lines 1–6 above), the Poets were on the ledge below and were walking straight into the sun. Now, having climbed the stairway and having walked half a league (about a mile and a half) and a bit more, at a very slow pace (lines 121–123), they are still walking straight into the sun. The fact that they could walk so far without a turning that would leave the sun on their right, certainly indicates that these first Cornices circle very slowly, being conceived on an enormous scale.

CANTO XVI

The Third Cornice—The Wrathful · Marco Lombardo

The Poets enter the acrid and blinding smoke in which *The Wrathful* suffer their purification. As Wrath is a corrosive state of the spirit, so the smoke stings and smarts. As Wrath obscures the true light of God, so the smoke plunges all into darkness. Within it, Dante hears souls singing *The Litany of the Lamb of God*. The Lamb, of course, is the symbol of the *Meekness of Divine Love*. As such, it is the opposite of Wrath. A further purification is implicit in the fact that the souls all sing as if with one voice, for Wrath is the sin that soonest breeds division among men, and only Spiritual Concord can reunite them.

Marco Lombardo hears Dante speak and calls to him. Invited by Dante, Marco accompanies the Poets to the edge of the smoke, discoursing on the causes of the modern world's corruption, which he locates in the usurpation of temporal power and wealth by the church. As Marco concludes, a light begins to appear through the smoke. Marco explains that it is the radiance of the Angel who waits ahead. He then turns back, for he is not yet fit to show himself to the Angel of the Lord.

No gloom of Hell, nor of a night allowed
  no planet under its impoverished sky,
  the deepest dark that may be drawn by cloud;   3

ever drew such a veil across my face,
  nor one whose texture rasped my senses so,
  as did the smoke that wrapped us in that place.   6

The sting was more than open eyes could stand.
  My wise and faithful Guide drew near me, therefore,
  and let me grasp his shoulder with my hand.   9

Just as a blindman—lest he lose his road
  or tumble headlong and be hurt or killed—
  walks at his guide's back when he goes abroad;   12

so moved I through that foul and acrid air,
  led by my sweet Friend's voice, which kept repeating:
  "Take care. Do not let go of me. Take care."   15

And I heard other voices. They seemed to pray
  for peace and pardon to the Lamb of God
  which, of Its mercy, takes our sins away.   18

They offered up three prayers, and every one
  began with *Agnus Dei,* and each word
  and measure rose in perfect unison.   21

"Master, do I hear spirits on this path?"
  I said. And he to me: "You do indeed,
  and they are loosening the knot of Wrath."   24

"And who are you, then, that you cleave our smoke,
  yet speak of us as if you still kept time
  by kalends?"—without warning, someone spoke   27

these words to me; at which my Lord and Guide
  said: "Answer. And inquire respectfully
  if one may find a way-up on this side."   30

And I: "O spirit growing pure and free
  to go once more in beauty to your Maker—
  you will hear wonders if you follow me."   33

"As far as is permitted me," he said,
  "I will. And if the smoke divide our eyes,
  our ears shall serve to join us in their stead."   36

So I began: "I make my way above
  still in these swathings death dissolves. I came here
  through the Infernal grief. Now, since God's love   39

incloses me in Grace so bounteous
  that he permits me to behold His court
  by means wholly unknown to modern use—   42

pray tell me who you were before you died,
  and if I go the right way to the pass
  that leads above. Your words shall be our guide."   45

"I was a Lombard. Marco was my name.
  I knew the ways of the world, and loved that good
  at which the bows of men no longer aim.   48

You are headed the right way to reach the stair
  that leads above," he added. And: "I pray you
  to pray for me when you have mounted there."   51

And I: "On my faith I vow it. But a doubt
  has formed within me and has swelled so large
  I shall explode unless I speak it out.   54

It was a simple doubt at first, but now
  it doubles and grows sure as I compare
  your words with what was said to me below.   57

The world, as you have said, is truly bare
  of every trace of good; swollen with evil;
  by evil overshadowed everywhere.   60

But wherein lies the fault? I beg to know
  that I may see the truth and so teach others.
  Some see it in the stars; some, here below."   63

A deep sigh wrung by grief, almost a moan
  escaped as a long "Ah!" Then he said: "Brother,
  the world is blind and you are its true son.   66

Mankind sees in the heavens alone the source
  of all things, good and evil; as if by Law
  they shaped all mortal actions in their course.   69

If that were truly so, then all Free Will
  would be destroyed, and there would be no justice
  in giving bliss for virtue, pain for evil.   72

The spheres *do* start your impulses along.
  I do not say *all,* but suppose I did—
  the light of reason still tells right from wrong;   75

and Free Will also, which, though it be strained
  in the first battles with the heavens, still
  can conquer all if it is well sustained.   78

You are free subjects of a more immense
  nature and power which grants you intellect
  to free you from the heavens' influence.   81

If, therefore, men today turn from God's laws,
  the fault is in yourselves to seek and find;
  and I shall truly explicate the cause: 84

From the hand of God, whose love shines like a ray
  upon it, even before birth, comes forth
  the simple soul which, like a child at play,   87

cries, laughs, and ignorant of every measure
  but the glad impulse of its joyous Maker,
  turns eagerly to all that gives it pleasure.   90

It tastes small pleasures first. To these it clings,
  deceived, and seeks no others, unless someone
  curb it, or guide its love to higher things.   93

Men, therefore, need restraint by law, and need
  a monarch over them who sees at least
  the towers of The True City. Laws, indeed,   96

there are, but who puts nations to their proof?
  No one. The shepherd who now leads mankind
  can chew the cud, but lacks the cloven hoof.   99

The people, then, seeing their guide devour
  those wordly things to which their hunger turns
  graze where he grazes, and ask nothing more.   102

The bad state of the modern world is due—
  as you may see, then—to bad leadership;
  and not to natural corruption in you.   105

Rome used to shine in two suns when her rod
  made the world good, and each showed her its way:
  one to the ordered world, and one to God.   108

Now one declining sun puts out the other.
  The sword and crook are one, and only evil
  can follow from them when they are together;   111

for neither fears the other, being one.
  Look closely at the ear, if still you doubt me,
  for by the seed it bears is the plant known.   114

Honor and Courtesy once made their home
  in the land the Adige and the Po water
  till Frederick came to loggerheads with Rome.   117

Now any man who has good cause to fear
   the sound of truth or honest company
   may cross it safely—he will find none there.   120

True, three old men are left in whom the past
   reproves the present. How time drags for them
   till God remove them to their joy at last—   123

Conrad da Palazzo, the good Gherard',
   and Guido da Castel, who is better named,
   in the fashion of the French, 'The Honest Lombard.'   126

Say, then, that since the Church has sought to be
   two governments at once, she sinks in muck,
   befouling both her power and ministry."   129

"O Marco mine," I said, "you reason well!
   And now I know why Levi's sons alone
   could not inherit wealth in Israel.   132

But who is this Gherard' in whom you say
   the past survives untarnished to reprove
   the savage breed of this degenerate day?"   135

"Your question seeks to test me," said Lombardo,
   "or else to trick me. How can you speak Tuscan
   and still seem to know nothing of Gherardo?   138

Just what his surname is, I do not know—
   unless he might be known as Gaia's father.
   Godspeed: this is as far as I may go.   141

See there across the smoke, like dawn's first rays,
   the light swell like a glory and a guide.
   The Angel of this place gives forth that blaze,   144

and it is not fit he see me." Thus he spoke,
and said no more, but turned back through the smoke.

NOTES

2. *no planet:* Dante, it must be remembered, considered the Moon (like the Sun) to be a planet.

15. *Take care. Do not let go of me. Take care:* Virgil's warning is especially apt at this point. Wrath is a bitter and a smoky passion that blinds the wrathful soul to reason. The Italian idiom *a perso i lumi degli occhii* (literally, "he has lost the lamps of his eyes") means that a man has lost his reason. Thus Virgil is warning Dante, allegorically, not to lose his Guiding Reason in the blind immoderations of Wrath.

19–20. *Agnus Dei:* The Litany of the Mass includes three prayers, each of which begins with *Agnus Dei*—"Lamb of God which taketh away the sins of the world." The first two add "have mercy upon us." The third adds "give us peace."

21. *in perfect unison:* Wrath is a discord that divides men. So, as part of their purification, these souls learn to unite in perfect concord.

27. *kalends:* The kalends were the first day of each Roman month. To reckon time by kalends, therefore, is to use mortal measures which are meaningless in the eternity of the dead.

27. *someone spoke:* Marco Lombardo, or Marco the Lombard. Nothing is definitely known of him, not even his exact name, for his own identification of himself may mean either "I am a man of Lombardy named Marco," or "I am Marco of the Lombardi family."

38. *these swathings death dissolves:* Mortal flesh. That Dante is alive and that he came by way of Hell are the wonders he promised to reveal to Marco in line 33. (Here, too, one may argue that he is comparing his eternal journey with the voyages of Marco Polo.)

51. *mounted there:* To Heaven, not to the next Cornice.

57. *what was said to me below:* Dante must surely mean what was said by Guido del Duca. Lombardo's theme certainly continues from what Guido had said.

63. *Some see it in the stars; some, here below:* The movements of the stars and planets, as surviving astrologists still believe, determine man's fate and compel his actions. *here below:* Despite the fact that Dante is in Purgatory, his words here must mean "in the world."

66. *and you are its true son:* I.e., "you have inherited its blindness."

70–72. The problem of Free Will is one of the knottiest in Christian theology. Dante is arguing that if a man's actions were entirely determined by the stars, he would have no control over what he does, and that he could not, therefore, justly be given eternal rewards for his virtues nor punishment for his sins.

98–99. *The shepherd who now leads mankind:* The Pope. In 1300 the Pope was Boniface VIII, Dante's supreme symbol of clerical corruption. *can chew the cud, but lacks the cloven hoof . . . :* Another mixed metaphor: the shepherd is presented as himself a sheep. Almost all commentators agree that chewing the cud signified spiritual reflection, and that the cloven hoof signifies the ability to distinguish between good and evil. *Cf.* Aquinas: *discrezionem boni et mali.*

105. *in you:* In mankind.

116. *the land the Adige and the Po water:* Lombardy.

117. *till Frederick came to loggerheads with Rome:* Frederick II engaged in a long and disastrous conflict with, successively, Popes Honorious III, Gregory IX, and Innocent IV.

121–122. *in whom the past reproves the present:* Their merit as survivors from a better age of honor and courtesy is a living reproof to the debased new age.

124. *Conrad* (Corrado) *da Palazzo:* A nobleman of Brescia (BRESH-ah). He held various high offices in Florence, Siena, and Piacenza between 1276 and 1289. According to one old commentator, there was a report that during a battle in which Conrad served as standard-bearer, both his arms were hacked off, but that he held the standard up by hugging it with his stumps until he died. The report is unconfirmed.

124. *Gherard':* Gherardo da Cammino, Captain-General of Treviso from 1283 till his death in 1306. Dante cites him as the type of the true noble in *Il Convivio* IV, 16, 114–123.

125. *Guido da Castel* (Castello): A nobleman of Reggio, famous

for his graciousness and liberality. Dante himself had been received by Guido with great honor.

126. *in the fashion of the French, "The Honest Lombard"*: The French called all Italians "Lombards" and believed all of them to be shrewd and unscrupulous usurers. To be thus called "honest" by them would be to win praise from the least likely source. (Dante's word is "simple"—i.e., not shrewd and unscrupulous—but "honest" is closer in English to what Dante intended.)

127. *Say, then*: Dante has asked to be shown the truth that he may teach it to others. Here, Marco is summing up with Dante's request in mind. "Say [to them] then [to sum up the whole thing]."

131. *why Levi's sons alone*: The Levites, the priests of Israel, were forbidden to inherit wealth, for the Lord was their inheritance, and except for their houses, they were commanded to depend on the tithes and offerings of the people. (See *Numbers* xviii, 20; *Joshua* xiii, 14; and *Deuteronomy* xviii, 2.) Dante has returned once more to his basic charge against the Church—that in massing wealth and power it lost spirituality and grew corrupt. (See *Inferno* XIX, 109–111.)

139. *Just what his surname is, I do not know*: Whoever Marco may be, it seems unlikely that he, in his turn, could speak Tuscan, know so much about Gherardo, and not know him as one of the famous da Cammino family. Dante probably has Marco phrase things in this way in order to bring in a reference to the daughter, Gaia (GUY-yah). Gaia seems to have left two reputations behind her, one for chastity, and one for sexual abandon. Dante has been developing the theme of the degeneration of the descendants of great and good men. It seems likely, therefore, that he thought of Gaia as a wanton, hence, as one more example of the degenerate age in which the daughter of great virtue flits through easy beds.

CANTO XVII

The Fourth Cornice—The Wrathful

THE REIN OF WRATH

The Ascent—The Angel of Meekness

The Poets emerge from the smoke and Dante is immediately en-
rapt by the visions that make up *The Rein of Wrath*. In succession
he beholds *The Destruction Caused by Wrath to Procne*, to *Haman*,
and to *Queen Amata*. Dante emerges from his trance to hear *The
Angel of Meekness* calling to him to show him the ascent, and the
Poets mount at once as the Beatitude, *Blessed are the Peacemakers*,
is sounded behind them.

They reach the top of the Ascent just as night falls, and though
they might normally continue along the level way Dante feels his
body so weighed down that he has to pause and rest.

As the Poets rest, Virgil gives Dante a *Discourse on Love*,
demonstrating to him that all actions spring from either *Natural*
or *Spiritual Love*, and that it is the various *Perversions of Love* that
lead to the sins that are punished in Purgatory.

Reader, if you have ever been closed in
  by mountain mist that left you with no eyes
  to see with, save as moles do, through the skin;   3

think how those dense damp vapors thinned away
  slow bit by bit till through them the sun's ball
  was once more dimly visible—thus you may,   6

and without strain, image from your own
  recalled experience how I came again
  to see the sun, which now was almost down.   9

Thus, matching steps with my true Guide once more,
  I passed beyond the cloud into those rays
  which lay already dead on the low shore.   12

O Fantasy, which can entrance us so
  that we at times stand and are not aware
  though in our ears a thousand trumpets blow!—   15

what moves you since our senses lie dead then?
  —A light that forms in Heaven of itself,
  or of His will who sends its rays to men.   18

A vision grew within me of the wrong
  she did who for her cruelty was changed
  into that bird which most delights in song;   21

and my imagination was so shut
  into itself that what I saw revealed
  could never have come to me from without.   24

Next, down like rain, a figure crucified
  fell into my high fantasy, his face
  fierce and contemptuous even as he died.   27

Nearby him great Ahasuerus stood,
  Esther his wife, and the just Mordecai
  whose word and deed were always one in good.   30

And as soap bubbles rise in air and seem
  full-bodied things, then rupture of themselves
  when the film about them breaks, just so that dream   33

vanished, and through my vision rose an image
  in which a maid cried: "O Queen! Queen no more!
  Your very being canceled by your rage!   36

All not to lose Lavinia? Ah, mother,
  now have you truly lost her. I am she,
    and mourn your death before I mourn another."   39

When strong light beats against a man's closed eyes
  his sleep is broken in him; yet, though broken,
    gives a last twitch before it wholly dies: 42

my vision fell from me exactly so
  the instant a new light beat on my face,
    a light outshining any that men know.   45

I was looking all about, as if to find
  where I might be, when a new voice that cried,
    "Here is the ascent" drove all else from my mind;   48

and kindled in my spirit such a fire
  to see who spoke, as cannot ever rest
    till it stand face to face with its desire.   51

But, as in looking at the sun, whose rays
  keep his form hidden from our stricken eyes—
    so I lacked power to look into that blaze.   54

"A spirit of Heaven guides us toward the height:
  he shows us the ascent before we ask,
    and hides himself in his own holy light.   57

He does for us what men in the world's uses
  do only for themselves; for who sees need
    and waits a plea, already half refuses.   60

To such sweet bidding let our feet reply
  by striving as they may before night fall;
    for then they may not, till day light the sky."   63

So spoke my Guide, and he and I as one
   moved toward the ascent; and soon as I had mounted
   the first step cut into that ramp of stone,   66

I felt what seemed to be a great wing fan
   my face and heard: "Blessèd are the peacemakers,
   who feel no evil wrath toward any man."   69

The last rays, after which night rules the air,
   were now so far above us that already
   the stars began to shine through, here and there.   72

"O strength, why do you melt away?" I said
   several times over to myself, for now
   it seemed my legs were turning into lead.   75

We had come to where the stair ascends no more
   and we were stuck fast on the topmost step
   like a vessel half drawn up upon the shore.   78

I waited with my head cocked to one side
   for any sound that might reveal the nature
   of the new ledge. Then, turning to my Guide,   81

I said: "Dear Father, what impurity
   is washed in pain here? Though our feet must stay,
   I beg you not to stay your speech." And he: 84

"That love of good which in the life before
   lay idle in the soul is paid for now.
   Here Sloth strains at the once-neglected oar.   87

But that you may more clearly know The Way,
   give your entire attention to my words;
   thus shall you gather good fruit from delay.   90

Neither Creator nor his creatures move,
  as you well know," he said, "but in the action
  of animal or of mind-directed love.   93

Natural love may never fall to error.
  The other may, by striving to bad ends,
  or by too little, or by too much fervor.   96

While it desires the Eternal Good and measures
  its wish for secondary goods in reason,
  this love cannot give rise to sinful pleasures.   99

But when it turns to evil, or shows more
  or less zeal than it ought for what is good,
  then the creature turns on its Creator.   102

Thus you may understand that love alone
  is the true seed of every merit in you,
  and of all acts for which you must atone.   105

Now inasmuch as love cannot abate
  its good wish for the self that loves, all things
  are guarded by their nature from self-hate.   108

And since no being may exist alone
  and apart from the First Being, by their nature,
  all beings lack the power to hate That One.   111

Therefore, if I have parsed the truth of things,
  the evil that man loves must be his neighbor's.
  In mortal clay such bad love has three springs: 114

some think they see their own hope to advance
  tied to their neighbor's fall, and thus they long
  to see him cast down from his eminence;   117

some fear their power, preferment, honor, fame
  will suffer by another's rise, and thus,
  irked by his good, desire his ruin and shame;   120

and some at the least injury catch fire
  and are consumed by thoughts of vengeance; thus,
  their neighbor's harm becomes their chief desire.   123

Such threefold love those just below us here
  purge from their souls. The other, which seeks good,
  but without measure, I shall now make clear.—   126

All men, though in a vague way, apprehend
  a good their souls may rest in, and desire it;
  each, therefore, strives to reach his chosen end.   129

If you are moved to see good or pursue it,
  but with a lax love, it is on this ledge—
  after a proper penance—you will rue it.   132

There is another good which bears bad fruit:
  it is not happiness, nor the true essence
  of the Eternal Good, its flower and root.   135

The love that yields too much to this false good
  is mourned on the three Cornices above us;
  but in what way it may be understood   138

as a tripartite thing, I shall not say.
  That, you may learn yourself upon our way."

NOTES

1–3. *as moles do, through the skin:* Dante follows a medieval belief
that the eyes of moles were completely sealed by a membranous cov-

ering through which they could see a diffused foggy light only. Here
the fog does for Dante what the skin covering was supposed to do
for the eyes of moles.

9. *the sun, which now was almost down:* It is near sunset of Easter
Monday, the second day on the mountain.

10. *matching steps . . . once more:* Through the smoke, Dante has
stumbled along holding on to Virgil's shoulder. Now, once more in
the light, he is able to match Virgil's pace.

12. *already dead on the low shore:* Dante, it must be remembered,
conceives Purgatory to be on a scale unmatched by any earthly
mountain. The sun, as seen from the mountain's base, would already
have set. At the poet's altitude, however, the sun is still in sight. Since
sunset would be at six o'clock on the earth's surface, it must be a bit
later than six now.

13–18. THE POWER OF FANTASY. Dante is about to describe
the Rein of Wrath, which consists of another set of visions. Typically,
he introduces the visions with a question on the nature of the imagi-
nation, and in developing his discussion makes clear, first, that the vi-
sions are from Heaven, and second, that he is utterly enrapt by them.

19–39. THE REIN OF WRATH. The three visions of the ru-
inous results of wrath may be taken as exemplifying wrath against
kin, against neighbor, and against God (and self).

The first vision (lines 19–21) shows Procne killing her own son
in wrath. The bird that most delights in song is the nightingale.
Dante probably intends Procne as "she . . . who was changed." See
IX, 15, note, which will also explain her act of great wrath.

The second vision (lines 25–30) is of the crucifixion of Haman,
the powerful minister of Ahasuerus, King of Persia. Enraged against
Mordecai, Haman persuaded Ahasuerus to decree the death of all the
Jews in Persia. A cross (as Dante envisions it, though more likely it
was a stake or a gibbet) was especially prepared for Mordecai. Queen
Esther, however, persuaded Ahasuerus of Haman's iniquity and the
decree was canceled. Not to waste a perfectly good cross, or perhaps
because he was confused by the number of people who were mak-
ing up his mind for him, Ahasuerus had Haman crucified in Morde-
cai's place. The basic story is told in *The Book of Esther.*

The third vision (lines 34–39) is of Amata killing herself for wrath. The incident is from the *Aeneid* XII, 595 ff. Lavinia, daughter of the Latian king, was betrothed to Turnus, a neighboring king. War broke out between Turnus and Aeneas, and Queen Amata, mother of Lavinia, hoped Turnus would kill the invader and marry Lavinia. When a false rumor of Turnus' death reached Amata, she hanged herself for rage at the thought that she had lost Lavinia beyond all hope. Aeneas did later kill Turnus in a duel. Lavinia's words in line 39—"and mourn your death before I mourn another"—are prophetic of the death of Turnus. Lavinia later married Aeneas.

The incident itself will not, however, explain Dante's full intent in citing it unless one remembers Dante's partisan identification with the Trojans. (See especially *Inferno* II, 13–30, and XXVI, 56–63 and notes.) Aeneas was God's chosen and was sent to Italy by Divine Will to found the Roman Empire as the seat of the True Church. It was God's will, therefore, that Aeneas marry Lavinia, daughter of Italy, and thus bring together God's two chosen races. Amata's wrath, therefore, was not only against herself but against God's decree.

47. *a new voice:* The Angel of Meekness.

49–51. Dante's phrasing should be understood in two senses (and both at once). The first: "I was filled with that yearning that allows a man no rest till he have his wish." The second: "I was filled with such yearning that I shall never rest until, this life ended, I rise to stand once more before the Angel."

64–66. *as one:* Virgil leading and Dante a step behind, as they have been going. Thus when Dante switches from the "he and I" of line 64, to the "I" of line 65, he is not being careless but, rather, precise. He mounts the steps a pace behind Virgil. (Reason goes first.)

69. *evil wrath:* One might think wrath inherently evil, and the adjective, therefore, redundant. Dante distinguishes here between Wrath as an evil thing, and Righteous Indignation as a just thing. (See *Inferno* VIII, 43, note.)

70–72. To read Dante is to educate the eye. The observation here is both subtle and exact. At high altitudes the setting sun's rays shoot up so steeply that the first stars begin to appear before the last light of the sun is gone. I do not know whether the phenomenon is observable from any earthly mountain, but it is easily observable in an airplane at high altitude.

77. *and we were stuck fast:* The Poets cannot ascend after darkness, but they have already finished the ascent to the Fourth Cornice. They are, therefore, free to continue on the level of the ledge. It is not darkness that stops them, but the contagion of Sloth that takes away their wills, though briefly. (See also XVIII, 87–90, and note to 87. And compare the pause they make in *Inferno* XI, where the stench of Lower Hell is so great the Poets must wait till their nostrils adjust to it.)

85–87. SLOTH. The central sin (there are three deadly sins below it and three above it) is Acedia (from L. *accidia,* from Gr. roots meaning "not caring") or Sloth. Sloth, however, must not be understood as physical laziness or slovenliness but as torpor of the soul which, loving the good, does not pursue it actively enough. Dante's condition in the Dark Wood of Error, from which he embarked on his long journey, is best conceived as a recognition of the slothful worldliness of his soul up to that time. The entire journey, in fact, is Dante's active pursuit of the true good, his own purgation from Acedia.

Acedia, however, is not simply the failure to perform good works for others, though it readily involves that failure. It is, more specifically, the failure to pay enough attention to the good, to make enough demands upon oneself. Were one to give all of his energy and attention to the pursuit of God's truth, good works would follow automatically. Acedia may consist in being too torpid to arrive at a vision of the good, or in achieving that vision but neglecting to pursue it.

90. *from delay:* Since Dante finds himself temporarily deprived of strength to continue, he seeks to win advantage from delay, thus showing a zeal of which the Slothful failed in their lives. (Here, also, compare *Inferno* XI.)

93. *animal love:* Blind instinct. *mind-directed love:* Those desires shared by the God-given light of reason.

95–96. Free will may err in three ways. First, by seeking bad goals (the self-love of Pride, which seeks to rise above others; of

Envy, which resents the rise of others; and of Wrath, which seeks revenge at the cost of others). Second, by too little zeal for the known good (Sloth). And third, by too much love for the good things of this world (Avarice, Gluttony, and Lust).

97–98. *the Eternal Good:* God. *secondary goods:* The pleasures of the earth given to man for his delight. To deny these is to reject God's bounty; to seek them immoderately is to abandon God for His gifts.

106–108. *love cannot abate:* The doctrine here is Aquinian. Nothing in creation seeks anything but what it takes to be the good of love. Even suicide is an act motivated by self-love, the suicide believing he does himself more good in escaping life than in enduring it.

124. *those just below . . . purge:* Those on the first three Cornices.

125. *The other:* The other kind of love.

132. *after a proper penance:* After a penitent turning to God, and after the delay in Purgatory for the period of time they made God wait. After due penance, due punishment.

CANTO XVIII

The Fourth Cornice—The Slothful

THE WHIP OF SLOTH · THE REIN OF SLOTH

Virgil continues his *Discourse on Love,* explaining *The Relation of Love and Free Will,* but warns Dante that Reason is limited. Dante must seek the final answer from Beatrice, for the question involves one of the mysteries of faith.

It is near midnight when Virgil concludes, and Dante is starting to drowse, when he is suddenly brought awake by a long train of souls who come running and shouting from around the mountain. They are *The Slothful,* the souls of those who recognized The Good but were not diligent in pursuit of it. As once they delayed, so now they are all hurry and zeal, and will not even pause to speak to the Poets.

Two souls run before the rest shouting aloud *The Whip of Sloth,* one citing Mary as an example of holy zeal, the other citing Caesar as an example of temporal zeal.

Virgil hails the racing souls to ask the nearer way to the ascent, but not even the news that Dante is still alive slows them. One soul, a former *Abbot of San Zeno,* shouts back an answer while still running.

Behind the train come two more souls shouting *The Rein of Sloth,* citing as examples of the downfall of the laggard, the Israelites in the desert, and those followers of Aeneas who remained in Sicily.

The souls pass from sight and hearing. Dante, his head full of confused thoughts, sinks into sleep. Instantly, his thoughts are transformed into *A Dream.*

His explanation at an end, My Guide,
  that lofty scholar, scrutinized my face
  as if to see if I seemed satisfied.   3

And I, my thirst already sprung anew,
  said nothing, thinking "He may well be tired
  of all this questioning I put him through."   6

But that true Father, sensing both my thirst
  and that I was too timid to reveal it,
  encouraged me to speak by speaking first.   9

I, therefore: "Master, in the light you shed
  my sight grows so acute that I see clearly
  all that your argument implied or said.   12

But, dear and gentle Father, please discourse
  more fully on that love in which you say
  all good and evil actions have their source."   15

And he: "Focus the keen eyes of your mind
  on what I say, and you will see made clear
  the error of the blind who lead the blind.   18

The soul, being created prone to Love,
  is drawn at once to all that pleases it,
  as soon as pleasure summons it to move.   21

From that which really is, your apprehension
  extracts a form which it unfolds within you;
  that form thereby attracts the mind's attention,   24

then if the mind, so drawn, is drawn to it,
  that summoning force is Love; and thus within you,
  through pleasure, a new natural bond is knit.   27

Then, just as fire yearns upward through the air,
  being so formed that it aspires by nature
  to be in its own element up there;   30

so love, which is a spiritual motion,
   fills the trapped soul, and it can never rest
   short of the thing that fills it with devotion.   33

By now you will, of course, have understood
   how little of the truth they see who claim
   that every love is, in itself, a good;   36

for though love's substance always will appear
   to be a good, not every impress made,
   even in finest wax, is good and clear."   39

"Your words and my own eager mind reveal
   exactly what Love is," I said, "but now
   there is an even greater doubt I feel: 42

if love springs from outside the soul's own will,
   it being made to love, what merit is there
   in loving good, or blame in loving ill?"   45

And he to me: "As far as reason sees,
   I can reply. The rest you must ask Beatrice.
   The answer lies within faith's mysteries.   48

Every substantial form distinct from matter
   and yet united with it in some way,
   has a specific power in it. This latter   51

is not perceivable save as it gives
   evidence of its workings and effects—
   as the green foliage tells us a plant lives.   54

Therefore, no man can know whence springs the light
   of his first cognizance, nor of the bent
   of such innate primordial appetite   57

as springs within you, as within the bee
  the instinct to make honey; and such instincts
  are, in themselves, not blamable nor worthy.   60

Now, that all later wills and this first bent
  may thrive, the innate counsel of your Reason
  must surely guard the threshold of consent.   63

This is the principle from which accrue
  your just deserts, according as it reaps
  and winnows good or evil love in you.   66

Those masters who best reasoned nature's plan
  discerned this innate liberty, and therefore
  they left their moral science to guide Man.   69

Or put it this way: all love, let us say,
  that burns in you, springs from necessity;
  but you still have the power to check its sway.   72

These noble powers Beatrice will comprehend
  as 'The Free Will.' Keep that term well in mind
  if she should speak of it when you ascend."   75

It was near midnight. The late-risen moon,
  like a brass bucket polished bright as fire,
  thinned out the lesser stars, which seemed to drown.   78

It traveled retrograde across that sign
  the sun burns when the Romans look between
  the Sards and Corsicans to its decline.   81

And he who made Piètola shine above
  all other Mantuan towns, had discharged fully
  the burden I had laid on him for love;   84

because of which I, being pleased to find
  such clear and open answers to my questions,
  was rambling drowsily within my mind.   87

I wakened in an instant to a pack
  of people running toward us, a great mob
  that broke around the mountain at my back: 90

as once, of old, wild hordes ran through the night
  along Ismenus' and Asopus' banks
  when Thebes invoked no more than Bacchus' might;   93

in such a frenzy, far as I could see,
  those who were spurred by good will and high love
  ran bent like scythes along that Cornice toward me.   96

They were upon us soon, for all that rout
  was running furiously, and out in front
  two spirits streaming tears were calling out: 99

"Mary *ran* to the hills"—so one refrain;
  and the other: "Caesar, to subdue Ilerda
  struck at Marseilles, and then *swooped* down
                                    on Spain."   102

"Faster! Faster! To be slow in love
  is to lose time," cried those who came behind;
  "Strive on that grace may bloom again above."   105

"O souls in whom the great zeal you now show
  no doubt redeems the negligence and delay
  that marred your will to do good, there below;   108

this man lives—truly—and the instant day
  appears again, he means to climb. Please show him
  how he may reach the pass the nearer way."   111

So spoke my Master, and one running soul
  without so much as breaking step replied:
  "Come after us, and you will find the hole.   114

The will to move on with all speed so fills us
  we cannot stop; we humbly beg your pardon
  if duty makes us seem discourteous.   117

I was abbot of San Zeno in the reign
  of the good emperor Frederick Barbarossa,
  of whom the Milanese still speak with pain.   120

And another with one foot now in the grave
  will shed tears for the monastery soon,
  and rue the evil orders he once gave.   123

For he has set his son up as the head—
  a man deformed in body, worse in mind,
  and bastard born—in its true Pastor's stead."   126

He had by then left us so far behind
  that if he said more, it was lost to me:
  but I was pleased to keep this much in mind.   129

My aid on all occasion, the prompt Master,
  said: "Look, for here come two who cry aloud
  the Scourge of Sloth, that souls may flee it faster." 132

At the tail end one runner cried: "They died
  before the Jordan saw its heirs, those people
  for whom the Red Sea's waters stood aside."   135

The other: "Those who found it too laborious
  to go the whole way with Anchises' son
  cut from their lives all that was glorious."   138

Then when those shades had drawn so far ahead
   that I could not make out a trace of them,
   a new thought seized upon me, and it bred   141

so many more, so various, and so scrambled,
   that turning round and round inside itself
   so many ways at once, my reason rambled;   144

I closed my eyes and all that tangled theme
   was instantly transformed into a dream.

NOTES

18. *the blind who lead the blind:* Virgil means here the teachers of Epicurean philosophy and their students, both spiritually blind in Dante's view in that they teach that all desire (i.e., all love, as Virgil calls it) is a good thing and should be gratified.

19 ff. VIRGIL'S DISCOURSE ON LOVE. The doctrine Dante puts into Virgil's mouth is typically medieval both in content and in the manner of its statement. The soul, Virgil posits, is made with a potential for love, i.e., it is naturally drawn to that which pleases it. Such love passes to action in three stages.

Lines 22–24 describe the first stage. The apprehensive faculty (the senses plus the intellect) observes *that which really is* (any object that has real existence) and extracts from it a *form* (not the thing, but what the mind conceives the thing to be). This *form* is registered upon the soul.

Lines 25–27 describe the second stage. If the soul is drawn to that form, it yields to it with a natural tie of love. It is in this way that the soul has contact with creation.

Lines 28–33 describe the third stage. Just as fire is so conceived and made by Nature that it naturally yearns to rise "up there" (i.e., to the Sphere of Fire) so the soul, by its very nature (its natural disposition to love) yearns for that which attracts it.

37–39. *love's substance:* Dante uses the philosophical term *matera,* i.e., matter, which may be taken to mean either "the thing loved" (which will always appear as a good to one who loves it), or "the natural substance of love," i.e., the soul's naturally created aptitude to love.

The Epicureans, according to Dante, err in not seeing that appearances may beguile the soul into loving a bad object (the Epicureans, of course, would reply that nothing that gives pleasure can be bad) and thus, that a force that is good in its potential may be exercised in such a way as to be evil in its action.

43–45. I have taken liberties here for the sake of clarity. The passage literally rendered would read: "If love is offered to us from outside, and the soul does not go with another foot (i.e., has no other way of choosing its course), then whether it goes rightly or wrongly is not a matter of its own merit."

49. *substantial form:* A scholastic term for "the essence of a thing." The substantial form of man is his soul, which is distinct from matter, yet united with it. Each substantial form has its specific tendencies, characteristics, and capacities which are visible only in its working and effects. Before what the Catholic Church declares to be the the age of reason (approximately age seven) these powers are simply innate and neutral. Thereafter, there develops within the soul a capacity to reason, and in order to gather the soul into a harmonious unit, innate reason must decide what may and what may not pass the threshold of the soul and be gathered into its love. With reason as the principle of conduct, the soul is then responsible for its actions.

67. *those masters:* Aristotle and Plato. Both based their moral philosophy upon free will.

75. *if she should speak of it:* Beatrice discusses Free Will in the Sphere of the Moon, *Paradiso* V, 19 ff.

76–81. Note that Dante does not say that the moon rose at midnight, but only that it was near midnight and that the moon was late-risen.

He then appends an astronomical figure too complicated to explain here in detail. In brief, the moon in its monthly retrograde motion is in the sign of the Zodiac (commentators dispute whether Dante means Scorpio or Sagittarius) in which the sun is when a Roman sees it set in a position between Sardinia and Corsica.

82. *Piètola:* A village near Mantua. One legend—and Dante obviously follows it—has it that Virgil was born in Piètola rather than in Mantua proper. Thus Piètola outshines all other Mantuan towns because it was Virgil's birthplace.

83–84. *had discharged fully:* The burden of all the doubts Dante has laid upon him.

87. *was rambling drowsily:* Mental laxness seems to be contagious on this Cornice. Dante, satisfied with what he has learned, does not answer with his usual eagerness, but lets his mind wander off. The appearance of the band of the Slothful, however, awakens him instantly, their presence and the nature of their sin reproaching Dante for his self-indulgence.

91–93. *Ismenus and Asopus:* Boetian rivers. The ancient Thebans ran on their banks at night invoking the aid of Bacchus when they needed rain for their vines. Dante makes a careful point in his phrasing: the Thebans exerted themselves for no more than such a pagan and earthly deity as Bacchus could give, but here the sinners strain for the Supreme Good.

96. *bent like scythes:* Bent so in the speed of their race.

97–102. THE WHIP OF SLOTH. The examples here are shouted by two of the sinners who run before the others. The first example of zeal (spiritual) is Mary's haste, after the Annunciation, to go visit Elizabeth in the hill country of Juda (*Luke* i, 39). The second (temporal) is Caesar's diligence in the conquest of Ilerda (the modern Spanish town of Lérida). He laid siege to Marseilles, left an army there under Brutus, and pushed by forced marches to take Ilerda.

Since all zeal must be either spiritual or temporal, two examples are enough to cover all possible categories.

109. *this man lives—truly:* Virgil is announcing the news that has amazed all other souls in Purgatory, but these souls are so intent on pursuing their purification that they pay no attention. Their attention is focused on the Supreme Good, and they shun the distraction of lesser things.

111. *the nearer way:* There is one ascent from each Cornice. Virgil's object on each ledge is to learn the short rather than the long

way round the circle to it. As it has been on every other ledge, the nearer way is to the right.

118. *San Zeno:* There are three churches of San Zeno in Verona, one of which has a monastery attached. The speaker has not been positively identified, but the Abbot of San Zeno through most of Barbarossa's reign was Gherardo II, who died in 1187.

119. *Frederick Barbarossa:* Frederick Redbeard. Frederick I, Emperor from 1152–1190. Dante calls him "good" because he pursued the good of the Empire. Frederick quarreled with Pope Alexander III and was excommunicated by him. Frederick then warred on the Pope's adherents in Lombardy. He took Milan in 1163, pulled down its walls, burned the city, ploughed the ruins, and sowed the ground with salt that nothing might grow there. After other bloody successes, his fortunes turned, and he had to kneel to Alexander for pardon. He drowned while crusading in the Holy Land.

121–126. *another with one foot now in the grave:* Alberto della Scala, Lord of Verona, who died in September of 1301. Thus, in 1300 he already had one foot in the grave. He had three natural sons, among them the famous Can Grande della Scala, who was Dante's host and protector in exile. Another was Giuseppe, and it was this son Alberto forced upon the monks as Abbot of San Zeno, a post he held from 1292 to 1313. The speaker, as former abbot, is especially indignant that an unworthy man should hold so high an office. Giuseppe was triply disqualified, being mentally incapable, physically deformed, and a bastard. Except by special dispensation, the Catholic Church does not grant ordination to the illegitimate; the candidate for ordination must of course be mentally qualified, and he must be free of physical deformities that would interfere with the performance of his duties. (A priest with a mutilated hand, for example, might not be able to celebrate the mass properly. Nor could a deaf priest hear confessions.)

127. *left us so far behind:* The sinner never slackened pace as he spoke.

129. *but I was pleased to keep this much in mind:* Dante seems to relish his chance to fire a shot at Alberto della Scala, certainly not as a personal attack on the father of his great protector, but generally

against all the temporal lords of Italy who used their power to corrupt the church by imposing their will and politics upon its offices.

131–138. THE REIN OF SLOTH. As two of the sinners ran ahead to shout the examples of the Whip, so two more run behind the train shouting the examples that constitute the Rein.

As usual, the first example of the destruction of the laggard is from sacred history. It reminds the sinners that though the Lord delivered Israel from Egyptian bondage, opening the Red Sea for their passage, the people still muttered and would not follow Moses (i.e., would not diligently pursue good); and that, therefore, the Lord doomed them to die in the wilderness. Of all Israel that crossed the Red Sea, only Joshua and Caleb reached the Promised Land of Jordan's waters. (*Numbers* xiv, 26–34; *Exodus* xiv, 10–20; *Deuteronomy* i, 26–36.)

The second example, from secular history, reminds the sinners of those followers of Aeneas who chose to live at ease in Sicily rather than follow him to the great end that had been promised. Thus they did not share in the glory of founding Rome.

Note that both incidents provide a parable of a promised joy (Heaven) lost by lack of zeal in following the clearly indicated road.

CANTO XIX

The Fourth Cornice—The Slothful

DANTE'S DREAM OF SIRENA

The Ascent—The Angel of Zeal

The Fifth Cornice—The Hoarders and Wasters
(The Avaricious)

Just before morning (when the truth is dreamed) Dante dreams of *The Siren* that lures the souls of men to incontinent worldliness. Hideous in her true form, the Siren grows irresistible in men's eyes as they look upon her. *A Heavenly Lady* races in upon the dream and calls to Virgil who, thus summoned, strips the Siren, exposing her filthy body. Such a stench rises from her, so exposed, that Dante wakens shuddering, to find Virgil calling him to resume the journey.

The Angel of Zeal shows them the passage, and when his wings have fanned the Poets, Dante casts off his depression and lethargy, and rushes up the remaining length of the passage.

Arrived at *The Fifth Cornice,* Virgil inquires the way of one of the souls of *The Hoarders and Wasters,* who lie motionless and outstretched, bound hand and foot, with their faces in the dust.

The soul of *Pope Adrian V* replies that, if they have incurred no guilt by Hoarding or Wasting, they may pass on to the right. Dante kneels in reverence to Adrian and is scolded for doing so. Adrian then dismisses Dante in order to resume his purification. Adrian's last request is that his niece, *Alagia,* be asked to pray for his soul.

At the hour when the heat of the day is overcome
  by Earth or at times by Saturn, and can no longer
  temper the cold of the moon; when on the dome   3

of the eastern sky the geomancers sight
  Fortuna Major rising on a course
  on which, and soon, it will be drowned in light;   6

there came to me in a dream a stuttering crone,
  squint-eyed, clubfooted, both her hands deformed,
  and her complexion like a whitewashed stone.   9

I stared at her; and just as the new sun
  breathed life to night-chilled limbs, just so my look
  began to free her tongue, and one by one   12

drew straight all her deformities, and warmed
  her dead face, till it bloomed as love would wish it
  for its delight. When she was thus transformed,   15

her tongue thus loosened, she began to sing
  in such a voice that only with great pain
  could I have turned from her soliciting.   18

"I am," she sang, "Sirena. I am she
  whose voice is honeyed with such sweet enticements
  it trances sailing men far out to sea.   21

I turned Ulysses from his wanderer's way
  with my charmed song, and few indeed who taste
  how well I satisfy would think to stray."   24

Her mouth had not yet shut when at my side
  appeared a saintly lady, poised and eager
  to heap confusion on the Siren's pride.   27

"O Virgil, Virgil! Who," she cried, "is this?"
  Roused by her indignation, Virgil came:
  his eyes did not once leave that soul of bliss.   30

He seized the witch, and with one rip laid bare
  all of her front, her loins and her foul belly:
  I woke sick with the stench that rose from there.   33

I turned then, and my Virgil said to me:
   "I have called at least three times now. Rise and come
   and let us find your entrance." Willingly   36

I rose to my feet. Already the high day
   lit all the circles of the holy mountain.
   The sun was at our backs as we took our way.   39

I followed in his steps, my brow as drawn
   as is a man's so bowed with thought he bends
   like half an arch of a bridge. And moving on,   42

I heard the words: "Come. This is where you climb."
   pronounced in such a soft and loving voice
   as is not heard here in our mortal time.   45

With swanlike wings outspread, he who had spoken
   summoned us up between the walls of rock.
   He fanned us with his shining pinions then,   48

affirming over us as we went by
   "Blessed are they that mourn—for they shall have
   their consolation given them on high."   51

"What ails you?" said my Guide. "What heavy mood
   makes you stare at the ground?" (We were by then
   above the point at which the Angel stood.)   54

And I: "An apparition clouds my spirit,
   a vision from a dream so strange and dreadful
   I cannot seem to leave off thinking of it."   57

"Did you see that ageless witch," he said, "for whom
   —and for no other—those above us weep?
   And did you see how men escape her doom?   60

Let it teach your heels to scorn the earth, your eyes
  to turn to the high lure the Eternal King
  spins with his mighty spheres across the skies."   63

As falcons stare at their feet until they hear
  the wished-for call, then leap with wings outspread
  in eagerness for the meat that waits them there;   66

so did I move: filled with desire, I ran
  up the remaining length of the rock passage
  to the point at which the next great Round began.   69

When I stood on the fifth ledge and looked around,
  I saw a weeping people everywhere
  lying outstretched and face-down on the ground.   72

"My soul cleaves to the dust," I heard them cry
  over and over as we stood among them;
  and every word was swallowed by a sigh.   75

"O Chosen of God, spirits whose mournful rites
  both Hope and Justice make less hard to bear,
  show us the passage to the further heights."   78

"If you have not been sentenced to lie prone
  in the bitter dust, and seek the nearest way,
  keep the rim to your right as you go on."   81

So spoke the Poet, and so a voice replied
  from the ground in front of us. I took good note
  of what its way of speaking did not hide.   84

I turned my eyes to Virgil then, and he
  gave me a happy sign of his permission
  to do what my eyes asked. Being thus free   87

to act according to my own intention,
  I moved ahead and stood above that soul
  whose speaking had attracted my attention,   90

saying: "O Soul in whom these tears prepare
  that without which no soul can turn to God,
  put off a while, I beg, your greater care,   93

to tell me who you were, why you lie prone,
  and if there is some way that I may serve you
  in the world I left while still in flesh and bone."   96

"Why Heaven makes us turn our backs shall be
  made known to you," the spirit said, "but first
  scias quod ego fui successor Petri.   99

Between Sestri and Chiaveri, flowing on
  through a fair land, there is a pleasant river
  from which the title of my line is drawn.   102

A single month, a month and some few days
  I came to know on my own weary body
  how heavily the Papal Mantle weighs   105

upon the wearer who would take good care
  to keep it from the mire; compared to that
  all other burdens are as light as air.   108

My conversion, alas, came late; for only when
  I had been chosen Pastor of Holy Rome
  did I see the falseness in the lives of men.   111

I saw no heart's rest there, nor ease from strife,
  nor any height the flesh-bound soul might climb,
  and so I came to love this other life.   114

My soul was lost to God until that moment,
  and wholly given over to avarice;
  such was my sin, such is my punishment.   117

The nature of avarice is here made plain
  in the nature of its penalty; there is not
  a harsher forfeit paid on the whole mountain.   120

We would not raise our eyes to the shining spheres
  but kept them turned to mundane things: so Justice
  bends them to earth here in this place of tears.   123

As Avarice, there, quenched all our souls' delight
  in the good without which all our works are lost,
  so, here, the hand of Justice clamps us tight.   126

Taken and bound here hand and foot, we lie
  outstretched and motionless; and here we stay
  at the just pleasure of the Father on High."   129

I had knelt to him. Now I spoke once more.
  That spirit sensed at once my voice was nearer
  and guessed my reverence. "Why do you lower   132

your knees into the dust?" he said to me.
  And I: "My conscience troubled me for standing
  in the presence of your rank and dignity."   135

"Straighten your legs, my brother! Rise from error!"
  he said. "I am, like you and all the others,
  a fellow servant of one Emperor.   138

It is written in holy scripture *Neque nubent;*
  if ever you understood that sacred text,
  my reason for speaking will be evident.   141

Now go your way. I wish to be alone.
  Your presence here distracts me from the tears
  that make me ready. And to your last question:

I have a niece, Alagia, still on earth.
  If she can but avoid the bad example
  those of our line have set, her native worth

will lead her yet the way the blessed go.
  And she alone remains to me below."

NOTES

1–3. An intricate passage based on the medieval belief that sunlight reflected from earth to the moon produced warmth on the moon, whereas sunlight reflected from the moon to the earth produced cold on the earth. *At the hour:* Before dawn. The accumulated heat of the day would have been dissipated through the long night and could no longer temper the cold of the moon. *overcome by Earth:* The last heat of the day is overcome by the night-chilled earth. *or at times by Saturn:* The times would be those in which Saturn draws close to the horizon. Saturn was believed to be a cold planet, as opposed to Mars, a hot planet.

5. *Fortuna Major:* A conjunction of the last stars of Aquarius and the first of Pisces, supposed to signify great good fortune. In this season these stars would be rising just before dawn, hence the sun is coming up behind them and their course will soon be drowned in light.

7 ff. DANTE'S DREAM. The Sirens were mythological creatures, usually of great beauty, and with the power of singing so entracingly that they charmed the souls of men. They were usually presented as luring sailors at sea to their destruction.

Dante's Sirena is a Christian adaptation. She symbolizes the three remaining sins (Greed, Gluttony, and Lust), which is to say, the abandonment to physical appetites. So in lines 58–60 Dante calls her "the ageless witch, for whom—and for no other—those above us [on the three remaining ledges] weep." Dante's description of her tells all the rest: she is deformed and hideous in herself but grows beautiful in the eyes of men, and few of those she lures to her pleasures ever stray from the kind of satisfaction she gives them. Only when a Heavenly Voice (the unidentified Saintly Lady of lines 26–30) summons Reason to strip Sensual Abandon of its false trappings, does man waken from his dream to realize what abomination has entranced him.

Note that she cannot be taken to symbolize the Pleasures of the Appetite (for those were given by God for man's joy in His creation), but the Abandonment of the Soul to Excessive Physical Appetite.

22. *I turned Ulysses:* In the Homeric version Ulysses escapes the Siren's blandishments by stuffing his ears with wax and having himself lashed to the mast of his ship. Dante may, perhaps, be following another version of the myth, but more probably he means to portray the Siren as a liar, an allegorically significant point.

26. *a saintly lady:* She may be Beatrice, or she may be Provenient Grace, but any identification is speculative.

43. *I heard the words:* They are spoken by the Angel of Zeal. Note that Dante is moving along bowed in thought and rather slowly, his spirit still weighed by the vision of the Siren, until they pass the Angel. Once the Angel of Zeal has fanned them with his wings, however (and by now the reader knows, without being told, that the fourth *P* has disappeared from Dante's brow), Virgil, as Dante's own Reason, tells him what he should do, and Dante immediately loses his heaviness, and hurries eagerly up the remaining passage to the next Cornice.

50. *blessed are they that mourn:* The Fourth Beatitude. "Blessed are they that mourn: for they shall be comforted." (*Matthew* iv, 5.)

73. *My soul cleaves to the dust:* Psalm CXIX.

76 ff. THE HOARDERS AND WASTERS. The sinfulness of Avarice is in the fact that it turns the soul away from God to an inordinate concern for material things. Since such immoderation can express itself in either getting or spending, the Hoarders and Wasters are here punished together and in the same way for the two extremes of the same excess, as in Hell.

84. *what its way of speaking did not hide:* The soul has said, "If you have not been sentenced to lie prone in the bitter dust." The impli-

cation is—and it is the first time the point has emerged clearly—that souls may pass through some of the Cornices without delay, if they are free of the taint of sin there punished. The speaker, his face in the dust, cannot know that Dante is a living man. He must have assumed, therefore, that Virgil's request for directions is that of a soul that has completed its purification on one of the lower Cornices, and that has no penance to do for Avarice. Dante, ever eager to grasp the nature of things, seizes upon the implication. In XIII, 133 ff., Dante makes it clear that he has penance to do for Pride, and some, though very little, for Envy. It is clear, therefore, that souls may be required to undergo penance on successive Cornices, and in XXI and XXII Statius confirms that fact. Now we know that souls may pass through some of the Cornices without delay.

99. *scias quod ego fui successor Petri:* "Know that I was Peter's successor." The speaker is Pope Adrian V. He died in 1276 after having been Pope for thirty-eight days.

101. *a pleasant river:* The river is the Lavagna. It flows between Sestri and Chiaveri, small coastal towns near Genoa. Adrian, born Ottobuono de' Fieschi, was of the line of the Counts of Lavagna.

139. *Neque nubent:* ". . . they neither marry [nor are given in marriage but are as the angels of God in heaven]" (*Matthew* xxii, 30). These were Christ's words when asked to which husband a remarried widow would belong in Heaven. Adrian obviously extends the meaning to include the cancellation of all earthly contracts, fealties, and honors. *Cf.* Cato's attitude toward Marcia in Canto I. It is well to remember, too, that the passing of the Christian marriage vow is "till death do us part."

145. *Alagia* (Ah-LAH-djah): Daughter of Niccolò di Tedisio di Ugone de' Fieschi (Oo-GO-ne day Fee-YEH-ski) and wife of Moroello (Moh-roh-ELL-oh) Malaspina, Marquis of Giovagallo (Djoe-vah-GAH-lo). Dante had been well received by Malaspina and knew and admired his wife for her good works.

CANTO XX

The Fifth Cornice—The Hoarders and Wasters
(The Avaricious)

THE WHIP OF AVARICE · THE REIN
OF AVARICE

Dante walks on after Adrian has dismissed him, wishing he might have continued the conversation, but bowing to Adrian's wish to resume his purification.

The Poets find the ledge so crowded with the souls of the Avaricious that only one narrow passage is left open to them. Dante hears a soul cry out *The Whip of Avarice,* a litany in praise of *Mary, Fabricius,* and *St. Nicholas.* The sinner identifies himself as *Hugh Capet* and proceeds to a *Denunciation of The Capetian Kings,* the dynasty he himself founded, but which has degenerated into a succession of kings distinguished only for their bloodthirsty avarice.

Hugh Capet then explains *The Rein of Avarice,* citing seven examples of the downfall of the Avaricious.

Dante has hardly left Capet when he feels the mountain shake as if stricken by *An Earthquake,* and he hears *A Shout of Triumph.* Dante is frightened but Virgil reassures him. The Poets move on at top speed, but Dante remains deep in thought, his mind pondering these new phenomena.

What's willed must bow to what is stronger willed:
  against my pleasure, to please him, I drew
  my sponge back from the water still unfilled.   3

I turned: my Guide set off along the space
  left clear next to the rock; for they who drain,
  slow tear by tear, the sin that eats the race   6

left little room along the outer edge.
  Thus, as one hugs the battlements in walking
  atop a wall, we moved along the ledge.   9

Hell take you, She-Wolf, who in the sick feast
   of your ungluttable appetite have taken
   more prey on earth than any other beast!   12

You Heavens, in whose turnings, as some say,
   things here below are changed—when will he come
   whose power shall drive her from the light of day?   15

We moved along with measured step and slow,
   and all my thoughts were centered on those shades,
   their tears and lamentations moved me so.   18

And walking thus, I heard rise from the earth
   before us: "Blessed Mary!"—with a wail
   such as is wrung from women giving birth.   21

"How poor you were," the stricken voice went on,
   "is testified to all men by the stable
   in which you laid your sacred burden down."   24

And then: "O good Fabricius, you twice
   refused great wealth that would have stained your honor,
   and chose to live in poverty, free of vice."   27

These words had pleased me so that I drew near
   the place from which they seemed to have been
                                                spoken,
   eager to know what soul was lying there.   30

The voice was speaking now of the largesse
   St. Nicholas bestowed on the three virgins
   to guide their youth to virtuous steadiness.   33

"O soul," I said, "whose words recite such good,
   let me know who you were, and why no other
   joins in your praises of such rectitude.   36

If I return to finish the short race
  remaining of that life that ends so soon,
  your words will not lack some reward of grace."   39

"Not for such comfort as the world may give
  do I reply," he said, "but that such light
  of grace should shine on you while yet you live.   42

I was the root of that malignant tree
  which cast its shadow on all Christendom
  so that the soil bears good fruit only rarely.   45

But if Douay and Lille and Bruges and Ghent
  were strong again, their vengeance would be swift;
  and that it may, I pray the King of Judgment.   48

I was Hugh Capet in my mortal state.
  From me stem all the Philips and the Louis'
  who have occupied the throne of France of late.   51

I was born in Paris as a butcher's son.
  When the old line of kings had petered out
  to one last heir, who wore a monk's gray gown,   54

I found that I held tight in my own hand
  the reins of state, and that my new wealth gave me
  such power and such allies at my command,   57

that my son's head, with pomp and sacrament
  rose to the widowed crown of France. From him
  those consecrated bones took their descent.   60

Till the great dowry of Provence increased
  my race so that it lost its sense of shame,
  it came to little, but did no harm at least.   63

That was the birth of its rapacity,
   its power, its lies. Later—to make amends—
   it took Normandy, Ponthieu, and Gascony.   66

Charles came to Italy, and—to make amends—
   he victimized Conradin. Then he sent
   Saint Thomas back to Heaven—to make amends.   69

I see a time, not far off, that brings forth
   another Charles from France. It shall make clear
   to many what both he and his are worth.   72

He comes alone, unarmed but for the lance
   of Judas, which he drives so hard he bursts
   the guts of Florence with the blow he plants.   75

He wins no land there; only sin and shame.
   And what is worse for him is that he holds
   such crimes too lightly to repent his blame.   78

The third, once hauled from his own ship, I see
   selling his daughter, haggling like a pirate
   over a girl sold into slavery.   81

O Avarice, what more harm can you do?
   You have taken such a hold on my descendants
   they sell off their own flesh and blood for you!   84

But dwarfing all crimes, past or yet to be,
   I see Alagna entered, and, in His Vicar,
   Christ Himself dragged in captivity.   87

I see Him mocked again and crucified,
   the gall and vinegar once more sent up.
   He dies again—with *live* thieves at His side.   90

I see another Pilate, so full of spite
  not even that suffices: his swollen sails
  enter the very Temple without right.   93

O God, my Lord, when shall my soul rejoice
  to see Thy retribution, which, lying hidden,
  sweetens Thine anger in Thy secret choice?   96

What you first heard me cry in adoration
  of that one only Bride of the Holy Ghost,
  which made you turn and ask an explanation,   99

is the litany we add to every prayer
  as long as it is day. When the sun sets
  we raise the counter-cry on the night air.   102

We cry then how Pygmalion of old
  was made a traitor, thief, and parricide
  by his insatiable sick lust for gold;   105

how Midas suffered when his miser's prayer
  was answered, and became forever after
  the legend of a ludicrous despair;   108

and then we tell how Achan, covetous,
  stole from the booty, for which Joshua's rage
  still falls upon him—so it seems to us.   111

We cry Sapphira's and her husband's blame;
  we praise the hooves that battered Heliodorus;
  then round the ledge runs Polymnestor's name,   114

foul to all time with Polydorus' blood.
  Then we conclude the litany crying: 'Crassus,
  you supped on gold—tell us, did it taste good?'   117

We wail or mutter in our long remorse
  according to the inner spur that drives us,
    at times with more, at others with less force: 120

thus I was not the only one who praised
  the good we tell by day; but, as it happened,
    the only one nearby whose voice was raised."   123

We had already left him to his prayers
  and were expending every ounce of strength
    on the remaining distance to the stairs,   126

when suddenly I felt the mountain shake
  as if it tottered. Such a numb dread seized me
    as a man feels when marching to the stake.   129

Not even Delos, in that long ago
  before Latona went there to give birth
    to Heaven's eyes, was ever shaken so.   132

Then there went up a cry on every side,
  so loud that the sweet Master, bending close
    said: "Do not fear, for I am still your Guide."   135

"Glory to God in the Highest!" rang a shout
  from every throat—as I could understand
    from those nearby, whose words I could make out.   138

We stood there motionless, our souls suspended—
  as had the shepherds who first heard that hymn—
    until the ground grew still and the hymn ended.   141

Then we pushed on our holy way once more,
  studying those prostrate souls who had already
    resumed their lamentation, as before.   144

I never felt my soul assaulted so—
  unless my memory err—as in that war
  ·between my ignorance and desire to know   147

the explanation of that shock and shout;
  nor dared I ask, considering our haste;
  nor could I of myself, looking about,   150

find anywhere the key to what I sought.
  So I moved on, timid and sunk in thought.

NOTES

2. *him:* Adrian. Dante's wish to know more had to bow to Adrian's greater wish to resume his purification. Thus, Dante had to withdraw the sponge of his desire to know, from the water of Adrian's presence, before he had absorbed all he wished for.

4–9. THE CROWDING OF THE LEDGE. The point, of course, is that Avarice is so common a sin that the ledge is jammed full of sinners, so many in fact that the space between their shades and the open side of the ledge is too narrow for safe passage. Virgil leads Dante, therefore, along the narrow space between the bodies and the inner cliff-face.

10–15. *She-Wolf:* See the three beasts encountered by Dante in *Inferno* I, 33 ff. *have taken more prey:* As in lines 4–9, above, Avarice has infected more souls than has any other sin. *when will he come:* Another reference to the mysterious Greyhound who will come to make the world pure again and who will drive the She-Wolf from the light of day, back into Hell. (See *Inferno* I, 95–104, and note.)

20–33. THE WHIP OF AVARICE. Once more the examples that make up the Whip are cried aloud by the sinners themselves. On this Cornice, however, all the sinners cry out the examples as impulse moves them, adding them as a litany to each prayer they recite as part of their penance. The prayer of this Cornice is, of course, from Psalm CXIX, "My soul cleaves to the dust." (See Canto XIX, 73.)

A further peculiarity of the Whip and the Rein on this ledge is that the sinners recite the Whip by day and the Rein by night.

The first example of the Whip (lines 20–24) praises the blessed poverty of Mary. So great was it that she gave birth to Jesus in a manger. Yet in such poverty she achieved blessedness in comparison with which all the possessions of the world are as baubles.

The second example (lines 25–27) praises the honorable poverty of Fabricius Caius Luscinus, Roman Consul in 282 B.C. and Censor in 275. He refused to deal in the bribes and gifts which were normally assumed to be perquisites of such high offices, and he died so poor that the state had to bury him, and had also to provide dowries for his daughters.

The third example (lines 31–33) cites Saint Nicholas, Bishop of Myra in Lycia, who was born rich and gave all his riches to the poor. A local minor nobleman found himself so poor that he could not provide dowries for his daughters. He was about to turn them over to a life of sin in order that they might make a living, when Nicholas heard of their plight and threw three bags of gold through the nobleman's window, one on each of three successive nights. Thus the father was able to buy husbands for the girls, and thus Nicholas guided their youth to "virtuous steadiness."

34–96. *Hugh Capet:* Dante seems to confuse Hugh, Duke of the Franks (died 956), and his son, Hugh Capet (King of France 987–996), into one person. Hugh Capet founded the Capetian dynasty of French kings, succeeding Louis V, the last of the Carlovingian line founded by Charlemagne.

Hugh Capet begins by replying to Dante's customary promise of earthly recollection, that he has little interest in any good the world can do him. Since he has been in Purgatory 344 years (by 1300), it seems reasonable enough to assume that he is well advanced in other worldliness.

He then laments the degeneracy of the line he himself founded and prays God's vengeance upon it soon, as it would already have fallen

had Flanders the power to avenge itself. Douay, Lille, Bruges, and
Ghent are the four principal cities of Flanders. Philip the Fair, King of
France, and his brother, Charles of Valois, warred on Flanders. In 1299
Charles negotiated the surrender of Ghent by making liberal
promises, which he later ignored, dealing harshly with the conquered.
The vengeance Hugh Capet prayed for as of 1300 had already taken
place by the time Dante wrote these lines, the Flemish having inflicted
a major defeat upon the French at the Battle of Courtrai in 1302.

50. *all the Philips and the Louis':* From 1060 to 1300 all the Kings
of France bore one or another of these names.

52. *a butcher's son:* Dante follows here a popular but erroneous
legend: the meat business was not that good in tenth-century
France. King Hugh Capet, as noted, was the son of Hugh Capet,
Duke of France, of Burgundy, and of Aquitaine, and Count of Paris
and of Orleans. The history that follows is full of similar confusions,
some of which may best be left to scholars, but some of which must
be explained for a basic understanding of the text.

53. *the old line of kings:* The Carlovingian dynasty.

54. *one last heir, who wore a monk's gray gown:* There is no evidence
that Charles of Lorraine, the last of the Carlovingians, took holy or-
ders. He died in prison, put there by Hugh Capet. Two sons born to
him while he was in prison were hustled away to Germany, where
they disappeared.

58. *my son's head:* The son of King Hugh Capet was Robert I,
but Dante is clearly having King Hugh speak now as if he were
Duke Hugh.

60. *those consecrated bones:* The Capetian kings. By the sacramen-
tal anointment which was part of the coronation, the King's person
became sacred.

61–63. *the great dowry of Provence:* Raymond Berengar was Count
of Provence. After the Count's death, Louis IX (St. Louis) married
the eldest of the Count's four daughters and Louis' brother, Charles
of Anjou, married one of the younger daughters. The brothers then
seized all of Provence, claiming it as their wives' dowry. *lost its sense of
shame:* Dante may have meant that in seizing Provence they acquired
a title so ancient that it wiped out the taint of low origin Dante as-

cribes to the Capets. The more obvious meaning is that in waxing great on so much wealth, they lost all sense of just reckoning.

65. *to make amends:* The triple repetition is meant as bitter irony; after each bad action the French kings "make amends" by doing something worse.

66. *Normandy, Ponthieu, and Gascony:* Philip II took Normandy from England in 1202. Philip the Fair took Ponthieu and Gascony from England in 1295.

67. *Charles:* Charles of Anjou, brother of Louis IX. When Clement IV excommunicated Manfred (see III, 103 ff., note), he summoned Charles to Italy and crowned him King of Sicily. In 1266 Charles defeated Manfred at Benevento. In 1268 he defeated Conradin, Manfred's nephew, at Tagliacozzo, and had him beheaded.

68–69. *sent Saint Thomas back to Heaven:* Dante is following an unfounded popular legend that Charles had Thomas Aquinas poisoned.

71. *another Charles:* Charles of Valois, brother of Philip the Fair. He was called Charles Sans Terre. Boniface VIII called him to Florence in 1301, presumably as peacemaker, but actually to destroy all who opposed Papal policy.

76. *He wins no land there:* A taunt at the fact that Charles had inherited no land. He will not improve his temporal state, says Hugh, and will only blacken his honor and his soul.

79. *The third:* The third Charles is Charles II of Anjou (Charles the Lame), King of Naples and of Apulia. He was born in 1243 and died in 1309. *once hauled from his own ship:* In June of 1284 the admiral of Peter III of Aragon sailed into the Bay of Naples. Charles, against express orders left by his father, allowed himself to be lured out to meet the Aragonese and was easily taken prisoner. Two hundred of his court were taken with him and were executed by the Aragonese to avenge the death of Conradin. Charles escaped with his life but remained a prisoner in Sicily until 1288.

80. *selling his daughter:* In 1305 Charles concluded a marriage contract between his very young daughter and Azzo (or Ezzo) VIII of Este, then 42. For the honor of marrying the king's daughter, Azzo settled for practically no dowry, and made very valuable gifts to his father-in-law.

85–93. *But dwarfing all crimes, past or yet to be:* The crime was the capture and humiliation of Pope Boniface VIII at the instigation of Philip the Fair. Philip had charged Boniface with heresy, and Boniface had prepared a bull excommunicating Philip. On September 7, 1303, before the bull could be published, Philip sent a large force to Alagna (now Anagni) under Guillaume de Nogaret and Sciarra (SHAH-rah) Colonna. They ransacked the palace and the cathedral treasury, and subjected Boniface to great indignities, threatening to haul him off in chains to execution. Boniface, then eighty-six, was released in a few days but his mind seems to have cracked, and he died of "hysterical seizures" in Rome within a few weeks, on October 12, 1303.

Dante's attitude in this matter is characteristic. Much as he loathed Boniface for his corruption of the Papacy, Dante saw the office itself as sacred, for Boniface was officially Christ's Vicar on Earth. Thus to offend his person was to offend the person of Christ Himself. King Philip's all-dwarfing crime, therefore, was against the very body of Christ.

90. *He dies again—with* live *thieves at His side:* Christ died between dead thieves who had been crucified with Him. In the person of Boniface, He "died" again, but with live thieves (de Nogaret and Colonna) at His side.

91. *another Pilate:* Philip. As Pilate turned Christ over to His tormentors, so Philip turned Him over—in the person of His Vicar—to de Nogaret and Colonna.

93. *enter the very Temple:* Philip out-Pilated Pilate by breaking into the Temple. The reference here is to Philip's suppression of the Knights Templars and the seizure of their lands and treasuries in 1314. He tortured those he captured and forced Pope Clement V to legalize the action (see VII, 109, note).

95–96. *which, lying hidden:* God's retribution. It lies hidden from men, but is known to God in His omniscient prevision, and will take place at His pleasure. His anger, therefore, is sweetened by the fact that His vengeance is already calculated and certain.

97–120. THE REIN OF AVARICE. The Rein of Avarice consists of seven examples of the downfall caused by Avarice. Note that although Dante divides Avarice into its two extremes of Hoarding and Wasting, the examples of the downfall of the Avaricious are all of what might be called Acquisitive Avarice.

(103–105) *Pygmalion:* Brother of Queen Dido. He killed King Sichaeus in the temple, stole his gold, and drove Dido into exile. Dante calls him a parricide because Sichaeus was not only his brother-in-law but his uncle. (He is not to be confused with the Pygmalion of Greek legend who fell in love with a statue.) Thus Avarice led him to damnation. If Pygmalion's crime is taken to be Treachery to his Host or Master, there is a strong probability (see *Inferno* XXXIII, 128–147) that his soul instantly descended to Ptolomea or Judaïca, while his body still lived.

(106–108) *Midas:* The famous King of Phrygia who did a favor for Bacchus and was promised the fulfillment of a wish. Midas wished for the power to change all things to gold at his touch. Bacchus granted the wish, but Midas began to starve since even his food turned to gold, and he had to beg Bacchus to take the power from him. The best-known version of the story is in Ovid's *Metamorphoses* XI, 85–145.

(109–111) *Achan:* After the fall of Jericho, Joshua commanded that all the booty should go into the Temple as the Lord's. Achan pilfered some treasures for himself and Joshua had him and his family stoned to death (*Joshua* vii, 1–26).

(112) *Sapphira and her husband:* They were entrusted to sell some property held in common by the apostles, but they returned only part of the sale price, representing it as the whole sum. When St. Peter reproved them for their fraud, they fell dead at his feet (*Acts* v, 1–11).

(113) *Heliodorus:* He was sent to Jerusalem by the King of Syria with orders to steal the Treasury but was driven from the Temple by the apparition of a great horse that battered him with its forefeet. "And it seemed that he that sat upon the horse had complete harness of good." (*II Maccabees* iii, 25.)

(114) *Polymnestor:* King of Thrace and a friend of King Priam. During the siege of Troy, Priam sent his youngest son, Polydorus, into Thrace for Polymnestor's protection. A considerable treasure ac-

companied the boy, and Polymnestor killed him for it as soon as Troy fell. Hecuba, mother of Polydorus, later avenged her son by blinding Polymnestor and killing him. *Aeneid* III, 19–68; *Metamorphoses* XIII, 429–575; and Euripides' *Hecuba,* all recount part of the story. (See also *Inferno* XXX, 16, note.)

(116) *Crassus:* Marcus Licinus Crassus (114–53 B.C.). Triumvir of Rome with Julius Caesar and Pompey, and infamous for his avarice, bribe taking, and plundering. He was taken in battle by the Parthians and his head was brought to King Hyrodes, who had molten gold poured into its mouth, thus mocking the memory of Crassus' bloody avarice by serving his severed head a last feast of gold.

130–132. *Not even Delos . . . Latona . . . Heaven's eyes:* Latona was pregnant by Jupiter and was chased from place to place by the jealous Juno. According to one legend, Jupiter caused an earthquake to raise the island of Delos from the bottom of the sea as a place of refuge for Latona. According to another, Delos was a floating island left over from the original division of the sea and the land and tossed about by waves until Jupiter fixed it in place for Latona. On Delos, Latona gave birth to Apollo (the Sun) and Diana (the Moon), hence, the twin eyes of Heaven. Dante regularly draws parallel-and-contrasting examples from both the Classical and the Judeo-Christian worlds. Note that in this example and the next he cites divine birth in both of those worlds.

140. *who first heard that hymn:* The shepherds of Bethlehem. It was first sung, according to *Luke* ii, 14, to announce the birth of Christ.

145–152. I have taken substantial liberties with these lines in trying to make Dante's intent clear. A literal rendering might read: "No ignorance ever with so much war [within me] made me so desirous to know—if my memory does not err in this—as I seemed to be at this time, pondering [the explanation of the earthquake and the shout]; nor, since we were hurrying so, did I dare ask; nor could I by myself see anything (that would explain them) there: thus I moved on, timid and deep in thought."

CANTO XXI

The Fifth Cornice—The Hoarders and Wasters
(The Avaricious)

STATIUS

Burning with desire to know the cause of the "shock and shout," Dante hurries after Virgil along the narrow way. Suddenly they are overtaken by a figure that salutes them. Virgil answers, and the new soul, taking the Poets to be souls who may not enter Heaven, expresses astonishment at finding them in this place.

Virgil explains his and Dante's state and asks the explanation of the earthquake and of the great cry. The new soul explains that these phenomena occur only when a soul arises from its final purification and begins its final ascent to Heaven. The newcomer then reveals that he is *Statius* and recites his earthly history, ending with a glowing statement of his love for the works of Virgil. To have lived in Virgil's time, says Statius, he would have endured another year of the pains he has just ended.

Virgil warns Dante, with a glance, to be silent, but Dante cannot suppress a half smile, which Statius notices, and asks Dante to explain. He thus learns that he is, in fact, standing in the presence of Virgil. Immediately he kneels to embrace Virgil's knees, but Virgil tells him to arise at once, for such earthly vanities are out of place between shades.

The natural thirst that nothing satisfies
  except that water the Samaritan woman
  begged of Our Lord, as St. John testifies,   3

burned me; haste drove me on the encumbered way
  behind my Guide, and I was full of grief
  at the just price of pain those spirits pay;   6

when suddenly—just as Luke lets us know
  that Christ, new risen from the tomb, appeared
  to the two travelers on the road—just so   9

as we moved there with bowed heads lest we tread
  upon some soul, a shade appeared behind us;
  nor did we guess its presence till it said: 12

"Brothers, God give you peace." My Guide and I
  turned quickly toward his voice, and with a sign
  my master gave the words their due reply.   15

Then he began: "May the True Court's behest,
  which relegates me to eternal exile,
  establish you in peace among the blest."   18

"But how, if you are souls denied God's bliss,"
  he said—and we forged onward as he spoke—
  "have you climbed up the stairs as far as this?"   21

My Teacher then: "You cannot fail to see,
  if you observe the Angel's mark upon him,
  that he will reign among the just. But she   24

whose wheel turns day and night has not yet spun
  the full length of the thread that Clotho winds
  into a hank for him and everyone.   27

Therefore, his soul, sister to yours and mine,
  since it cannot see as we do, could not
  climb by itself. And, therefore, Will Divine   30

has drawn me out of the great Throat of Woe
  to guide him on his way, and I shall lead him
  far as my knowledge gives me power to go.   33

But tell me, if you can, what was the shock
  we felt just now? And why did all the mountain
  cry with one voice down to its last moist rock?"   36

He struck the needle's eye of my desire
  so surely with his question, that my thirst,
  by hope alone, lost something of its fire.   39

The shade began: "The holy rules that ring
  the mountain round do not permit upon it
  any disordered or unusual thing,   42

nor any change. Only What Heaven draws
  out of itself into itself again—
  that and nothing else—can be a cause.   45

Therefore, there never can be rain nor snow,
  nor hail, nor dew, nor hoarfrost higher up
  than the little three-step stairway there below.   48

Neither dense clouds nor films of mist appear,
  nor lightning's flash, nor Thaumas' glowing daughter,
  who shifts about from place to place back there;   51

nor can dry vapors raise their shattering heat
  above the top of these three steps I mentioned
  upon which Peter's vicar plants his feet.   54

Shocks may occur below, severe or slight,
  but tremors caused by winds locked in the earth
  —I know not how—do not reach to this height.   57

It trembles here whenever a soul feels
  so healed and purified that it gets up
  or moves to climb; and then the great hymn peals.   60

The soul, surprised, becomes entirely free
    to change its cloister, moved by its own will,
    which is its only proof of purity.   63

Before purgation it does wish to climb,
    but the will High Justice sets against that wish
    moves it to will pain as it once willed crime.   66

And I, who in my torments have lain here
    five hundred years and more, have only now
    felt my will free to seek a better sphere.   69

It was for that you felt the mountain move
    and heard the pious spirits praise the Lord—
    ah may He call them soon to go above!"   72

These were the spirit's words to us, and mine
    cannot express how they refreshed my soul,
    but as the thirst is greater, the sweeter the wine.   75

And my wise Leader: "Now I see what snare
    holds you, how you slip free, why the mount trembles,
    and why your joint rejoicing fills the air.   78

Now it would please me greatly, if you please,
    to know your name and hear in your own words
    why you have lain so many centuries."   81

"In the days when the good Titus, with the aid
    of the Almighty King, avenged the wounds
    that poured the blood Iscariot betrayed,   84

I lived renowned back there," replied that soul,
    "in the most honored and enduring name,
    but still without the faith that makes us whole.   87

My verses swelled with such melodious breath
　that, from Toulouse, Rome called me to herself,
　and there I merited a laurel wreath.　　　　　　90

Statius my name, and it still lives back there.
　I sang of Thebes, then of the great Achilles,
　but found the second weight too great to bear.　　93

The sparks that were my seeds of passion came
　from that celestial fire which has enkindled
　more than a thousand poets; I mean the flame　　96

of the *Aeneid,* the mother that brought forth,
　the nurse that gave suck to my song. Without it
　I could not have weighed half a penny's worth.　　99

And to have lived back there in Virgil's time
　I would agree to pass another year
　in the same banishment from which I climb."　　102

Virgil, at these last words, shot me a glance
　that said in silence, "Silence!" But man's will
　is not supreme in every circumstance:　　　　105

for tears and laughter come so close behind
　the passions they arise from, that they least
　obey the will of the most honest mind.　　　108

I did no more than half smile, but that shade
　fell still and looked me in the eye—for there
　the secrets of the soul are most betrayed.　　111

"So may the road you travel lead to grace,"
　he said, "what was the meaning of the smile
　that I saw flash, just now, across your face?"　　114

Now am I really trapped on either side:
  one tells me to be still, one begs me speak.
  So torn I heave a sigh, and my sweet Guide   117

understands all its meaning. "Never fear,"
  he says to me, "speak up, and let him know
  what he has asked so movingly to hear."   120

At which I said: "Perhaps my smiling thus
  has made you marvel, Ancient Soul; but now
  listen to something truly marvelous: 123

this one who guides my eyes aloft is he,
  Virgil, from whom you drew the strength to sing
  the deeds of men and gods in poetry.   126

The only motive for my smiling lay
  in your own words. If you conceived another,
  as you love truth, pray put the thought away."   129

He was bending to embrace my Teacher's knee,
  but Virgil said: "No, brother. Shade you are,
  and shade am I. You must not kneel to me."   132

And Statius, rising, said: "So may you find
  the measure of the love that warms me to you
  when for it I lose all else from my mind,   135

forgetting we are empty semblances
  and taking shadows to be substances."

NOTES

1. *The natural thirst:* "All men naturally desire knowledge."
(Aristotle, *Metaphysics* I, 1.) *that nothing satisfies:* "In acquiring

knowledge, there always grows the thirst for more." (*Il Convivio* IV, 12.)

2–3. *that water the Samaritan woman begged:* At Jacob's Well, Jesus asked the Samaritan woman for a drink, and she showed surprise that a Jew should make such a request of her, but Jesus replied that had she known who he was, she would have asked him for a drink and he would have given her the living water of the truth. "The woman saith unto him, Sir, give me this water that I thirst not. . . ." (*John* iv, 6–15.)

7. *as Luke lets us know:* "And behold two of them [James and John] went that same day to a village called Emmaus. . . . And it came to pass that, while they communed together and reasoned, Jesus himself drew near, and went with them." (*Luke* xxiv, 13–15.)

11. *a shade appeared:* The shade is Statius, for whom see note to lines 82 ff.

14–15. *with a sign . . . due reply:* There were regular formulas for greeting and reply among monks of the Middle Ages. Most commonly, "God give you peace" or "God's peace be with you," would be answered. "And with thy spirit." Virgil's answer is not verbal. He replies with what must have been a gesture of benediction.

23. *the Angel's mark:* The three remaining *P*'s on Dante's brow, which identify him as a saved soul, i.e., as one who will enter Heaven when he has completed his purification.

24–27. *she:* Lachesis. She is the Fate (or Parca) who spins the Thread of Life. Her sister Clotho winds each man's thread about her distaff, forming it into a hank begun at each man's birth. The third sister, Atropos, cuts the thread at the end of the man's life. Virgil means simply that Dante is not yet dead, i.e., his thread has not been cut. (The Poets are on the western side of the mountain with the sun in the east, and Dante casts no identifying shadow.)

36. *cry with one voice down to its last moist rock:* I.e., "Down to the shore where the reeds grow." "Rock" is rhyme-forced. Dante says, literally, "down to its moist feet," and the shore is described not as rocky but as muddy.

40 ff. STATIUS' REPLY. Virgil has asked the reason for the earthquake and the shout. Statius begins his elaborate reply in good scholastic form by explaining the principles on which the answer

must be based, and having stated them in brief, he goes on to develop each in detail.

The first principle is that nothing on the mountain is subject to change except within itself, for nothing there is subject to external forces. Every soul in Purgatory is effectively in Heaven, and beyond the Gate evil does not exist.

The second principle follows from the first. The soul issues from the hand of God. When the soul goes from Purgatory to Heaven, therefore, it is not entering from outside. Heaven is simply receiving its own again. Only that motion of Heaven's receiving its own from itself to itself can, therefore, be a *cause* on the mountain, "cause" being "that which gives rise to an effect."

48. *the little three-step stairway:* The three steps that lead to the Gate of Purgatory mark the highest point to which the weathers of the world (literally and in every extended sense) can reach. Above them, all that is, is from God.

50. *Thaumas' glowing daughter:* Iris, the rainbow. Daughter of the Centaur Thaumas and of Electra. Her sisters were the Harpies. Like her sisters, she was a messenger of the Gods and came and went by way of the rainbow, with which she became identified.

The rainbow is an especially apt symbol of mutability. Note, too, that it always appears *away* from the sun, never between the sun and the observer. Taking Iris to represent changeableness and the sun to represent God, one may pursue a number of interesting allegories.

52. *dry vapors:* For Dante's theory of wet and dry vapors as the origin of storms see *Inferno* XXIV, last note. The theory is from Aristotle. Wet vapors cause rain, hail, dew, and hoarfrost, as specified in lines 46–47. Dry vapors, if they are free, produce lightning and thunder. If, however, they enter the earth as winds and are locked inside, they cause earthquakes. But such terrestrial earthquakes (lines 55–60) cannot be felt above the three steps at the Gate.

58. *whenever a soul feels:* Once again the point is made that the Purgatorial souls are free of external restraints. Each decides within itself when it is free to move up.

59. *that it gets up:* If the soul has been crawling with the Proud,

seated with the Envious, or lying with the Avaricious, its moment of purity is achieved when it feels the will to get up.

60. *or moves to climb:* If the soul has been circling with the Wrathful, the Slothful, the Gluttonous, or the Lustful, it would not need to get up: its moment of purity would be achieved when it feels moved to stop circling and to move toward the ascent. *to climb:* Statius must mean "to climb to Paradise" rather than merely to a higher ledge. As Dante has already hinted, and as Statius soon demonstrates, a soul may pass unchecked through those ledges that punish sins of which it is not guilty. Thus on completing a given penance, a soul may move on to another, or directly to Paradise. There is no conclusive evidence that the mountain shakes and the hymn peals only when souls achieve their final purification, but the very scale of the celebration suggests that it is reserved for graduation exercises only. If the shock and shout occurred every time a soul moved from one ledge to another, there is every likelihood that Dante would have touched things off every time he passed up one of the stairways, or every time an Angel removed one of his *P's*.

62. *cloister:* An especially apt choice in that "cloister" implies (a) confinement, (b) confinement of one's own free will, and (c) a life ordered by strict rules of worship and discipline. Dante, because "soul" is feminine in Italian, uses "convent."

64–66. *wish . . . will:* I am not happy about these terms, but they are the only ones I could make work within prosodic necessity. The intended distinction is between "impulse" (the *relative will* of scholastic philosophy) and what might be called "innate desire" (the *absolute will* of scholastic philosophy). Thus the passage in extended paraphrase: "Before purification it does have a relative will to climb, but the absolute will that High Justice sets against that relative will, gives the soul the same sort of will to suffer penitential pain that it once had [in life] toward the crime it now expiates." (Compare the state of the Infernal souls who cross Acheron driven by their own absolute will to yearn for what they fear.)

82 ff. *Statius:* Publius Papinius Statius (c. 45–96 A.D.) is a central figure of the *Purgatorio* and an especially complex one. He remains with Dante till the very end of the ascent. Thus Dante completes his

climb to the presence of Beatrice (Divine Love) in the company of Virgil as Human Reason, and of Statius, who must be taken as a symbol of the soul's triumphant redemption.

Thus Statius has a major role, though his known history hardly serves to explain it. In life he was a Latin poet much admired by Dante, though it is difficult to see why Dante, himself so stylistically sparse, should admire a writer as prolix as was Statius. Statius' main work was the *Thebaid,* an epic of the Seven against Thebes (so line 92: "I sang of Thebes"). He was engaged in an epic of the Trojan War, the *Achilleid,* at his death (so line 93, "but found the second weight too great to bear," i.e., he died bearing it). An earlier collection of poems, the *Silvae,* came to light after Dante's time.

Statius was born in Naples and lived in Rome. Dante confused him in part with Lucius Statius Ursulus, a rhetorician of Toulouse, and has Statius give his birthplace accordingly in line 89.

Why Dante should have chosen Statius to represent the triumph of the purified soul is a matter open to any careful reader's speculation. The very fact that so little is known of Statius' life may be a point in favor, for it leaves Dante free to attribute qualities to Statius without embarrassment from history. (There is, for example, no slightest historical evidence that Statius turned Christian.)

If, as seems likely, Dante himself invented this legend, its own elements best explain it, for so interpreted, Statius becomes a symbolic figure joining the Roman and the Christian past, a theme always dear to Dante. Thus Statius may be seen as a lesser Virgil and a greater; a less perfect writer, but a greater soul in the gift of Christ's redemption. Thus he may be taken as springing from that cardinal point in Church history at which the greatness of the Roman past and the glory of the Christian present are joined. So Dante may now climb guided not only by Virgil (as Human Reason, Philosophy, and the Classic Virtues of Ancient Rome) but by Statius (these same qualities transformed by faith and thus nearer to God). Between Virgil and Statius, that is, Dante now climbs in the company of the total Roman tradition.

Dramatically, of course, the possibilities inherent in presenting Statius to Virgil must have been especially inviting.

82. *the good Titus:* Roman Emperor 79–81 A.D. In 70 A.D. in the reign of his father, Vespasian, Titus besieged and took Jerusalem. Thus, with God's help, Rome avenged the death (the wounds) of Christ. So Dante, within his inevitable parochialism, chose to take that passage of history. The Jews, one may be sure, found less cause for rejoicing in the goodness of Titus.

86. *in the most honored and enduring name:* Of poet.

CANTO XXII

The Ascent to the Sixth Cornice

The Sixth Cornice—The Gluttons

THE TREE · THE WHIP OF GLUTTONY

The Poets have passed the Angel who guards the ascent, and Dante has had one more *P* removed from his forehead. So lightened, he walks easily behind Virgil and Statius despite their rapid ascent, listening eagerly to their conversation.

Virgil declares his great regard for Statius, and Statius explains that he was on the Fifth Cornice for Wasting rather than for Hoarding. He adds that he would certainly have been damned, had Virgil's poetry not led him to see his error. For Virgil, he acknowledges, not only inspired his song, but showed him the road to faith, whereby he was baptized, though secretly, for fear of the persecutions—a lukewarmness for which he spent four hundred years on the Fourth Cornice.

Statius then names his favorite poets of antiquity and asks where they are. Virgil replies that they are with him in Limbo. He then cites many who have not been mentioned before as being among his eternal companions.

At this point the Poets arrive at *The Sixth Cornice* and, moving to the right, come upon *An Enormous Tree* laden with fruits. From its foliage a voice cries out the examples of abstinence that constitute *The Whip of Gluttony*.

We had already left behind by now
   the Angel who directs to the Sixth Round.
   He had erased a stigma from my brow,   3

and said that they who thirst for rectitude
   are blessèd, but he did not say "who hunger"
   when he recited that Beatitude.   6

I, lighter than on any earlier stairs,
   followed those rapid spirits, and I found it
   no strain at all to match my pace to theirs.   9

Virgil began: "When virtue lights in us
   a fire of love, that love ignites another
   within the soul that sees its burning. Thus,   12

ever since Juvenal came down to be
   one of our court in the Infernal Limbo,
   and told me of your great regard for me,   15

my good will toward you has been of a sort
   I had not felt for any unseen person;
   such as will make the climb ahead seem short.   18

But tell me—and if I presume too much
   in slackening the rein this way, forgive me
   as a friend would and answer me as such: 21

how, amid all the wisdom you possessed—
   and which you won to by such diligence—
   could Avarice find a place within your breast?"   24

At these words Statius let a brief smile play
   across his lips, and fade. Then he replied:
   "I hear love's voice in every word you say.   27

Often, indeed, appearances give rise
   to groundless doubts in us, and false conclusions,
   the true cause being hidden from our eyes.   30

Seeing me on the ledge from which I rose,
   you have inferred my sin was Avarice;
   an inference your question clearly shows.   33

Know then that my particular offense
  was all too far from Avarice: I wept
  thousands of months for riotous expense.   36

Had I not turned from prodigality
  in pondering those lines in which you cry,
  as if you raged against humanity: 39

'To what do you not drive man's appetite
  O cursèd gold-lust!'—I should now be straining
  in the grim jousts of the Infernal night.   42

I understood then that our hands could spread
  their wings too wide in spending, and repented
  of that, and all my sins, in grief and dread.   45

How many shall rise bald to Judgment Day
  because they did not know this sin to grieve it
  in life, or as their last breaths slipped away!   48

For when the opposite of a sin, as here,
  is as blameworthy as the sin itself,
  both lose their growth together and turn sere.   51

If, then, I lay so long in my distress
  among the Avaricious where they weep,
  it was to purge the opposite excess."   54

"But when you sang of the fierce warfare bred
  between the twin afflictions of Jocasta,"
  the singer of the sweet *Bucolics* said,   57

"from what you said when Clio tuned your strain,
  it would not seem that you had found the faith
  without the grace of which good works are vain.   60

If that be so, what sun or beacon shone
    into your mist that you set sail to follow
    the Fisherman?" And that long-waiting one: 63

"You were the lamp that led me from that night.
    You led me forth to drink Parnassian waters;
    then on the road to God you shed your light.   66

When you declared, 'A new birth has been given.
    Justice returns, and the first age of man.
    And a new progeny descends from Heaven'—   69

you were as one who leads through a dark track
    holding the light behind—useless to you,
    precious to those who followed at your back.   72

Through you I flowered to song and to belief.
    That you may know all, let me stretch my hand
    to paint in full what I have sketched in brief.   75

The world, by then, was swollen with the birth
    of True Belief sown by those messengers
    the Everlasting Kingdom had sent forth.   78

Those words of yours I quoted, so agreed
    with the new preachers', that I took to going
    to where they gathered to expound the Creed.   81

In time, they grew so holy in my eyes
    that in the persecutions of Domitian
    the tears burst from me when I heard their cries.   84

And long as I remained upon the vexed
    shores of that life, I helped them, and they taught me,
    by their strict ways, to scorn all other sects.   87

Before my poem sang how the Greeks drew near
  the Theban rivers, I had been baptized,
  but kept my faith a secret, out of fear,   90

pretending to be pagan as before;
  for which lukewarmness I was made to circle
  the Ledge of Sloth four hundred years and more.   93

Now may you please to tell me—you who rent
  the veil that hid me from this good I praise—
  while we have time to spare in the ascent,   96

where is our ancient Terence now? and where
  Caecilius, Varro, Plautus?—are they damned?
  and if they are, what torments must they bear?"   99

—"All these are there with Persius and the rest,
  myself among them, who surround that Greek
  who outsucked all men at the Muses' breast.   102

All walk the first ledge of the dark of Hell;
  and we speak often of the glorious mountain
  on which the Nine who suckled us still dwell.   105

Euripides is with us, Antiphon,
  Athenian Agathon, Simonides,
  and many more who wore the laurel crown.   108

And there, of your own people, one may see
  Ismene, mournful as she was before,
  Deiphyle, Argia, Antigone,   111

Hypsipyle, who led to Langia's water,
  Thetis, Deidamia with her sisters,
  and there, too, one may see Tiresias' daughter."   114

We stepped from the walled stairs to level ground,
  and both the Poets now had fallen still,
  attentive once again to look around.   117

Of the day's handmaids, four had fallen back,
  and now the fifth stood at the chariot's pole,
  pointing the bright tip on its upward track,   120

when Virgil said: "I think we ought to go
  with our right shoulders to the outer edge,
  circling the slope as we have done below."   123

So custom served to guide us, and we went
  as Virgil said, with all the more assurance
  since Statius' silence gave us his consent.   126

They walked ahead and I came on behind
  treasuring their talk, which was of poetry,
  and every word of which enriched my mind.   129

But soon, in mid-road, there appeared a tree
  laden with fragrant and delicious fruit,
  and at that sight the talk stopped instantly.   132

As fir trees taper up from limb to limb,
  so this tree tapered down; so shaped, I think,
  that it should be impossible to climb.   135

From that side where the cliff closed-off our way
  a clear cascade fell from the towering rock
  and broke upon the upper leaves as spray.   138

The poets drew nearer, reverent and mute,
  and from a center of the towering tree
  a voice cried: "You shall not eat of the fruit!"   141

Then said: "Mary thought more of what was due
  the joy and honor of the wedding feast
  than of her mouth, which still speaks prayers
                               for you.   144

Of old, the mothers of Rome's noble blood
  found joy in water. And great wisdom came
  to holy Daniel in despising food.   147

Bright as pure gold was mankind's state at first:
  then, hunger seasoned acorns with delight,
  and every rill ran sweet to honest thirst.   150

No wine nor meat were in the wilderness.
  Honey and locusts—that and nothing more
  nourished the Baptist in his holiness;   153

and to that fact is his great glory due,
  as the Gospel clearly testifies to you."

NOTES

1–6. *We had already . . . :* The Poets, now three, are climbing the stairway to the Sixth Cornice, having passed the Angel posted at the entrance to the Ascent. Since this Angel must represent the virtue opposite both Avarice and Prodigality, he may best be called the Angel of Moderation.

    The Angel has lightened Dante's soul by striking away one more *P,* and has speeded the Poets on their way by reciting a Beatitude, but with an interesting variation. The whole Beatitude would be *Beati qui esuriunt et sitiunt justitiam*—"Blessed are they who hunger and thirst after righteousness." But the Angel left out *esuriunt* ("they hunger") and said only "Blessed are they who thirst after righteousness." The "who hunger" will be spoken by the next Angel; appropriately, for the Gluttons. Dante was forced into some such device if he was to make six Beatitudes do for seven Cornices. Certainly, the aptness of his invention under such pressures is the mark of his structural genius.

11. *that love ignites another:* Cf. *Inferno* V, 103: "Love which permits no loved one not to love. . . ."

13. *Juvenal:* Decius Junius Juvenal, satiric poet born about 47 A.D., died about 130 A.D. His long life almost entirely overlapped that of Statius. Since both lived in Rome, and both were poets (Juvenal mentions Statius in his *Seventh Satire*), he would be a natural choice as the bearer of tidings of Statius.

17. *for any unseen person:* For any person one has not met.

18. *such as will make the climb ahead seem short:* Since it will be passed in such happy company.

27 ff. STATIUS' REPLY. Statius smiles briefly at Virgil's error in forgetting that Avarice and Prodigality are twin sins, both of which absorb the soul into an immoderate concern for material matters. (Cf. Wordsworth, "Getting and spending we lay waste our powers.") Statius then explains that he was not a miser but a waster, and that his sin was riotous expense.

He then pays tribute to Virgil, explaining that it was a passage from the *Aeneid* (as he quotes in lines 40–41) that led him to correct his ways, else he would at that moment be in Hell rolling the enormous weights that the Hoarders and Wasters send crashing against one another there. There is no historic evidence either that Statius was a wasteful spender or that he turned Christian. On the contrary, Juvenal's *Seventh Satire* mentions Statius as being so poor that he would have starved without a patron.

Dante's reasons for both these inventions will have to be inferred from the text itself. Obviously, in making Statius' sin wasteful spending, Dante makes an opportunity to discuss Wasting along with Hoarding as related extremes of Avarice. Even more obviously, Statius could not be in Purgatory at all unless Dante established him as a Christian.

40–41. *To what do you not drive . . . . :* These lines are from the *Aeneid* (III, 56–57)—*quid non mortalia pectora cogis Auri sacra fames* ("to what do you not drive mortal appetites, o sacred [godlike] hunger for gold?") In the Italian, Dante seems to have rendered these lines: "Why do you not control mortal appetites, O sacred hunger for gold?" rendering Virgil's *quid* as "why" instead of as "to what" and thereby not only praising gold-hunger, but making it responsible for the control of avarice. The hunger could, of course, be called "sacred" in that it is God-given, whereby only its excesses would be evil.

No lines in the *Divine Comedy* have called forth more critical argument. Did Dante make a ludicrous mistake? Was he so familiar with the text that he rendered it carelessly in a sleepy moment? Has the text been corrupted? Was he indulging in a sermonizer's license to twist the text to some obscure purpose? Was he using "sacred" in a special reverse way meaning "cursed," a usage still current in some parts of Italy? All these are puzzles for scholars. Dante is probably reading into Virgil an idea of Aristotelian moderation.

42. *the grim jousts:* Of the Hoarders and Wasters in the Fourth Circle of Hell (*Inferno* VII).

46. *rise bald to Judgment Day:* Cf. *Inferno* VII, 56–57, where Dante says of the Hoarders and Wasters:

> one crew will stand tight-fisted, the other stripped
>
> of its very hair at the bar of Judgment Day.

49–51. *when the opposite of a sin . . . is as blameworthy:* On this Cornice, as noted, Hoarding and Wasting are the two opposite faces of Avarice and are equally blameworthy. The opposites of Pride, Envy, and Anger, on the other hand, are the virtues of Humility, Caritas, and Meekness. The force of "when" is exactly in the fact that not every opposite is blameworthy.

55–57. *the twin afflictions of Jocasta:* Eteocles and Polynices, the twin sons of Oedipus by his own mother, Jocasta. When they succeeded to the throne of Thebes they agreed to rule in alternating years, the nonruling brother to pass the year in exile. Eteocles occupied the throne the first year and then refused to surrender it when Polynices came to claim it. Thereupon there broke out the war of the Seven against Thebes which Statius celebrated in his *Thebaid*. *the singer of the sweet Bucolics:* Virgil. So identified in preparation for the reference to *Eclogue* IV in line 67. This is the first time Virgil has been cited as the author of any work but the *Aeneid*.

58. *when Clio tuned your strain:* I.e., in the *Thebaid,* which Statius began with an invocation to Clio, the Muse of History. Virgil is saying that there is no sign in Statius' work to indicate that he had turned Catholic (as, in fact, he almost certainly had not).

59–60. *the faith without the grace of which good works are vain:* Virgil is citing the doctrine that there can be no salvation except through the Catholic Church. The doctrine has only very recently been modified and was the object of some controversy in the United States in the late 1940's.

61. *what sun:* Divine Illumination. *or beacon:* Power of Reason. (Probable interpretations only.)

63. *the Fisherman:* St. Peter.

64. *You were the lamp:* Allegorically, Statius was guided by Human Reason.

67. *A new birth . . . :* These are the words of the Sybil in Virgil's *Eclogue* IV, 5–7, from his *Bucolics.* Virgil, as a courtier, was celebrating the birth of a son to the well-placed Asinius Pollio. Medieval readers were quick to interpret the lines as a prophecy of the birth of Christ, thus giving rise to the legend of Virgil as a powerful soothsayer and magician.

77. *those messengers:* The Apostles.

88–90. *drew near the Theban rivers:* The ninth book of the *Thebaid* relates the arrival of the Greeks under Adrastus to the Theban rivers, the Ismenus and the Asopus. The *Thebaid* consists of twelve books in all. Thus Statius would have had to write something more than three books (plus his work on the *Achilleid*) without letting slip any slightest indication that he was a Christian. Such a lack is sufficiently explained historically by the fact that there is no slightest evidence that Statius was converted. Within Dante's legend, however, that lack is further evidence of the Sloth of Statius, for which he spent more than four hundred years on the Fourth Cornice.

Statius must also have spent a considerable time in Ante-Purgatory or at the Mouth of the Tiber, or both, for he had been dead for 1,204 years by 1300. If "over four hundred years" plus "over five hundred years" is taken to equal as much as "about a thousand" there are still two centuries unaccounted for. Statius died at fifty-four. If he had been made to wait in Ante-Purgatory for as long as his entire life, there would still remain a century and a half unaccounted for. Some of that time may have been spent in doing minor penances on the other ledges, but he probably spent most of it at the Mouth of the Tiber waiting for the Angel Ferryman's approval.

95. *this good I praise:* The True Faith.

97–99. *Terrace . . . Caecilius, Varro, Plautus:* All those here mentioned were Latin poets of the third and second centuries B.C. Since all of them died before Christ, none could have won to salvation.

100. *Persius:* Latin poet, 34–62 A.D.

101. *that Greek:* Homer.

104. *the glorious mountain:* Parnassus.

105. *the Nine:* The Muses, Here, as in line 102, they are conceived as the mothers at whose breasts poets sucked the milk of inspiration. Homer, who outsucked all others, is, therefore, the foremost poet.

106–108. *Euripides . . . Antiphon . . . Agathon, Simonides:* All those here mentioned were Greek poets of the Golden Age.

109 ff. *of your own people:* Virgil means "of the people you wrote about in *Thebaid.*" All those listed may be taken as characters of the poem, only two of whom here require further explanation: *Ismene, mournful as she was:* Daughter of Oedipus and Jocasta, sister of Antigone and of Eteocles and Polynices. She had good reason to mourn, having witnessed the death of all her family and of her betrothed, and having been sentenced to death by Creon. *who led to Langia's water:* When the Seven Heroes who fought against Thebes were dying of thirst on their march through Boetia, Hypsipyle showed them the way to a spring called Langia. For the rest of her story see XXVI, 94–96, note.

118–120. THE TIME. In Canto XII Dante has established the fact that he means the hours when he speaks of the "handmaids of the day." Here he presents them as directing the chariot of the sun in turn, each handing over her position at the chariot's pole to her successor. Four have already fallen back. It is, therefore, at least four hours since dawn (which was at 6:00 A.M.). The fifth hour is now pointing the bright tip of the chariot's pole (bright because it is approaching noon) toward the zenith. It is therefore, between 10:00 and 11:00 A.M.

133 ff. THE TREE. The description of this tree has led to many strange speculations. A number of the early commentators thought of it as growing upside down and it is so illustrated in some old manuscripts. I take Dante's central idea to be of an unclimbable tree with a great spreading top.

140 ff. THE WHIP OF GLUTTONY. It is prefaced (line 141) by a voice that cries from amid the luscious fruits, denying them to the sinners. Note how much the phrasing suggests God's first command prohibiting the Fruit of Knowledge.

The voice then cites great examples of abstinence and moderation. It cites first (lines 142–144) the example of Mary at the marriage feast at Cana in Galilee (cf. XIII, 28–30) and how she thought only of the good of others, not of her own appetite.

The voice then cites (lines 145–146) the matrons of ancient Rome. It was the custom during the Republic for noble matrons not to drink wine. Thus they "found joy in water."

The third example (lines 146–147) is based on *Daniel* i, 8 and 17. Daniel determined not to defile himself with the king's wine and meat . . . "and Daniel had understanding in all visions and dreams."

The fourth example (lines 148–150) cites mankind's earliest and most natural state, when men lived in accord with nature and had not developed the cookery that leads men to gluttonous feasting, nor the wine (distilled spirits were not developed till the eighteenth century) that leads to drunkenness. Then, according to the voice, acorns and water were enough to delight men.

The final example (lines 151–155) cites John the Baptist, who ate only honey and locusts in the desert (*Matthew* iii, 4) and won thereby to the glory the Gospel attests (*Matthew* xi, 11, and *Luke* vii, 28).

CANTO XXIII

The Sixth Cornice—The Gluttons

Dante stares up into the tree to see who has spoken but he is called away by Virgil who leads on, talking to Statius, while Dante walks behind, drinking in their conversation. Suddenly, from behind him, Dante hears a psalm, and turning, he sees a band of *Gluttons* overtaking them, souls so emaciated that one can read in their sunken eyes and in the lines of the cheeks and nose the word *"Omo."*

After some difficulty Dante recognizes one of the hideously wasted souls as his old friend *Forese* who had died only five years before, but who had been advanced into Purgatory and directly to this Cornice by the prayers of his widow, Nella.

In praising Nella for her devotion, Forese takes occasion to deliver a rather salty *Invective Against the Women of Florence* for their immodest dress and behavior.

In answer to Forese's plea (for the souls have all seen Dante's shadow), Dante explains how he has mounted into Purgatory and with whom he is traveling.

In hope of seeing who had cried those words
  I drew near and peered up at the green boughs
  like one who wastes his lifetime stalking birds.   3

At that, my more-than-father said: "My son,
  come now, for we must portion out more wisely
  the time allotted us." And he moved on.   6

I looked down and turned round to join those sages
  in the same instant. And their talk was such
  that every step I took paid double wages.   9

Then suddenly at my back I heard the strain
  of *Labia mea, Domine,* so sung
  that it was both a hymn and cry of pain.   12

"Father," I said, "What is this sound?" And he:
  "Spirits who, circling so, loosen perhaps
  the knot of debt they owe Eternity."   15

As pilgrims wrapped in holy meditation,
  when they encounter strangers on the way,
  look, but do not pause for conversation;   18

so from behind us, turning half about
  to stare as they went by, a band of souls
  came up and passed us, silent and devout.   21

The sockets of their eyes were caves agape;
  their faces death-pale, and their skin so wasted
  that nothing but the gnarled bones gave it shape.   24

I doubt that even Erysichthon's skin,
  even when he most feared that he would starve,
  had drawn so tight to bone, or worn so thin.   27

"Behold," I thought, although I did not speak,
  "the face of those who lost Jerusalem
  when Miriam ripped her son with her own beak."   30

Their eye pits looked like gem-rims minus gem.
  Those who read OMO in the face of man
  would easily have recognized the *M*.   33

Who could imagine, without knowing how,
  craving could waste souls so at the mere smell
  of water and of fruit upon the bough?   36

I was still wondering how they could have grown
  so thin and scabby (since what famished them
  had not yet been made clear to me), when one   39

turning his eyes from deep inside his skull,
  stared at me fixedly, then cried aloud:
  "How have I earned a grace so bountiful?"   42

I never would have recognized his face,
  but in his voice I found that which his features
  had eaten from themselves without a trace.   45

That spark relit my memory and, in awe,
  I understood beneath those altered features
  it was Forese's very self I saw.   48

"Ah, do not stare," he pleaded, "at my hide,
  bleached like a leper's by these flaming scabs,
  nor at the fleshless bones I bear inside;   51

but tell me all about yourself, and who
  these two souls are that bear you company;
  and tell me with all haste, I beg of you."   54

"I wept to see your face once when it lay
  in death," I said, "and I weep no less now
  to see what pain has wasted it away;   57

in God's name tell me how. Do not demand
  I speak while still bemused, for he speaks badly
  whose mind is too full to be at command."   60

And he: "From the Eternal Counsel flow
  the powers whereby the water and the tree
  we have just passed, emaciate us so.   63

All those who sing while weeping in their pain
  once loved their stomach-sacs beyond all measure.
  Here, thirst and hunger wring them clean again.   66

Hunger and thirst that nothing can assuage
  grow in us from the fragrance of the fruit
  and of the spray upon the foliage.   69

And not once only as we round this place
  do we endure renewal of our pain.
  —Did I say 'pain'? I should say 'gift of grace.'   72

For the same will that drives us to the Tree
  drove Christ on gladly to cry 'Eli! Eli!'
  when he paid with his blood to set us free."   75

And I to him: "Forese, from the day
  in which you changed worlds for the better life,
  less than five years, as yet, have passed away.   78

If your ability to sin had fled
  before the hour of that sublime sweet sorrow
  that weds us back to God, among his blessèd,   81

how have you reached so high in the great climb?
  I thought to find you still below, with those
  who sit and wait, repaying time for time."   84

"My Nella's flood of tears," he answered me,
  "Have borne me up so soon to let me drink
  the blessed wormwood of my agony.   87

Her sighs and prayers were heard where Love abounds:
  they raised me from the slope where I lay waiting
  and set me free of all the other Rounds.   90

The dearer and more pleasing in God's sight
  is the poor widow of my love, as she
  is most alone in doing what is right.   93

For the Barbagia of Sardinia breeds
  chaste women as compared to that Barbagia
  in which I left her to her widow's weeds.   96

O my dear brother, what is there to say?
  In vision I already see a time—
  and it is not far distant from this day—   99

in which the pulpit shall denounce by writ
  the shameless jades that Florentines call ladies,
  who go about with breasts bare to the tit.   102

What Moslem woman ever has required
  a priestly discipline, or any other,
  before she would go decently attired?   105

But if the chippies only could foresee
  swift Heaven's punishment, they'd have their mouths
  already open to howl misery.   108

For if what we foresee here does not lie,
  they shall be sad before those sons grow beards
  who can be soothed now with a lullaby.   111

Now, brother, answer in your turn. You see
  your shadow there, and how these other souls
  are staring at the spot along with me."   114

I then: "If you call back to mind from here
  my past life in your company, yours in mine,
  memory will seem too great a load to bear.   117

I was recalled from such ways by that one
  who leads me here, and just the other day
  when that one's sister (pointing to the Sun)   120

was at the full. Through the profoundest night
  of final death he led me in this flesh
  which follows him to find the final Right.   123

From there with many a sweet encouragement
  he led me upward and around the mountain
  which straightens in you what the world has bent.   126

And he has pledged himself to go with me
  until I stand by Beatrice, above.
  Then I must do without his company.   129

The one who pledges this (and as I spoke
  I pointed to him standing there) is Virgil.
  The other is the shade of him who woke   132

to blessedness just now when every rim,
  the mountain round, shook in releasing him."

NOTES

11. *Labia mea, Domines:* "O Lord, open Thou my Lips, and my mouth shall pour forth Thy praise." From the Fifty-first Psalm of the Vulgate. The psalm is part of the service of Lauds for Tuesdays, and the time is now Easter Tuesday. A second aptness is in the mention of lips being opened for praise, rather than for eating and drinking.

21. *silent and devout:* Virgil (lines 14–15) seems to have implied that the souls go circling the ledge endlessly uttering their mixed hymn and lament. Here they are presented as silent and devout. The only possible inference seems to be that they circle the ledge in devout and silent meditation until they reach the tree, and then cry aloud.

25. *Erysichthon:* Erysichthon mocked the goddess Ceres by felling an oak in her sacred grove, and Ceres visited an insatiable hunger upon him. He ate up all his own substance, sold his daugh-

ter in order to buy more food, consumed that, and finally devoured his own limbs. (*Metamorphoses* VIII, 726–881.) He does admirably as the archetype of gluttony, for the glutton consumes his soul just as Erysichthon consumed his body.

29–30. *who lost Jerusalem . . . Miriam:* Josephus (*Jewish Wars* VI, 3) relates that when Titus was besieging Jerusalem in 70 A.D. (see XXI, 82, note), the people were so reduced by hunger that a woman named Mary or Miriam, the daughter of Eleazar, killed her son, cooked him, and ate half his body. *with her own beak:* As if she were a bird of prey, a creature reduced from all humanity. So gluttony reduces the soul.

32. *Those who read OMO in the face of man:* A medieval notion held that the Creator had signed His creation (thoughtfully anticipating the Latin alphabet) *OMO DEI,* "Man [is] of God"; the eyes forming the two *O*'s, the brows, nose, and cheekbones forming the *M,* the ears the *D,* the nostrils the *E,* and the mouth the *I.* Dante mentions only the *OMO,* making the point that these souls were so emaciated that one could readily see the *M.*

34. *without knowing how:* Dante's wonderment here concerns the nature of souls. How can insubstantial spirits become so hideously wasted by the craving aroused by the mere smell of food and water? (One need only inhale the moist air near a fountain or waterfall to know what Dante means by the "smell" of water.) In XXV the question arises again and is answered in detail.

42. *How have I earned a grace so bountiful?:* The grace of seeing Dante again.

46. *That spark:* The soul's voice.

48. *Forese:* Forese (For-RAY-zeh) Donati died 28 July 1296. Gemma Donati, Dante's wife, was Forese's kinswoman. Forese was the brother of Corso Donati, head of the Black Guelphs, and Dante was a passionate White, but before politics separated them they had been warm friends. Forese had been something of a poet, and he and Dante had exchanged rhymed lampoons in one of which Dante had accused him of Gluttony; and of Pride and Prodigality as well.

70. *And not once only:* In XXIV, 104, Dante sights a second tree, and in XXIV, 115–117 we are told that this second tree sprawled from yet a third, which is the original Tree of Knowledge from which Eve and then Adam ate. (The third tree is not described here except as growing "further up the slope." Dante finds it in the Terrestrial Paradise, Canto XXXII, 37–60.)

74. *drove Christ on gladly to cry 'Eli! Eli!':* At the ninth hour of his agony Christ cried, *Eli, Eli, lama sabachthani?*—"My God, my God, why hast thou forsaken me?" (*Matthew* xxvii, 46.) Dante does not mean that Christ rejoiced in his final despair but, rather, that foreseeing it, he still went gladly toward it. The desire of these sinners to endure their terrible suffering is thus compared to Christ's eagerness to endure the pain that would redeem the souls of men.

76–84. DANTE'S QUESTION. Dante's phrasing is difficult here. It must be understood to be Dante's personal knowledge that Forese did not give up gluttony until he was too weak to eat any more, *i.e.,* in his final hour. Then only did he achieve the sweet sublime sorrow of repentance. But since he died in 1295, only five years before the present meeting, Dante would have expected to find him outside The Gate, his purifying pains delayed for as long as he made God wait. So line 84, "repaying time for time."

85. *Nella:* Forese's wife Giovanna, a name whose affectionate diminutive is Giovanella, whence Nella. Dante clearly offers her as the type of the good Christian wife. Her virtue puts all the more to shame the decadence of the other women of Florence.

90. *set me free of all the other Rounds:* Nella's prayers have not only moved Forese out of Ante-Purgatory, but have freed him of all the pains of the Rounds below, on which he might have suffered (if

Dante's charge in his rhymed lampoons had any substance) for Pride and Prodigality.

94. *the Barbagia of Sardinia:* Barbagia, a wild region in the Sardinian mountains, was dominated by the Barbacini, a bandit clan said to have been landed by the Vandals. They were reputed to be savages and idolaters. St. Gregory speaks of them as living like animals. Other medieval sources report their women as going half-naked; and inevitably some later sources (Dante's son Pietro among them) drop the "half" and report the Barbagian women to be naked savages. Thus, Forese is saying that the naked savages of the Sardinian Barbagia are chaste as compared to the women of that other Barbagia, *i.e.,* Florence, Barbagia-on-the-Arno.

109. *For if what we foresee here does not lie:* As usual, it does not, the calamities here foreseen, as of 1300, having already befallen Florence by the time Dante wrote this prophecy. In November of 1301 (see XX, 70–78) Charles de Valois entered Florence and sowed disaster. In 1302 Rinier da Calboli introduced his reign of terror (XIV, 58 ff.), and a great famine occurred in the same year. In 1303 Florence was interdicted, and shortly thereafter a bridge collapsed, killing many people. (See also *Inferno* XVI, 7–12.) It would take about fifteen years for male children to progress from lullabies to beards, and by 1315 Florence had more than enough to mourn.

120. *that one's sister (pointing to the Sun):* The Moon. As Diana, she was said to be the sister of Apollo, the Sun. (See note to XX, 130–132.) Dante is, of course, referring to the moon of the night of Holy Thursday when he was in the Dark Wood of Error (*Inferno* I).

121–122. *the profoundest night of final death:* Hell.

CANTO XXIV

The Sixth Cornice—The Gluttons

THE TREE OF KNOWLEDGE ·
THE REIN OF GLUTTONY

The Poets move on as Dante continues his talk with Forese, who
identifies many of the souls of the Gluttons, among them *Bona-
giunta of Lucca.* Bonagiunta mutters a prophecy concerning
Dante's future meeting with *Gentucca.* He then questions Dante
about *The Sweet New Style* and ends by concluding that had he
and the others of his school of poetry grasped the principle of
natural expression, they would have written as well as do the
poets of Dante's school.

All the other souls speed ahead, but Forese remains to proph-
esy the death of his brother, *Corso Donati,* leader of the Black
Guelphs. Then he speeds away and soon disappears.

The Poets move on and come to *The Tree of Knowledge* from
which a voice cries *The Rein of Gluttony,* citing *Eve, The Centaurs,*
and *The Army of Gideon.* Having skirted the tree carefully, warned
away by the voice, the Poets move ahead and meet *The Angel of
Abstinence,* who shows them to the ascent.

Talk did not slow our steps, nor they in turn
　　our talk, but still conversing we moved on
　　like ships at sea with a brisk wind astern.　　　　　　　3

And all those shades, looking like things twice dead,
　　were drinking in through their sepulchral eyes
　　the awe of seeing me as I had been bred.　　　　　　　6

And I, continuing as I had begun,
　　said: "His ascent, I think, is somewhat slower
　　than it would be but for that other one.　　　　　　　9

—But where now is Piccarda? Do you know?
  And is there anyone of special note
  among these people who stare at me so?"   12

"My sister, who was good as she was fair,
  and fair as good, sits crowned on High Olympus,
  rejoicing in eternal triumph there."   15

Thus he began. Then: "To identify
  anyone here is certainly permitted,
  for abstinence has milked our features dry.   18

This" (and he pointed to him) "dearest brother,
  was Bonagiunta of Lucca. That behind him,
  his face more sunken in than any other,   21

once fathered Holy Church. Of Tours his line;
  and here in the long fast he expiates
  Bolsena's eels and the Vernaccia wine."   24

Then he named many others, one by one,
  at which I saw not one black look among them,
  but all seemed pleased at being thus made known.   27

Ubaldino della Pila hungered there,
  and Boniface, shepherd to all those bellies—
  they were so starved they used their teeth on air.   30

I saw my Lord Marchese. Before he died
  he drank with somewhat less thirst at Forlì,
  yet no man ever saw him satisfied.   33

As one who notes one face especially
  among a crowd, I noted him of Lucca
  who seemed most to desire a word with me.   36

He muttered something, and I seemed to hear
  the word "Gentucca" issue from the wound
  where most he felt High Justice pluck him bare.   39

"Spirit," I said, "since you seem so intent
  on talking to me, do so audibly,
  and speaking so, make both of us content."   42

"Though men may mock my city," he replied,
  "she who will teach you how to treasure it
  is born there, though she is not yet a bride.   45

This presage you shall take with you from here,
  and if you misconstrued what I first muttered
  the facts themselves, in time, will make it clear.   48

But is this really the creator of
  those new *canzoni,* one of which begins
  'Ladies who have the intellect of Love'?"   51

And I: "When Love inspires me with delight,
  or pain, or longing, I take careful note,
  and as he dictates in my soul, I write."   54

And he: "Ah, brother, now I see the thong
  that held Guittone, and the Judge, and me
  short of that sweet new style of purest song.   57

I see well how your pens attained such powers
  by following exactly Love's dictation,
  which certainly could not be said of ours.   60

And if one scan the two styles side by side,
  that is the only difference he will find."
  With that he fell still, as if satisfied.   63

Just as the cranes that winter by the Nile
  form close-bunched flights at times, then, gathering
                                  speed,
  streak off across the air in single file;   66

so all the people there faced straight ahead,
  and being lightened by both will and wasting,
  quickened their paces, and away they sped.   69

And as a runner who must take a rest
  lets his companions pull ahead and walks
  till he has eased the panting in his chest;   72

just so Forese let that blessed train
  outdistance him, and held his pace to mine,
  and said to me: "When shall we meet again?"   75

"I do not know how long my life will be,"
  I said, "but I cannot return so soon
  but what my wish will reach the shore before me;   78

for from that city where I came to life
  goodness is disappearing day by day;
  a place foredoomed to ruin by bloody strife."   81

"Take heart," he said, "for I see him whose crime
  exceeds all other's dragged at a beast's tail
  to where sin lasts beyond the end of time.   84

At every stride the beast goes faster, faster,
  until its flashing hooves lash out, and leave
  the foul ruin of what was once its master.   87

Those Spheres (and he looked toward the Heavens
                                  here)
  will not turn far before what I have said,
  and may not add to now, shall be made clear.   90

Now I must leave you far behind: your pace
  has cost me a considerable delay;
  and time is precious to us in this place."   93

At times during a horse charge, one brave knight
  will spur ahead, burning to claim the honor
  of having struck the first blow in the fight;   96

just so his lengthened stride left us behind,
  and I trailed on, accompanied by those two
  who were such mighty marshals of mankind.   99

And when, in such haste, he had pulled ahead
  so far that I could only make him out
  as I could understand what he had said;   102

we turned a corner and there came in sight,
  not far ahead, a second tree, its boughs
  laden with fruit its foliage bursting bright.   105

Sometimes when greedy children beg and screech
  for what they may not have, the one they cry to
  holds it in plain sight but beyond their reach   108

to whet their appetites: so, round that tree,
  with arms raised to the boughs, a pack of souls
  begged and was given nothing. Finally   111

they gave up and moved on unsatisfied,
  and we drew close in our turn to that plant
  at which such tears and pleadings were denied.   114

"Pass on. Do not draw near. The tree whose fruit
  Eve took and ate grows further up the slope,
  and this plant sprouted from that evil root."   117

—Thus, from the boughs, an unknown voice called
                    down.

And thus warned, Virgil, Statius, and myself
  drew close, and hugged the cliff, and hurried on.   120

"Recall," the voice went on, "those cursed beasts
  born of a cloud. When they had swilled the wine,
  Theseus had to slash their double breasts.   123

Recall those Jews who once showed Gideon
  how to abandon all to thirst, whereat
  he would not lead them down the hills to Midian."   126

So we strode on along the inner way
  while the voice cried the sins of Gluttony
  which earn, as we had seen, such fearful pay.   129

Then the road cleared, and with more room for
                    walking
  we spread out, and had gone a thousand paces
  in meditation, with no thought of talking;   132

when suddenly a voice cried, startling me
  as if I were a panic-stricken colt:
  "What are you thinking of alone, you three?"   135

I looked up to see who had spoken so:
  no man has ever seen in any furnace,
  metal or glass raised to so red a glow.   138

"If your wish is to ascend," I heard one say,
  "this is the place where you must turn aside.
  All you who search for Peace—this is the way."   141

His glory blinded me. I groped and found
  my Teacher's back and followed in his steps
  as blind men do who guide themselves by sound.   144

Soft on my brow I felt a zephyr pass,
　soft as those airs of May that herald dawn
　with breathing fragrances of flowers and grass;　　　147

and unmistakably I felt the brush
　of the soft wing releasing to my senses
　ambrosial fragrances in a soft rush.　　　150

And soft I heard the Angel voice recite:
　"Blessèd are they whom Grace so lights within
　that love of food in them does not excite　　　153

excessive appetite, but who take pleasure
　in keeping every hunger within measure."

NOTES

6.　*as I had been bred:* In the flesh of the first life.

8.　*His ascent, I think, is somewhat slower:* Dante is speaking of Statius, continuing his answer to Forese's question from the last Canto. Statius is now free to ascend to the top of the Mount, and thence to Heaven, but is slowing his ascent in order to be with Virgil that much longer. Were Statius to climb with the speed of the almost-weightless (for, barring last rites, his soul is now purified and free) he would have to leave Virgil, who is still slowed by his need to keep pace with Dante, who is still slowed by his flesh.

Clearly, however, Dante is making an exception to the rule of his own great concept, for Statius is delaying his ascent to God (making God wait) in favor of Virgil. Such a choice would certainly emerge as sinful were Dante to apply his own rule impartially, and in Canto XXX Dante himself receives a substantial tongue-lashing from Beatrice when he mourns the disappearance of Virgil.

10.　*Piccarda:* Sister of Forese. She took vows as a nun but was later forced by her other brother, Corso, into a political marriage in violation of her vows. Dante will meet her in the lowest sphere of Paradise.

14. *High Olympus:* Heaven. Another of Dante's easy adaptations of pagan themes and concepts to Christian belief.

16. *Thus he began. Then:* As at many other points in *The Divine Comedy,* Dante has asked two questions. "Thus he began" signifies that the preceding speech was in answer to the first question (line 10). "Then" begins the answer to the second (lines 11–12).

17. *is certainly permitted:* Their emaciation being such that they could never be recognized by their appearances.

19. *(and he pointed to him):* Dante seems to have discovered this device at the end of the last Canto, and to have become so taken by it that he uses it three times in thirty-one lines.

20. *Bonagiunta of Lucca:* See below, note to line 35.

20–21. *That* [one] *behind him . . . :* Simon de Brie, of Tours, Pope from 1281–1285 as Martin IV. Italians, with their normal proprietary arrogance toward Vatican matters, frowned at the thought of a French Pope, but generally granted him to be a good one, though gluttonous. Since in Dante the punishment is always meant to fit the crime, the fact that his face is more sunken-in than any other, would indicate that he was, in life, the most gluttonous of all. Or it may indicate that his exalted position as Pope made his gluttony that much more sinful.

24. *Bolsena's eels and the Vernaccia wine:* The eels of Lake Bolsena, near Viterbo, are still especially prized. Vernaccia is a rich, sweet white wine of the mountains near Genoa. Eels were prepared by dropping them alive into a vat of wine. The eels, thus pickled alive, died and were roasted. Martin IV gorged incessantly on such eels and died of an attack brought on by overindulgence.

28. *Ubaldino della Pila:* A knight of the Ubaldini. Brother of the Cardinal of the Ubaldini who is roasting in Hell with Farinata, among the Epicureans (*Inferno* X). Another brother was Ugolino d'Azzo, who is mentioned with great honor in XIV. Ubaldino was the father of Archbishop Ruggieri who is serving as lunch for Ugolino in the cooler of Hell (*Inferno* XXXII–XXXIII). He was a great feaster and entertainer, once playing host for several months— in necessarily lavish style—to the Pope and his whole court.

29. *Boniface:* Archbishop of Ravenna, 1274–1294. He was rather

more drawn to political than to spiritual affairs. Dante's charge against him involves a word play I could not render without taking considerable liberties. Literally: "Who pastured so many people with his crozier [*i.e.*, shepherd's staff]." But there is the spiritual pasturage the archbishop should provide for his flock of souls, and there is the material pasturage that filled the bellies of all the retainers Boniface kept about him as political boss of his district and its patronage. Thus the essential sarcasm of Dante's charge is that Boniface was shepherd to the bellies rather than to the souls of his archdiocese. There is no evidence outside of Dante that Boniface was a glutton.

31. *my lord Marchese:* Messer Marchese of Forlì, Podestà of Faenza in 1296. He once asked what the people thought of him. When told they spoke of nothing but his incessant drinking, he replied that they should remember he was always thirsty.

35. *him of Lucca:* Bonagiunta (Bon-ah-DJOON-tah) degli Overardi. Poet and orator of some repute in Lucca, but one whose language Dante condemns in *De Vulgari Eloquentia* I, xiii. He was a famous glutton and tippler. Died 1297.

38. *Gentucca:* Is probably best taken as the name of a lady Dante met when he went to live with a friend at Lucca, probably about 1314–1316.

38–39. *the wound where most he felt High Justice pluck him bare:* Another of Dante's mixed metaphors. "Pluck him bare" can only be understood as "waste him away." "The wound" where he would most feel his wasting is his mouth, now reduced to a wound in his ruined face, but originally the part of him through which he sinned.

43. *Though men may mock my city:* Dante is certainly not more scornful of Lucca than of the other cities of Tuscany. Throughout the *Comedy* he enjoys taking pot shots at all of them.

44. *she:* Gentucca. In 1300 she had been born and was living in Lucca but as a girl not yet married.

49–51. Literally: "But tell me if I truly behold him who brought forth the new rhymes beginning . . ." The line quoted is the first line of a *canzone* of the *Vita Nuova* (XIX).

Bonagiunta already knows who Dante is. His phrasing is not, therefore, for identification. He has just prophesied a Platonic love into which Dante will enter with Gentucca. His thoughts turn naturally to the past Platonic love that Dante celebrated in his *Vita Nuova*. As a poet himself, Bonagiunta would be interested in discussing the "sweet new style" with its foremost practitioner.

49–62. BONAGIUNTA AND THE SWEET NEW STYLE. Bonagiunta, Guittone d'Arezzo (who first perfected the form of the Italian sonnet), and Jacopo da Lentino (known as "Il Notaro," i.e., The Judge)—a Sicilian poet to whom Dante gives some qualified praise in *De Vulgari Eloquentia* (I, xxi)—were all practitioners of a kind of conventionalized verse modeled after the most decadent phase of Provençal poetry. They flourished in the first half of the thirteenth century. Dante was a prime mover in the later "sweet new style" of more natural expression. In lines 55–57 Bonagiunta regrets that his school failed to discover the principle of the sweet new style, for only the adherence to that principle of natural expression, he adds (lines 61–62), distinguishes the one style from the other. His implication is that, had his school observed that principle, he and his fellows would have written as well as the new poets, being their equals in all else. And with this final wishful assertion, Bonagiunta seems satisfied, and says no more.

It is possible to interpret Bonagiunta's remarks as a lament over his failure to discover the new style and thereby to write better, but the first interpretation seems firmer.

64–66. Compare Dante's description of the Carnal, *Inferno* V, 46–47.

68. *being lightened by both will and wasting:* Sin is equated to heaviness and purity to lightness throughout the *Comedy*. These souls are made lighter both by their own will to endure the purifying penance and by the wasting that resulted from it. Dante seems to imply that an emaciated incorporeal essence weighs less than a normal one. If so, the explanation must lie in one of the mysteries of faith.

76–81. DANTE'S ANSWER TO FORESE. Forese, moved by love, has expressed his longing to see Dante again, but obviously he cannot until Dante is dead. To a soul in Purgatory, to be sure, death is not a tragedy but an arrival. Yet Forese phrases his question delicately, aware that he is speaking to a living man. Dante, on the other hand, understands Forese's intent, and answers without circumlocution: however soon his return to the second life, his wish will be there before him.

78. *the shore:* Of Purgatory. Dante will have some time to spend on the Cornice of Pride (and perhaps of Wrath), but he may yet overtake Forese in the final ascent.

79. *that city:* Florence.

82. *him:* Corso Donati. Forese's brother and head of the Black Guelphs. It was Corso who persuaded Boniface VIII to send Charles of Valois to Florence in 1300. Thus the crimes of Charles are indirectly his. In 1309 Corso tried a coalition that would make him the supreme authority in Florence, but the Blacks, whom he had done so much so bloodily to put into power, discovered his plot and condemned him to death. He fled but was pursued and killed. Dante follows an account (line 83) that has him dragged to death by his horse.

84. *where sin lasts beyond the end of time:* Hell.

88. *Those Spheres:* Of Heaven, as indicated by the parenthetical stage direction.

90. *and may not add to now:* Forese has already overstayed and must rejoin his band.

92. *a considerable delay:* In matching his pace to Dante's when he should be speeding toward his expiation with the other spirits.

100–105. These two tercets present fairly typical problems of Dantean interpretation. In 100–102 Dante says he can follow Forese with his eyes only as he could follow in his mind (i.e., understand) what Forese had said. Hence if Forese was still remotely in sight, it would follow that Dante had some glimmer of the meaning of his prophecy. If, on the other hand, Dante meant he could not grasp the prophecy at all, Forese must have disappeared.

At that very instant, however (103–105) the Poets round a bend in the cliff. If they are that close to a turning (and the circles at this altitude would turn on a shortened radius), Forese must have long since disappeared around the bend. It must follow, therefore, that Dante means he had no idea whatever of the meaning of Forese's prophecy—as, in fact, he could not have known in 1300 how Corso would die in 1309.

104. *a second tree:* Various attempts have been made to relate this tree to the first, as they must, indeed, be related since from one the Whip of Gluttony is spoken, and from the other, the Rein. This one, we are told by the voice, is sprung from the same root as the Tree of Knowledge from which Eve ate. Among other things, therefore, it is the Tree of Death. By simple opposites the other may be argued to be the Tree of Life. Or the two may be seen as the Tree of Mortal Woe (death included) and the Tree of Eternal Life, the former containing the voice of the ruin brought on by sin, the latter the voice of the eternal joy that arises from obedience.

115–126. THE REIN OF GLUTTONY. (115–117) The first admonition cites the downfall of Eve (aptly cited from an offshoot of the original tree). Gluttony, in Dante's view, is sinful because it rejects God in favor of appetite: the Glutton thinks of his belly rather than of his soul. Eve's act is, therefore, the supreme Gluttony in that it lost God to all mankind until the coming of Christ. In Dante's geography, the Garden of Eden stands at the top of the Mount of Purgatory. Thus the tree from which Eve ate, and from whose roots this tree springs, must stand above it.

(121–123) The second admonition cites the drunkenness of the Centaurs and the grief to which it brought them. Invited to a wedding feast by the neighboring Lapithae, the Centaurs became so drunk they tried to make off with the bride, whereupon Theseus and the Lapithae seized arms and killed great numbers of the Centaurs. The Centaurs are spoken of as "born of a cloud" (line 122) because they were supposed to have been sired by Ixion upon the cloud Nephele whom Jupiter had formed into the likeness of Juno, beloved of Ixion. They are said to have double breasts (line 123) because of their two natures, half-horse and half-human.

(124–126) The third admonition is based on *Judges* vii, 5–6. When Gideon was leading the army of the Jews against Midian, he was instructed by the Lord to lead his men to the river and to watch how they drank. Those who threw aside all caution at the sight of water and plunged their faces into the river, were to be set aside. Those who stayed alert despite their thirst, drinking cautiously by scooping the water up in their hands and remaining watchful, were to be chosen. Three hundred were so chosen, and with them alone Gideon moved down to victory.

127. *the inner way:* Along the cliff-face.

130–131. *the road cleared, and with more room . . . :* One must remember that the tree grows in the middle of the ledge. The Voice had warned the Poets not to draw near. Since the ledge is narrow and the tree spreads wide, the Poets had to draw far to one side along the inner cliff-face, naturally drawing close together. Now, with the road cleared, they once more draw apart for better walking.

135. *alone:* As Dante has made clear, the souls in Purgatory go normally in great bands. Three alone is an exception the Angel could not fail to note.

135–155. THE ANGEL OF ABSTINENCE. The combined fieriness and softness of the Angel of Abstinence makes him an especially memorable figure, and an especially appropriate one, his office considered. The fieriness of his aura may be taken to symbolize raging appetite, perhaps prefiguring the Fire of *Luxuria* (lust) of the next Canto; his softness to symbolize the sweetness of abstinence in its conquest of such fire.

His blessing to the Poets is based on the second half of the Fifth Beatitude, the first half of which was recited by the Angel of Moderation on the ledge just below. (See opening lines of XXII.) That Angel had left out "who hunger" in his version of the Beatitude. The Angel leaves out "who thirst" but puts in "who hunger."

CANTO XXV

Departure from the Sixth Cornice—The Ascent

THE DISCOURSE OF STATIUS

The Seventh Cornice—The Lustful

THE WHIP OF LUST

It is 2:00 P.M. as the Three Poets leave the Cornice of the Gluttonous and begin their hurried *Ascent to the Seventh Cornice.*

Dante, burning with eagerness to ask how the Gluttons could give the appearance of advanced starvation despite the fact that they are airy bodies and do not need food, fears to speak but is finally encouraged to do so by Virgil. Dante immediately offers his question, and Virgil, as an act of courtesy, invites Statius to answer it. The rest of the rapid ascent is then occupied by *The Discourse of Statius on the Nature of the Generative Principle, The Birth of the Human Soul,* and *The Nature of Aerial Bodies.*

By the time Statius is finished, the Poets have reached the Seventh Cornice. There, enwrapped in sheets of flame, the souls of *The Lustful* sing over and over the hymn *Summae Deus Clementiae.* At each conclusion of the hymn, they cry out in praise of an example of High Chastity. These examples form *The Whip of Lust.* It is in this way, singing and praising as they move through the flames, that the Lustful perform their purification.

It was an hour to climb without delay.
  Taurus succeeded to the Sun's meridian,
  and Scorpio to Night's—a world away; 3

thus, as a man spurred on by urgent cause
  will push ahead, no matter what appears
  along the way inviting him to pause— 6

just so we filed, one of us at a time,
  into the gap, and started up those stairs
  whose narrowness divides all those who climb.   9

And as a little stork, eager to fly
  but afraid to leave the nest, will raise a wing
  then let it fall again—just such was I,   12

the will within me now strong and now weak,
  eager to ask, but going only so far
  as to make me clear my throat, and then not speak.   15

The pace was swift: nor did my Sweet Lord slow
  his stride, but said: "I see the bow of speech
  drawn back to the very iron. Let it go."   18

My doubts resolved, I did not hesitate
  to use my mouth. "How can they grow so thin,"
  I said, "who need no food in their new state?"   21

"Recall Meleager wasting as the brand
  wasted in fire," he said, "and you will find
  the matter not so hard to understand.   24

Or think how your least move before a glass
  is answered by your image, and what seemed hard
  is bound to grow much clearer than it was.   27

But this wish burns you, I know, and to put out
  all of its flames, I shall beg Statius now
  to be the one to heal the wounds of doubt."   30

"If, in your presence," Statius first replied,
  "I explain eternal things, let my excuse
  be only that your wish be not denied."   33

And then to me: "Son, let it be your task
  to hear and heed my words, and they will be
  a light upon the 'how' of what you ask.   36

Perfect blood—that pure blood that remains
  as one might say, like food upon the table,
  and never goes to slake the thirsty veins—   39

acquires, within the heart, formative power
  over all human organs; as that which flows
  into the veins forms *them*. It is once more   42

changed in the heart, then flows down to that place
  the better left unmentioned. Thence, it drips
  over another blood in its natural vase.   45

There, the two commingle; and one blood shows
  a passive bent, while the other blood is active,
  due to the perfect place from which it flows.   48

So joined, the active force within the latter
  first clots, then quickens what it has made firm
  of the former blood to serve as working matter. 51

The active force has now become a soul
  like that of a plant, but with the difference
  that this begins where that achieves its goal. 54

Soon, like some sea-thing, half-beast and half-weed,
  it moves and feels. It then begins to form
  those powers of sense of which it is the seed.   57

Now, my son, the formative power expands
  and elongates within, till every member
  takes form and place as nature's plan commands. 60

But how this animal-thing grows human powers
  you do not yet see; and this very point
  has led astray a wiser head than yours.   63

By him, the *possible intellect* was thought
  (since it occupied no organ) to be disjoined
  from the *vegetative soul*—and so he taught.   66

Open your heart to the truth I shall explain,
  and know that at the instant articulation
  has been perfected in the foetal brain,   69

that instant the First Mover turns to it.
  And there, rejoicing at such art in nature,
  breathes into it a new and powerful spirit.   72

All that is active there, this spirit draws
  into itself, forming a single soul
  that lives, and feels, and measures its own cause.   75

(Consider, if you find these words of mine
  too strange to understand, how the sun's heat
  joined to the sap of the vine turns into wine.)   78

Then when Lachesis' flax is drawn, it frees
  itself from flesh, but takes with it the essence
  of its divine and human faculties—   81

its lower powers grown passive now and mute;
  but memory, intelligence, and will
  more active than they were, and more acute.   84

Miraculously then, by its own will,
  it falls at once to one or the other shore.
  There it first learns its way, for good or ill.   87

And once inclosed in that new atmosphere,
   the *formative power* rays out, as it did first
   in shaping the bodily parts it left back there.   90

Then, as the air after a rain will glow
   inside itself, reflecting an outer ray,
   and clothe itself in many colors—so   93

wherever the soul may stop in its new hour,
   the air about it takes on that soul's image.
   Such is the virtue of the *formative power.*   96

Thereafter, in the same way one may see
   flame follow fire wherever it may shift,
   the new form follows the soul eternally.   99

From air it draws its visibility. Hence,
   it is called a *shade.* And out of air it forms
   the organs of sight, speech, and every sense.   102

Thus are we able to speak and laugh. And thus
   are we able to weep such tears and breathe such sighs
   as you have seen and heard, passing among us.   105

As desire, or other feelings move us, so
   our shades change their appearances. And that
   is the cause of what amazed you just below."   108

—We had come, by then, to the last turn of the stairs
   from which we bore to the right along the cornice,
   and our minds were drawn already to other cares.   111

Here, from the inner wall, flames blast the ledge,
   while from the floor an air-blast bends them back,
   leaving one narrow path along the edge.   114

This path we were forced to take as best we might,
  in single file. And there I was—the flames
  to the left of me, and the abyss to the right.   117

My Leader said: "In this place, it is clear,
  we all must keep a tight rein on our eyes.
  To take a false step would be easy here."   120

"*Summae Deus clementiae,*" sang a choir
  inside that furnace, and despite my road
  I could not help but look into the fire.   123

Then I saw spirits moving through the flames,
  and my eyes turned now to them, now to my feet,
  as if divided between equal claims.   126

When they had sung the hymn, those souls in pain
  cried out in full voice: "*Virum non cognosco.*"
  Then, softly, they began the hymn again.   129

That done, they cried: "Diana kept to the wood,
  and drove Helicé from her when that nymph
  had felt Venus's poison in her blood."   132

Then, once again, the hymn swelled from their choir;
  and after it they praised husbands and wives
  who were chaste as virtue and marriage vows
                          require.   135

And in this way, I think, they sing their prayer
  and cry their praise for as long as they must stay
  within the holy fire that burns them there.   138

Such physic and such diet has been thought fit
  before the last wound of them all may knit.

NOTES

1. *It was an hour to climb without delay:* Afternoon. Hence there was no time to waste, for darkness will come soon.

2–3. *Taurus succeeded to the Sun's meridian:* The sun is in the sign of Aries, which is succeeded by the sign of Taurus. If Taurus has replaced the sun at the meridian, the sun must have moved lower toward the west. And since the signs of the Zodiac each represent two hours (twelve of them for twenty-four hours), it must be two hours past noon. *and Scorpio to Night's—a world away:* Night is personified here. A world away (above Jerusalem). Night would have reached its meridian point (midnight) in the sign of Libra, but has now passed on and Scorpio is the ruling sign. It is, therefore, 2:00 A.M. in Jerusalem.

7. *one of us at a time:* The probable order is: Virgil, Statius, Dante. (*Cf.* XXVI, 1.)

9. *whose narrowness divides all those who climb:* A clear allegorical meaning not to be overlooked here, is that each soul must ultimately climb to salvation alone, inside itself, no matter how much assistance it may receive from others. Another would be the soul's loneliness in meeting sexual temptation.

10–15. *eager . . . afraid:* Dante is burning to ask how such insubstantial entities as shades, who need no physical nourishment, could have every appearance of advanced starvation, as is the case with the souls of the Gluttonous. This eagerness to ask, along with the need to hurry on, is implicit in all of Dante's phrasing in lines 1–6.

17–18. *the bow of speech . . . . :* Dante's speech is conceived to be a bow that he has bent back to the very iron (the head) of the arrow, in his eagerness to let fly, but which he has been afraid to release.

22. *Meleager:* Son of Oeneus, King of Calydon, and of Althaea. When he was born, the Fates threw a branch into the fire and decreed that he should live until fire had consumed it. Althaea pulled it out of the fire and hid it.

When he had grown, Meleager fell in love with Atalanta, famous for the story of the golden apples. He slew a great bear for her and gave her the skin. His own brothers stole the skin from Atalanta and

Meleager, in his rage, killed them. Althaea thereupon brought the fatal branch out of hiding and threw it into the fire. As the flames consumed it, Meleager's life was consumed.

29. *I shall beg Statius now:* Some commentators see Virgil's action in calling upon Statius as signifying that Human Reason has begun to surrender its function to the redeemed soul. Certainly, however, there is nothing in what Statius goes on to say, that lies beyond the province of Virgil as Human Reason. Statius's long reply, in fact, would have been taken as a scientific disquisition in Dante's time.

Virgil's action is better taken, I believe, as a courtesy to Statius. Rather than have Statius stand by while Virgil lectures on matters that Statius knows perfectly well, Virgil invites Statius to take over the lecture—a courtesy to a visiting professor. Statius returns the courtesy by pointing out that he can say nothing not known to Virgil, but undertakes the lecture because Virgil has been so gracious in requesting that he do so.

36. *the 'how':* Dante had asked (line 20): "How can they grow so thin?"

34–108. THE DISCOURSE OF STATIUS. The long discourse into which Statius launches cannot fail to present unusual difficulties to modern readers, yet it is worth special attention as an illustration of what Dante meant by "Science," as a series of outdated but interesting theories, and especially as an example of how carefully Dante led up to and then introduced his inquiries into the nature of things as an important part of the total scheme of the *Commedia*.

The discourse may be divided into three parts: I. The Nature of the Generative Principle; II. The Birth of the Human Soul; and III. The Nature of Aerial Bodies. An extended paraphrase is perhaps the best way to deal with the complexities of the discourse.

I. *The Nature of the Generative Principle:*

31–39. Dante's concept of blood includes not only blood as we understand it, but a pre-substance (perfect blood) some of which flows into the veins (i.e., the arteries), but some of which remains apart (like food left untouched and in its original state).

40–42. This perfect blood enters the heart (without entering into the general circulation of the bloodstream) and acquires the power (which we now associate with the genes) to determine the development of the bodily organs and members. Similarly, the blood that flows into the "veins" has the power to determine *their* form and function. *formative power:* a technical term from Scholastic philosophy. It may be thought of as "the generative principle." It is derived entirely from the male parent.

43–45. Within the heart of the father, this "perfect blood" undergoes a change into sperm. It then flows down to the male organs ("better left unmentioned") and, in the act of conception, drips over the blood of the female in the womb ("another blood in its natural vase").

46–48. These two bloods commingle. One of them (the female blood) is passive, i.e., it is menstrual, tending to flow away rather than to take form. The other (the male blood), because of the perfect place from which it flows (the heart), is active, i.e., it seeks to generate form.

49–51. The active blood then causes the passive blood to clot. It thus forms it into solid and workable matter, which it then quickens into life. Conception has taken place.

II. *The Birth of the Human Soul:*

52–54. With conception the soul is born, not as a coinheritance from the mother and father, but from the active force (the formative power) of the father-blood alone, the maternal blood providing only the matter for the formative power to work on. (Dante's views here are pure Aquinian doctrine.)

This newly formed soul is like that of a plant (vegetative only), but with the difference that the plant soul is fully formed at this stage, whereas the human soul is only beginning.

55–57. From this plantlike state (possessing only "vegetative faculties") the soul grows capable of elementary motion and sensation (the "sensitive faculties"). It has achieved the state of some "sea-thing." Dante says not "sea-thing" but "sea-fungus." He probably meant some coelenterate, such as the hydra, sea anemone, or jellyfish. In Dante's time such life-forms were believed to be single living masses without differentiated organs of any sort.

58–60. From this "sea-thing" stage, the *formative power* of the soul (from the father) moves within the maternal material shaping each organ and member into its form and place in human anatomy, according to nature's plan.

61–63. One must still ask how this animal foetus acquires the power of human reason (in Scholastic phrasing, "the possible intellect"). And here, before propounding the true doctrine as he sees it, Statius pauses to refute the teaching of Averroës ("a wiser head than yours"), who erred on this point.

64–66. To grasp the importance to Dante's doctrine of the error of Averroës, one must understand that in Scholastic teaching the soul possesses (1) the *vegetative faculty,* which is to say it lives, (2) the *sensitive or perceiving faculty,* which is to say it feels and receives impressions, and (3) the *reflective faculty,* called the *possible intellect,* which is to say it has the power of reasoning from the known to the unknown, and of extracting forms and concepts from nature.

The vegetative and sensitive faculties receive particular impressions only. The organ of those faculties, common to both man and beast, is the brain. Where then was the organ of the higher intellectual faculty, the possible intellect?

Since he could find no such organ, Averroës postulated a generalized universal rationality from which all men could draw rational faculties during their lives, but which was lost to them at death. It must follow, therefore, that no individual and rational soul could be summoned to eternal judgment, since the soul would have lost its possible intellect (rationality) at death. Church scholars would necessarily be required to reject such a doctrine since it denied the very basis of free will and of just reward and punishment.

67–75. Having refuted error, Statius then explains the truth: the instant the brain is fully formed in the human foetus, God turns to it in his joy at the art of nature in forming so perfect a thing, and breathes into it a powerful spirit peculiar to man. This God-infused spirit draws all the life forces (vegetative, sensitive, and rational) into a single soul. Note especially, in reply to Averroës, that the soul so formed is individualized, self-measuring, and, therefore, self-responsible.

76–78. Statius then compares the change wrought by the new

spirit with the way the heat of the sun is transformed into the quickened wine when joined to the relatively inert sap of the vine.

III. *The Nature of Aerial Bodies:*

79–81. Then when Lachesis (the Fate who draws out the flaxen thread of life—see XXI, 24–27, note) measures the end of the mortal life, the soul goes free of the flesh but takes with it, by virtue of that essence God breathed into it, all of its faculties both human (vegetative and sensitive) and divine (rational).

82–84. These lower (vegetative and sensitive) faculties grow passive and mute after death, since they have left behind the organs whereby they functioned. The higher faculties, however, since they are God-inspired and now free of their mortal involvement in materiality, become more active and acute.

85–87. At the instant of death the soul miraculously falls, by an act of its own will, either to the shore of Hell for damnation, or to the mouth of the Tiber to await transport to Purgatory.

88–90. As soon as the soul feels itself inclosed in the new atmosphere of the afterlife, the *formative power* from the heart of the father (line 40) sends out its rays, as it first did through the matter of the maternal blood to shape the living organs of the body.

91–93. The process is compared to the way the sun's rays (a force from without) work upon moist air to form a rainbow (within the air). Note that the power of the Sun's rays is, allegorically, from God the Father, just as the formative power of the soul is from the mortal father, and that both work upon passive matter to give it form.

94–96. Wherever (i.e., on whichever shore, as in line 86) the soul lights, the inclosing air takes on the image of that soul by virtue of the soul's indwelling formative power.

97–99. Then, ever after, and just as flame follows fire, the new form follows the soul, wherever it may move.

100–102. This new form is called a *shade* because it is made of insubstantial air, and because out of air it forms all the organs of sense.

103–105. Not only is the shade able to receive sensory impressions, but to produce sounds and appearances that can be registered by mortal senses. (As well as by other shades, as the narrative has made clear at many points.)

106–108. The appearance of the shade, moreover, conforms in detail to the inner feelings of the soul. Thus, if God fills the souls of the gluttonous with a craving for food which is then denied them, their shades appear to wither and starve, their outward appearance conforming to their inner state. It is this phenomenon that amazed Dante on the ledge below. (Note, too, the difference made clear here between men and shades. Men may appear virtuous by hiding their inner evil desires, and thus practice fraud. But shades cannot hide their inner workings: as they are within themselves, so must they appear. This doctrine applied retrospectively, especially to the souls in Hell, will immediately suggest another dimension to be considered when reading Dante's descriptions of the souls he meets there.)

119. *we all must keep a tight rein on our eyes:* On the narrative level, Virgil means simply, we must watch our dangerous path with great care. On the allegorical level, however, he can certainly be read to mean that lust (the excess of love) is the most readily inviting sin, but that it is as dangerous as a fall off the cliff, and that all men must guard their souls against it and refuse, like the souls of the Carnal now in Hell, to "abandon reason to their appetites." It was a convention of the "sweet new style," moreover, that love always enters through the eyes.

121. *"Summae Deus clementiae":* God of clemency supreme. These words are the beginning of the old hymn (now revised) which was sung at Matins on Saturday. The hymn is a prayer for chastity, begging God, of his supreme clemency, to burn lust from the soul and to leave the suppliant chaste.

128 ff. THE WHIP OF LUST. The Whip of Lust consists of examples of chastity which are called forth in praises by the sinners themselves, one example being cried forth at each completion of the Hymn they sing endlessly. The first example (Holy chastity) is, as always, from the life of Mary. The second (Natural chastity) cites Diana. In subsequent intervals between the hymn-singing, the sinners cry out the praise of various husbands and wives (not specified

by Dante) who were chaste as required by natural virtue and the sacramental vows of matrimony. They might be called examples of Catholic chastity.

128. *"Virum non cognosco"*: "I know not a man." These words were spoken by Mary at the Annunciation. Gabriel had said, "Behold, thou shalt conceive in thy womb, and bring forth a son." Mary replied, "How shall this be, seeing I know not a man?" (*Luke* i, 26–38.)

130 ff. *"Diana kept to the wood . . ."*: In order to preserve her virginity, Diana lived in the woods and became a huntress. One of her attendant nymphs, Helicé, felt the urging of lust (the *poison of Venus,* as opposed to love itself, which would also be from Venus, but not as poison) and gave herself to Jove. After she had been driven away by Diana, Helicé was changed into a bear by Juno. Jove, who semed systematically incapable of keeping his wife under control where his philandering was concerned, made his new she-bear a questionable sort of recompense by placing her in the sky as Ursa Major, the Big Dipper. (Ovid, *Metamorphoses* II, 401–530.)

CANTO XXVI

The Seventh Cornice—The Lustful

THE REIN OF LUST

Dante's shadow falls on the wall of flame and it is noticed by the souls of the Lustful who approach (without leaving the flames) to question him. Dante's answer, however, is interrupted by the approach of a second band of souls from the opposite direction. These are *The Sodomites*. The two bands of souls exchange brief embraces and then cry out *The Rein of Lust* as they move on, drawing rapidly apart.

The first group again approaches Dante and the soul of *Guido Guinizelli* speaks to him. Dante pays high homage to Guinizelli and discusses with him the growth of the Sweet New Style.

With a final request for a prayer for his soul, Guido withdraws and Dante then addresses *Arnaut Daniel,* who answers in the *langue d'oc,* and also begs that Dante say a prayer for him. His petition made, Daniel disappears into the purifying flame.

So, one before the other, we moved there
  along the edge, and my Sweet Guide kept saying:
  "Walk only where you see me walk. Take care."   3

The Sun, already changing from blue to white
  the face of the western sky, struck at my shoulder,
  its rays now almost level on my right;   6

and my shadow made the flames a darker red.
  Even so slight an evidence, I noticed,
  made many shades that walk there turn their head.   9

And when they saw my shadow, these began
  to speak of me, saying to one another:
  "He seems to be no shade, but a living man!"   12

And some of them drew near me then—as near
   as they could come, for they were ever careful
   to stay within the fire that burned them there.   15

"O you who trail the others—with no desire
   to lag, I think, but out of deference—
   speak to me who am burned by thirst and fire.   18

Not I alone need what your lips can tell:
   all these thirst for it more than Ethiopes
   or Indians for a drink from a cold well: 21

how is it that you cast a shadow yet,
   making yourself a barrier to the Sun,
   as if death had not caught you in its net?"   24

—So one addressed me. And I should have been
   explaining myself already, but for a new
   surprising sight that caught my eye just then;   27

for down the center of that fiery way
   came new souls from the opposite direction,
   and I forgot what I had meant to say.   30

I saw them hurrying from either side,
   and each shade kissed another, without pausing,
   each by the briefest greeting satisfied.   33

(Ants, in their dark ranks, meet exactly so,
   rubbing each other's noses, to ask perhaps
   what luck they've had, or which way they should go.)   36

As soon as they break off their friendly greeting,
   before they take the first step to pass on,
   each shade outshouts the other at that meeting.   39

"Sodom and Gomorrah," the new souls cry.
    And the others: "Pasiphaë enters the cow
    to call the young bull to her lechery."   42

As if cranes split into two flocks, and one
    flew to the Rhipheans, one to the sands,
    these to escape the ice, and those the Sun—   45

so, then, those shades went their opposing ways;
    and all returned in tears to their first song,
    and each to crying an appropriate praise.   48

Then those who came my way drew close once
                                                        more—
    the same shades that had first entreated me.
    They seemed as eager to hear me as before.   51

I, having had their wish presented twice,
    replied without delay: "O souls assured—
    whenever it may be—of Paradise,   54

I did not leave my limbs beyond the flood,
    not green nor ripe, but bear them with me here
    in their own jointure and in their own blood.   57

I go to be no longer blind. Above
    there is a lady wins us grace, and I,
    still mortal, cross your world led by her love.   60

But now I pray—so may it soon befall
    you have your greater wish to be called home
    into that heaven of love that circles all—   63

tell me, that I may write down what you say
    for all to read, who are you? and those others
    who move away behind you—who are they?"   66

Just as our mountaineers, their first time down,
  half-wild and shaggy, gape about the streets
  and stare in dumb amazement at the town—   69

just such a look I saw upon those shades;
  but when they had recovered from their stupor
  (which from a lofty heart the sooner fades),   72

the first shade spoke again: "Blessèd are you
  who for a better life, store in your soul
  experience of these realms you travel through!   75

Those souls you saw going the other way
  grew stained in that for which triumphant Caesar
  heard his own legions call him "Queen" one day.   78

Therefore their band, at parting from us, cries
  'Sodom!'—as you have heard—that by their shame
  they aid the fire that makes them fit to rise.   81

We were hermaphroditic in our offenses,
  but since we did not honor human laws,
  yielding like animals to our lusting senses,   84

we, when we leave the other band, repent
  by crying to our shame the name of her
  who crouched in the mock-beast with beast's intent.   87

And now you know our actions and our crime.
  But if you wish our names, we are so many
  I do not know them all, nor is there time.   90

Your wish to know mine shall be satisfied:
  I am Guido Guinizelli, here so soon
  because I repented fully before I died."   93

In King Lycurgus' darkest hour, two sons
  discovered their lost mother: I was moved
  as they had been (but could not match their actions)   96

when I heard his name, for he had fathered me
  and all the rest, my betters, who have sung
  sweet lilting rhymes of love and courtesy.   99

Enraptured, I can neither speak nor hear
  but only stare at him as we move on,
  although the flames prevent my drawing near.   102

When at last my eyes had fed, I spoke anew;
  and in such terms as win belief, I offered
  to serve him in whatever I could do.   105

And he to me then: "What you say has made
  such a profound impression on my mind
  as Lethe cannot wash away, nor fade.   108

But if the words you swore just now are true,
  let me know why you show by word and look
  such love as I believe I see in you?"   111

And I to him: "Your songs so sweet and clear
  which, for as long as modern usage lives,
  shall make the very ink that writes them dear."   114

"Brother," he said, "that one who moves along
  ahead there," (and he pointed) "was in life
  a greater craftsman of the mother tongue.   117

He, in his love songs and his tales in prose,
  was without peer—and if fools claim Limoges
  produced a better, there are always those   120

who measure worth by popular acclaim,
  ignoring principles of art and reason
  to base their judgments on the author's name.   123

So, once, our fathers sent Guittone's praise,
  and his alone, bounding from cry to cry,
  though truth prevails with most men nowadays.   126

And now, if you enjoy such privilege
  that you are free to go up to that cloister
  within which Christ is abbot of the college,   129

say an Our Father for me in that host,
  as far as it may serve us in this world
  in which the very power to sin is lost."   132

With that, perhaps to yield his place with me
  to someone else he vanished through the fire
  as a fish does to the dark depths of the sea.   135

I drew ahead till I was by that shade
  he had pointed to, and said that in my heart
  a grateful place to feast his name was laid.   138

And he replied at once and willingly:
  "Such pleasaunce have I of thy gentilesse,
  that I ne can, ne will I hide from thee.   141

Arnaut, am I, and weepe and sing my faring.
  In grievousnesse I see my follies past;
  in joie, the blistful daie of my preparing.   144

And by the eke virtue, I thee implour,
  that redeth thee, that thou amount the staire,
  be mindful in thy time of my dolour."   147

Then he, too, hid himself within the fire
  that makes those spirits ready to go higher.

NOTES

4–8. *changing from blue to white . . . the western sky:* It is now 4:00
P.M., or a bit later, of the third day on the mountain. At that hour of
a clear day Dante sees the sun as washing the blue out of the west-
ern sky and turning it whiter and brighter than the east. *struck at my
shoulder . . . now almost level on my right:* If the circumference of the
mountain is taken as a compass rose, the Poets have moved beyond
WNW and are moving toward W. The sun is in about the same po-
sition in the sky and getting low (perhaps a bit less than 30°), and
Dante says its rays are almost level. In point of fact, the mean distance
of the sun from the earth is approximately 93,000,000 miles and to
be level with it at one-third of its altitude, Dante would have to be
about 30,000,000 miles up: an altitude that makes it a considerable
mountain even as hyperbole goes. In any case, the shadow of Dante's
body falls on the wall of flame to his left, where it is noticed by many
of the shades within the fire. This fact, too, is certainly impossible:
Dante is treating the wall of flame as if it were a fog bank.

20–21. *all these:* All these others who walk with me here. *Ethiopes
or Indians:* Dante thought of Ethiopia and India as nothing but
parched and burning wastes.

29 ff. THE SODOMITES. The first shades Dante met on this
Cornice walked along bearing to the right (from east to west, the di-
rection of the sun, and the natural way of going on the mountain).
These new souls, to Dante's surprise, walk in the opposite direction,
i.e., against the natural way. They are The Sodomites. (See further
note to 37–42, below.)

31. *them:* Both bands of sinners.

32. *and each shade kissed another:* In accordance with the Apos-
tolic admonition: "Salute one another with a holy kiss." (*Romans*
xvi, 16.) These holy kisses not only remind them of the libidinous
kisses of their sin, but help expiate it. *without pausing:* Throughout,
Dante is moving behind Virgil and Statius as rapidly as possible

along that dangerous path. Thus, all his exchanges with these sinners are carried on at a fast walk, the Sodomites walking the opposite way and soon passing from view, the other shades retaining their same relative positions to Dante in their course along the ledge.

37–42. THE REIN OF LUST. The Rein consists here of a single admonition against *unnatural lust,* and of another against *natural lust.*

(40) *Sodom and Gomorrah:* Ancient cities destroyed in a rain of fire from Heaven as punishment for the fact that homosexuality was a general practice in them.

(41–42) *Pasiphaë:* Daughter of Apollo by the nymph Perseis. Wife of King Minos of Crete. Poseidon sent Minos a black bull to be offered as a sacrifice, but Minos put it in his herd. For revenge, Poseidon made Pasiphaë fall in love with the bull. She had Daedalus make a cunning effigy of a cow with wicker or wooden ribs, over which a cowhide was spread. She then crouched inside in order to be possessed by the bull. The Minotaur (see *Inferno* XII, 12–18, note) was born of the union. Thus, lust gave birth to a monster.

Note that Dante reserves "sodomy" specifically for "homosexuality." In modern usage "sodomy" includes "sexual relations with animals." Parsiphaë's example, though it may seem unnatural enough to us, does not violate natural law, but only human law. See 82–84, note, below.

43–45. *the Rhipheans:* The Rhiphean Mountains, a mythical range that occurs "somewhere in the north" on some old maps. Dante's phrasing is best understood to mean north in a generic sense. *the sands:* Of the African desert. Note that Dante does not say cranes actually behave in this way (he could not fail to know that cranes do not migrate both north and south in the same season), but only that it is *as if* cranes did so behave. Clearly the figure relates to the cranes of *Inferno* V, 46–47, thereby suggesting both a parallelism and a contrast.

46–48. *their opposing ways:* The Sodomites go away from Dante. The others continue along in his direction. *their first song: Summae Deus clementiae. each . . . an appropriate praise:* The appropriate praises are the miscellaneous exhortations from The Whip of Lust. The sinners sing their hymn, then shout a praise, then sing again. After the first hymn they praise Mary. After the second, Diana. After the third, and before starting the cycle over, each cites his own example of chastity, probably an example that stands directly opposite his particular sin.

55. *beyond the flood:* Across the sea. Hence, in the world.

59. *a lady:* Dante could mean either Beatrice or the Virgin Mary.

63. *that heaven . . . that circles all:* The Empyrean. *of love:* Note the special aptness of "holy love" to the state of these sinners whose crime was unholy love.

77–78. *Caesar . . . "Queen":* Suetonius (*Caesar* 49) reports Caesar's homosexual relation with Nicomedes, the conquered King of Bithynia, and that he was called "The Queen of Bithynia" for it, his soldiers singing a lampoon that ran:

> *Gallias Caesar subegit, Nicomedes Caesarem;*
> *Ecce Caesar nunc triumphat, qui subegit Gallias;*
> *Nicomedes non triumphat, quit subegit Caesarem.*

The point of the lampoon lies in a pun on the word *subegit*—"put under" or "conquered." Thus:

> Caesar put Gaul under; Nicomedes, Caesar.
> Now behold Caesar triumphant who put Gaul under,
> But now Nicomedes who put Caesar under.

80–81. *by their shame they aid the fire:* To do its purifying work. The pains of Purgatory are willed joyously by those who endure them. Both the flame and the shame therefore are a gladly offered penance. In Dante's view, the fire itself would be meaningless (and Infernal rather than Purgatorial) without the shame (a true act of contrition).

82–84. *hermaphroditic:* Heterosexual. These sinners were guilty of abandoning themselves, to lust, but not of mating with their own sex. *human law:* Those restraints that govern human but not animal behavior, and which are the functions of intelligence and of a moral sense. To lose those restraints is to be bestial, and therefore the example of Pasiphaë in the Rein of Lust.

87. *the mock-beast:* The "cow" in which Pasaphaë crouched, and which consisted of a hide stretched over a framework.

92. *Guido Guinizelli:* Guido di Guinizelli de' Principi (GWEE-doh dee Gwee-nee-TZEH-lee day PREEN-chee-pee). Vernacular poet of the mid-thirteenth century, esteemed as a forerunner of the sweet new style. Died 1276. *here so soon:* Since Guido had been dead only twenty-four years by 1300, his full repentance spared him a long delay.

94–96. *Lycurgus' darkest hour:* Hypsipyle, wife of Jason, to whom she had borne twin sons, Thoas and Euneus, was captured by pirates and sold to Lycurgus, King of Nemea. She was appointed nurse of the king's infant son.

When she met the parched heroes who fought against Thebes (XXII, 112, note) she put the baby down on the grass long enough to point out the spring called Langia. While she was gone, the infant was bitten by a poisonous snake. Lycurgus condemned her to death for negligence, and she was on the point of being executed when her sons (they had been sent to Nemea by Dionysus) discovered her, rushed to embrace her, and won her release.

Dante's point is that he felt upon discovering the identity of Guinizelli as the twins had felt on discovering their lost mother. He adds, however, that he could not match their actions in racing to embrace her, for he was prevented by the fire. (Note, also, that in basing his figure on an incident narrated in the *Thebaid,* Dante is once more registering the presence of Statius.) Statius' earlier feeling for Virgil forms another parallel.

98. *my betters:* There is some disagreement as to whether or not Dante meant to rate himself among the six greatest poets of all time in narrating his reception in Limbo. Considering his confessed pride, and his willingness to point out how well he can accomplish certain poetic feats that no other has equaled (see *Inferno* XXV, 91–99, and XXXII, 7–9), I believe Dante knew very well how good he was, and that he had few betters. This phrasing, therefore, is best taken as a compliment to the generation of poets that preceded him, its tone set by his wish to honor Guido Guinizelli. One must also recognize, however, that Dante distinguished between *poeti* (poets) and *rimatori* (versifiers). Here, "betters" could mean "as versifiers."

113. *modern usage:* Of writing about love in the spoken tongue

rather than in Latin or in elaborate euphuisms. The Sweet New Style.

119–120. *Limoges produced a better:* Girault de Bornelh, of Limoges, a rival poet.

121–123. I have all but abandoned Dante's phrasing here in attempting to convey his meaning. Literally rendered, the passage reads: "They turn their faces to rumor (i.e., to what is being said, i.e., to reputation) more than to the truth (of merit in the writing) and so they fix their opinions before they have heeded art or reason."

124. *Guittone:* See XXIV, 56, and note. *our fathers:* Dante says *antichi,* the primary meaning of which is "the ancients" but which can also mean simply "gone by." Guittone died in 1294, and Guinizelli, though only thirty-two years old, in 1276.

131. *as far as it may serve:* The souls in Purgatory cannot yield to temptation, for their power to sin has been taken from them. Thus the supplication "and lead us not into temptation but deliver us from evil" could not apply to them. One could argue, too, that Purgatorial souls do not need their "daily bread," but "bread" can, of course, be taken to mean "spiritual sustenance." In any case, the point is that not all of the Lord's Prayer is apt to the state of the Purgatorial souls.

136–139. *that shade he had pointed to:* Arnaut Daniel, Provençal poet of the second half of the twelfth century. He was especially given to intricate rhyme structures and elaborate phrasing and is generally credited with having invented the sestiná. Many commentators have wondered why Dante held him up for such high praise, for his work seems rather more elaborate than compelling to most readers. Perhaps it was Dante's particular passion for elaborate structural relations and for such devices as the *UOM* of Canto XII that drew him to Daniel.

140–147. DANIEL'S REPLY. Daniel replies, in the original, not in Italian, but in the *langue d'oc,* the Provençal tongue in which he wrote. Since some obvious shift of language is necessary here, and since Daniel's would seem an antique and a courtly tongue to Dante, I have rendered his lines into what can best be called a desperate attempt at bastard Spenserian. *faring:* going. *blistful:* blissful. *redeth:* leads. *amount:* mount.

CANTO XXVII

The Seventh Cornice—The Angel of Chastity

THE WALL OF FIRE

The Earthly Paradise—The Angel Guardian

A little before sunset of the third day on the Mountain the Poets come to the further limit of the Seventh Cornice and are greeted by *The Angel of Chastity,* who tells them they must pass through the wall of fire. Dante recoils in terror, but Virgil persuades him to enter in Beatrice's name.

They are guided through the fire by a chant they hear coming from the other side. Emerging, they find it is sung by *The Angel Guardian* of the Earthly Paradise, who stands in a light so brilliant that Dante cannot see him. (It is probably here that *The Last* P is stricken from Dante's brow. Or perhaps it was consumed by the fire.)

The Angel hurries them toward the ascent, but night overtakes them, and the Poets lie down to sleep, each on the step on which he finds himself. (For Statius it will be the last sleep, since there is no night in Heaven.) There, just before Dawn, Dante has a prophetic *Dream of Leah and Rachel,* which foreshadows the appearance, above, of Matilda and Beatrice.

Day arrives; the Poets rise and race up the rest of the ascent until they come in sight of *The Earthly Paradise.* Here *Virgil Speaks His Last Words,* for the Poets have now come to the limit of Reason, and Dante is now free to follow his every impulse, since all motion of sin in him has been purged away.

As the day stands when the Sun begins to glow
  over the land where his Maker's blood was shed,
  and the scales of Libra ride above the Ebro,   3

while Ganges' waters steam in the noonday glare—
　　so it stood, the light being nearly faded,
　　when we met God's glad Angel standing there　　　6

on the rocky ledge beyond the reach of the fire,
　　and caroling *"Beati mundo corde"*
　　in a voice to which no mortal could aspire.　　　9

Then: "Blessèd ones, till by flame purified
　　no soul may pass this point. Enter the fire
　　and heed the singing from the other side."　　　12

These were his words to us when we had come
　　near as we could, and hearing them, I froze
　　as motionless as one laid in his tomb.　　　15

I lean forward over my clasped hands and stare
　　into the fire, thinking of human bodies
　　I once saw burned, and once more see them there.　　　18

My kindly escorts heard me catch my breath
　　and turned, and Virgil said: "Within that flame
　　there may be torment, but there is no death.　　　21

Think well, my son, what dark ways we have trod . . .
　　I guided you unharmed on Geryon:
　　shall I do less now we are nearer God?　　　24

Believe this past all doubt: were you to stay
　　within that womb of flame a thousand years,
　　it would not burn a single hair away.　　　27

And if you still doubt my sincerity,
　　but reach the hem of your robe into the flame:
　　your hands and eyes will be your guarantee.　　　30

My son, my son, turn here with whole assurance.
  Put by your fears and enter to your peace."
  And I stood fixed, at war with my own conscience.   33

And seeing me still stubborn, rooted fast,
  he said, a little troubled: "Think, my son,
  you shall see Beatrice when this wall is past."   36

As Pyramus, but one breath from the dead,
  opened his eyes when he heard Thisbe's name,
  and looked at her, when the mulberry turned red—   39

just so my hard paralysis melted from me,
  and I turned to my Leader at that name
  which wells forever in my memory;   42

at which he wagged his head, as at a child
  won over by an apple. Then he said:
  "Well, then, what are we waiting for?" and smiled.   45

He turned then and went first into the fire,
  requesting Statius, who for some time now
  had walked between us, to bring up the rear.   48

Once in the flame, I gladly would have cast
  my body into boiling glass to cool it
  against the measureless fury of the blast.   51

My gentle father, ever kind and wise,
  strengthened me in my dread with talk of Beatrice,
  saying: "I seem already to see her eyes."   54

From the other side, to guide us, rose a paean,
  and moving toward it, mindless of all else,
  we emerged at last where the ascent began.   57

There I beheld a light that burned so brightly
  I had to look away; and from it rang:
  "Venite benedicti patris mei."   60

"Night falls," it added, "the sun sinks to rest;
  do not delay but hurry toward the height
  while the last brightness lingers in the west."   63

Straight up through the great rock-wall lay the way
  on such a line that, as I followed it,
  my body blocked the sun's last level ray.   66

We had only climbed the first few stairs as yet
  when I and my two sages saw my shadow
  fade from me; and we knew the sun had set.   69

Before the vast sweep of the limned horizon
  could fade into one hue and night win all
  the immeasurable air to its dominion,   72

each made the step on which he stood his bed,
  for the nature of the Mount not only stopped us
  but killed our wish to climb, once day had fled.   75

As goats on a rocky hill will dance and leap,
  nimble and gay, till they find grass, and then,
  while they are grazing, grow as tame as sheep   78

at ease in the green shade when the sun is high
  and the shepherd stands by, leaning on his staff,
  and at his ease covers them with his eye—   81

and as the herdsman beds down on the ground,
  keeping his quiet night watch by his flock
  lest it be scattered by a wolf or hound;   84

just so we lay there, each on his stone block,
  I as the goat, they as my guardians,
    shut in on either side by walls of rock.   87

I could see little ahead—rock blocked the way—
  but through that little I saw the stars grow larger,
    brighter than mankind sees them. And as I lay,   90

staring and lost in thought, a sleep came on me—
  the sleep that oftentimes presents the fact
    before the event, a sleep of prophecy.   93

At the hour, I think, when Venus, first returning
  out of the east, shone down upon the mountain—
    she who with fires of love comes ever-burning—   96

I dreamed I saw a maiden innocent
  and beautiful, who walked a sunny field
    gathering flowers, and caroling as she went: 99

"Say I am Leah if any ask my name,
  and my white hands weave garlands wreath on
                          wreath
    to please me when I stand before the frame   102

of my bright glass. For this my fingers play
  among these blooms. But my sweet sister Rachel
    sits at her mirror motionless all day.   105

To stare into her own eyes endlessly
  is all her joy, as mine is in my weaving.
    She looks, I do. Thus live we joyously."   108

Now eastward the new day rayed Heaven's dome
  (the sweeter to the returning wanderer
    who wakes from each night's lodging nearer home), 111

and the shadows fled on every side as I
  stirred from my sleep and leaped upon my feet,
  seeing my Lords already standing by.   114

"This is the day your hungry soul shall be
  fed on the golden apples men have sought
  on many different boughs so ardently."   117

These were the very words which, at the start,
  my Virgil spoke to me, and there have never
  been gifts as dear as these were to my heart.   120

Such waves of yearning to achieve the height
  swept through my soul, that at each step I took
  I felt my feathers growing for the flight.   123

When we had climbed the stairway to the rise
  of the topmost step, there with a father's love
  Virgil turned and fixed me with his eyes.   126

"My son," he said, "you now have seen the torment
  of the temporary and the eternal fires;
  here, now, is the limit of my discernment.   129

I have led you here by grace of mind and art;
  now let your own good pleasure be your guide;
  you are past the steep ways, past the narrow part.   132

See there the sun that shines upon your brow,
  the sweet new grass, the flowers, the fruited vines
  which spring up without need of seed or plow.   135

Until those eyes come gladdened which in pain
  moved me to come to you and lead your way,
  sit there at ease or wander through the plain.   138

Expect no more of me in word or deed:
  here your will is upright, free, and whole,
  and you would be in error not to heed   141

whatever your own impulse prompts you to:
  lord of yourself I crown and mitre you."

NOTES

1–4. *As the day stands:* Meaning of this passage: It is shortly before sunset of the third day on the Mountain. Dante's details here are the reverse of those given at the opening of II, which see. *the land where his Maker's blood was shed:* Jerusalem. *the Ebro:* For Spain.

6. *God's glad Angel:* The Angel of Chastity. He is standing on the narrow rocky path outside the wall of fire.

8. *Beati mundo corde:* "Blessed are the pure in heart [for they shall see God]." (*Matthew* v, 8.)

10–12. THE WALL OF FLAMES. It is, of course, the fire in which the Lustful are purified. It is also the legendary wall of fire that surrounded the Earthly Paradise. Note that all souls must pass through that fire. The readiest interpretation of that fact is that every soul must endure some purification before it can approach God (theoretically, a soul could climb Purgatory and endure no pain but this). Since no man's soul is perfect in its love, moreover, it must endure the fire that purifies impure love. Additionally, the allegorical intent may be that no man is entirely free of Lust. Having reached the Earthly Paradise, the soul has reached the Perfection of the Active Life. Below, its motion has been *toward* perfection. Now, after a few final rituals, the soul *becomes* perfect, and therefore changeless.

16. *I lean forward over my clasped hands:* Dante's hands must be clasped a bit below the waist. It is an odd posture, but it is also oddly Dantean.

17–18. *bodies I once saw burned:* Dante must mean as a witness at an execution. Burnings at the stake generally took place in public squares. They were a rather common spectacle. Dante's sentence of exile, it is relevant to note, decreed that he was to be burned if taken on Florentine territory.

23. *Geryon:* The Monster of Fraud. See *Inferno* XVII, 1 ff., note.

37–39. *Pyramus . . . Thisbe:* Famous tragic lovers of Babylon. Ovid (*Metamorphoses* IV, 55–166) tells their story. At a tryst by a mulberry (which in those days bore white fruit) Thisbe was frightened by a lion and ran off, dropping her veil. The lion, his jaws bloody from a recent kill, tore at the veil, staining it with blood. Pyramus, arriving later, saw the stained veil, concluded that Thisbe was dead, and stabbed himself. Thisbe, returning, found him and cried to him to open his eyes for his Thisbe. At that name Pyramus opened his eyes, looked at her, and died. Thisbe, invoking the tree to darken in their memory, thereupon stabbed herself. (*Cf.* Shakespeare's *Romeo and Juliet*.) The mulberry roots drank their blood and the fruit turned red ever after.

40. *my hard paralysis melted:* Note how Dante describes his emotions throughout this passage. He is afraid, to be sure. But the fear is of his human body and habit. His soul yearns forward, but his body will not obey until Reason has overcome mortal habit.

58. *a light:* This is the Angel Guardian of the Earthly Paradise. He corresponds to the Angel guarding the Gate. At every other ascent in Purgatory, Dante has met one angel. Here, he meets two, one on either side of the fire. It is the song of this Angel that has guided the Poets through the flames. In all probability, too, it is this Angel that strikes away the final *P* from Dante's brow (or perhaps it was consumed in the fire). It is unlikely that the final *P* was removed by the Angel of Chastity, since the Poets had not yet been through the fire, i.e., had not really crossed all of the Cornice.

60. *Venite benedicti patris mei:* "Come ye blessèd of my Father." (*Matthew* xxv, 34.)

68. *my shadow:* Virgil and Statius, of course, cast none.

94. *At the hour . . . when Venus, first returning:* Venus is in the sign of Pisces, which immediately precedes Aries, in which sign the sun now is. It is, therefore, Venus Morningstar. Thus it is the hour before dawn, in which the truth is dreamed.

97–108. DANTE'S DREAM. Leah and Rachel were, respectively, the first- and second-born daughters of Laban and the first and second wives of Jacob. Many authors before Dante had interpreted them as representing the Active and the Contemplative Life of the Soul. Leah's white hands *(le belle mani)* symbolize the Active Life, as Rachel's eyes (lines 104–108) symbolize the Contemplative Life.

Since it is the truth Dante is dreaming, these figures must foreshadow others, as the eagle of his earlier dream (IX, 19 ff.) represented Lucia. Thus Leah prefigures Matilda, who will appear soon, and Rachel prefigures Beatrice, who will appear soon thereafter. But just as the eagle is not to be confused with Lucia, so Leah and Rachel are not to be narrowly identified with Matilda and Beatrice except as allegorical dream equivalents, for Matilda and Beatrice may very well be taken, as part of their total allegory, to represent the Active and the Contemplative Life of the Soul.

127 ff. *"My son," he said:* These are Virgil's last words, for the Poets have now reached the extreme limit of Reason's (and Art's) competence. Virgil continues awhile with Dante into the Earthly Paradise (walking, one should note, behind rather than ahead of Dante) but he has no more to say. A little later in fact (XXIX, 55–57) when Dante turns to Virgil out of old habit as if for an explanation of the strange and marvelous sights he comes on, he receives in answer only a look as full of awe as his own. And later yet (XXX, 43 ff.), when Dante turns from Beatrice to look for him, Virgil has vanished.

For Virgil has now performed all that he had promised at their first meeting *(Inferno* I, 88 ff.), and Dante's soul is now free to obey its every impulse, for it now contains nothing but Good.

143. *I crown and mitre you:* Crown as king of your physical self and mitre (as a bishop) as lord of your soul. Dante has not, by much, achieved the full lordship of his soul, but he has achieved as much as Virgil (Reason) can confer upon him. A bishop's mitre, though it confers great authority, does not confer final authority. And a king, for that matter, may still be subject to an emperor, as he certainly would be, in Dante's view, to God.

CANTO XXVIII

The Earthly Paradise—Lethe

It is the morning of the Wednesday after Easter, Dante's fourth day on the Mountain, and having been crowned Lord of Himself by Virgil, Dante now takes the lead for the first time, wandering at his leisure into *The Sacred Wood of the Earthly Paradise* until his way is blocked by the waters of *Lethe*.

His feet stopped, Dante sends his eyes on to wander that Wood and there suddenly appears to him a solitary lady singing and gathering flowers. She is *Matilda,* who symbolizes *The Active Life of the Soul.*

In reply to Dante's entreaty, Matilda approaches to the other bank of the river. So standing, three paces across from him, she offers to answer all that Dante wishes to ask. Dante replies that he is in some confusion about the sources of the wind and the water of the Earthly Paradise. Matilda promises to dispel the mists from his understanding and proceeds to explain in great detail *The Natural Phenomena of the Earthly Paradise,* which is to say, the source of the wind, the vegetation, and the water. She further explains the special powers of the water of *Lethe* and of *Eunoë* and concludes with some remarks on the errors of the ancient poets in the location of the Earthly Paradise. At her last words, Dante turns to his two ancient poets to see how they are taking her remarks. Finding them smiling, he turns back once more to Matilda.

Eager now to explore in and about
  the luxuriant holy forest evergreen
  that softened the new light, I started out,   3

without delaying longer, from the stair
  and took my lingering way into the plain
  on ground that breathed a fragrance to the air.   6

With no least variation in itself
  and with no greater force than a mild wind,
    the sweet air stroked my face on that sweet shelf,   9

and at its touch the trembling branches swayed,
  all bending toward that quarter into which
    the holy mountain cast its morning shade;   12

yet not so far back that in any part
  of that sweet wood the small birds in the tops
    had reason to stop practicing their art;   15

but bursting with delight those singing throngs
  within their green tents welcomed the new breeze
    that murmured a sweet burden of their songs   18

like that one hears gathering from bough to bough
  of the pine wood there on Chiassi's shore
    when Aeolus lets the Sirocco blow.   21

I had already come, slow bit by bit,
  so far into that ancient holy wood
    I could not see where I had entered it;   24

when I came upon a stream that blocked my way.
  To my left it flowed, its wavelets bending back
    the grasses on its banks as if in play.   27

The purest waters known to man would seem
  to have some taint of sediment within them
    compared to those, for though that holy stream   30

flows darkly there, its surface never lit
  in its perpetual shade by any shaft
    of sun or moon, nothing could hide in it.   33

My feet stopped, but my eyes pursued their way
  across that stream, to wander in delight
  the variousness of everblooming May.   36

And suddenly—as rare sights sometimes do,
  the wonder of them driving from the mind
  all other thoughts—I saw come into view   39

a lady, all alone, who wandered there
  singing, and picking flowers from the profusion
  with which her path was painted everywhere.   42

"Fair lady who—if outward looks and ways
  bear, as they ought, true witness to the heart—
  have surely sunned yourself in Love's own rays, 45

be pleased," I said to her, "to draw as near
  the bank of this sweet river as need be
  for me to understand the song I hear.   48

You make me see in my imagining
  Persephone as she appeared that day
  her mother lost a daughter; she, the Spring."   51

As a dancer, keeping both feet on the ground
  and close together, hardly putting one
  before the other, spins herself around—   54

so did she turn to me upon the red
  and yellow flowerlets, virgin modesty
  making her lower her eyes and bow her head. 57

And she did all I asked, for she came forward
  till I not only heard the melody
  of what she sang, but made out every word.   60

And when she stood where the bright grasses are
  bathed and bent by the waves of the clear river,
  she raised her eyes—and gave my soul a star.   63

I cannot think so glorious a ray
  shot out of Venus' eyes that time her son
  wounded her inadvertently in play.   66

There, on the other bank, smiling she stood
  and gathered to her arms more of the flowers
  that sprang up without seeds in that high wood.   69

The stream between us was three paces wide,
  but the Hellespont where Persian Xerxes crossed
  to leave a dire example to all pride,   72

in its raging between Sestos and Abydos,
  caused less hate in Leander than this in me,
  for not dividing so that I might cross.   75

"You are newcomers, and perhaps you find
  because I smile," she said, "here in this place
  chosen to be the nest of humankind,   78

some doubt that makes you wonder at the sight.
  To pierce such mists as gather on your thoughts
  the psalm, *Delectasti me,* will give you light.   81

And you in front who first entreated me,
  speak if you would know more. I came prepared
  to answer you as fully as need be."   84

"The way the wood hums and the waters flow,"
  I said then, "are at odds with the conclusions
  I drew from what I heard a while ago."   87

"I shall explain from what cause," she replied,
  "these things that have confused your mind proceed,
  and thus brush its obscuring mist aside.   90

That Highest Good which only Itself can please
  made man good, and for goodness, and I gave him
  this place as earnest of eternal peace.   93

But man defaulted. All too brief his stay.
  Defaulted, and exchanged for tears and toil
  his innocent first laughter and sweet play.   96

When vapors of the earth and water meet
  a storm is born, below there. Now these vapors
  reach up, as far as possible, toward heat.   99

To guard man from such warring elements
  this mountain soared so high that no earth vapor
  could rise above the gate of penitence.   102

Now since the air revolves in one conjoint
  and perfect circuit with The Primal Motion,
  unless its wheel is broken at some point;   105

here at this altitude, where it goes round
  in its pure state, it strikes the foliage
  which, being dense, is made to give off sound.   108

The stricken plant impregnates the pure air
  with its particular powers, which are then borne
  on the great wheel and scattered everywhere;   111

and the other earth, according to the powers
  of soil and climate in its various zones,
  conceives and bears its various fruits and flowers.   114

When this is understood there, no man need
  believe it strange when plants take root and spring
  out of the earth without apparent seed.   117

Know, too, the sacred soil on which you stand
  is bursting-full of species of all sorts,
  and bears fruits never picked by human hand.   120

The water you see here is from no source
  that needs replenishment from cloudy vapors,
  like streams that rise and fall: with constant force   123

it leaves a fountain that receives again,
  from God's Will, every drop that it pours forth
  to the two streams it sends across this plain.   126

On this side, it removes as it flows down
  all memory of sin; on that, it strengthens
  the memory of every good deed done.   129

It is called Lethe here: Eunoë there.
  And one must drink first this and then the other
  to feel its powers. No sweetness can compare   132

with the savor of these waters. And although
  you may at once, and with no more instruction,
  drink your soul's fill from the eternal flow,   135

let me bestow one thing more for good measure.
  Though I exceed my promise, I cannot think
  what I add now will meet with your displeasure.   138

Those ancients who made songs to celebrate
  man's Age of Gold, placed probably on Parnassus
  this perfect garden of his first pure state.   141

Here mankind lived its innocent first days.
  Here is the Eternal Spring and every fruit.
  This is the nectar that the poets praise."   144

She paused, I turned around to face my lords,
  the poets whose strains had honored ancient song,
  and saw they had received her final words   147

with smiles that lingered yet upon their faces;
  then turned back to that lady of glad graces.

NOTES

3. *softened the new light:* In its green shade. It is the morning of the Wednesday after Easter, the beginning of Dante's fourth day on the Mountain, and the last of his Divine Journey, for he will complete his tour of Heaven in less than a day. *I started out:* Note that for the first time it is Dante who leads the way in his new state as "king of himself."

11. *that quarter:* The West.

20. *the pine wood there on Chiassi's shore:* Chiassi (now Classe) was the seaport of Ravenna in 1300. It is now a desolate place left behind by the recession of the Adriatic.

21. *Aeolus:* In ancient mythology the god who kept the winds in his cave and controlled their blowing. *the Sirocco:* The South Wind, which in Italy is the wind from Africa.

36. *everblooming May:* See line 143. It is eternally springtime in the Earthly Paradise.

40. *a lady, all alone:* Matilda. She may be taken, as foreshadowed in Dante's dream of Leah and Rachel, to symbolize the Active Life of the Soul. She is the innocence that guides Dante through the Earthly Paradise to Beatrice. Thus, she is the intermediary between Human Reason and the various manifestations of Beatrice as Divine Love, Faith, the Contemplative Life of the Soul, and the Church Triumphant, among others.

There has been a great deal of speculation among commentators concerning her possible historical identity. Dante clearly treats her as someone he recognizes at once, for he does not ask her name. And later (XXXIII, 119) when her name is mentioned, he asks none of his usual questions about her identity.

Nevertheless there seems to be no point in trying to identify her with any historic person. The allegorical point may very well be that, having achieved the Earthly Paradise by his own active pursuit of the Good, Dante instantly recognizes the Active Life of the Soul. He has, moreover, just had a prophetic dream of her coming.

45. *sunned yourself in Love's own rays:* In the light of God.

50. *Persephone:* Daughter of Demeter (whose name signifies "Mother Earth"), the goddess of vegetation. One day, as Persephone was gathering flowers in a field, she was carried off to the lower world of Hades (with the consent of Zeus, her father). At the insistence of Demeter, Zeus sent Hermes to fetch her back. Persephone, however, had eaten a quarter of a fateful pomegranate and, in consequence, could only return for three quarters of each year, being forced to return to the lower world for the fourth quarter.

Thus Persephone represents the vegetative cycle, spending spring, summer, and fall with Demeter (as Mother Earth) but descending to the lower world (into the ground) for the winter. When she is in the lower world she rules beside her husband as the goddess of the dead, but she forever returns to her mother as the virgin daughter (spring). Matilda not only reminds Dante of Persephone, but of Persephone as she was in that original springtime before she was carried off to the lower world.

51. *she, the Spring:* The flowers fell from Persephone's arms when Hades abducted her. Dante certainly means "the Spring" both as those lost flowers, and as the unchanging springtime of the world's first innocence. The myth, of course, is obviously concerned with the idea of virgin innocence, and as obviously related to the Christian myth of the *Fall*.

65–66. *Venus'* . . . *her son:* Cupid was playing with his mother one day when one of the arrows in his quiver scratched her breast by accident and she was smitten with love of Adonis, the son of

Myrrha by her own father (see *Inferno* XXX, 38, and note). Ovid tells the story in *Metamorphoses* X, 525 ff.

69. *that sprang up without seeds:* Here, in XVII, 115 ff., and below in 109–111, 114–117, and 118–119, Dante refers to seeds and to plants springing up without seed. At this point he seems quite clearly to intend, as suggested by *Genesis,* that the newly created earth brought forth of itself. At other times he seems to intend something like the distribution of plants by wind-borne seeds. I have not been able to satisfy myself on the exact nature of his theory on this plant. Note that he does not deny that most earthly plants grow from seed, but declares that *some* plants spring up without apparent seed. He could mean that *new species* arise in consequence of wind-borne influences from the Earthly Paradise, thereafter reproducing themselves from their seed.

70. *three paces:* May symbolize the three steps to true repentance (contrition, confession, and the rendering of satisfaction), thereby repeating the motif of the three steps that lead to the Gate.

71. *Hellespont:* Now called the Dardanelles, the strait between Europe and Asia Minor. It is famous for its raging currents. *Xerxes:* Son of Darius, the Persian king. In 485 B.C. Xerxes crossed the Hellespont on a bridge of ships to invade Greece. Decisively defeated in a sea battle off Salamis, Xerxes fled back across the Hellespont undone, thus leaving to all posterity a dire example of the downfall of pride.

73–74. *Sestos and Abydos:* Cities on the Hellespont in, respectively, Greece and Asia Minor. The Hellespont is about a mile wide between them. *Leander:* A young man of Abydos who fell in love with Hero, a priestess of Aphrodite at Sestos. Because of her position and of family opposition, they could not marry but decided to meet clandestinely every night, Leander swimming to her across the Hellespont, guided by a light from Hero's tower. One night the light blew out and Leander lost his direction, was carried off by the current, and drowned. The next morning Hero found his body washed ashore and threw herself into the current. The story of Hero and Leander has been told by countless poets, none of whom thought to provide him with a rowboat.

78. *the nest of humankind:* The Earthly Paradise is the Garden of Eden.

81. *Delectasti me:* Psalm XCII, "I will triumph in the works of Thy hands." Matilda's phrase is from verse 4: "For Thou, Lord, hast made me glad through Thy work" *(Quia delectasti me, Domine, in factura tua).* The light the psalm will give, of course, is the fact that Matilda smiles for sheer joy in God's works.

87. *what I heard a while ago:* In XXI, 40–57, Statius told Dante that no rain nor snow could fall, nor any variation in the weather occur above the Gate. Dante's confusion arises from the fact that he cannot see how to take the wind he feels, nor the waters he sees flowing, except as products of earthly weathers.

91. *That Highest Good which only Itself can please:* Two ideas central to Dante's thinking are expressed in this phrasing.

The first is Dante's idea of purification. God is conceived as perfect goodness. As such, He can be pleased only by perfect goodness. In that estate He made man. And to that spiritual state man, since the Fall, must strive to return in order to regain God, who will take to Himself only the perfection He originally created.

The second, basic to all Dante's conception of the Earthly Paradise (and later of Heaven) is that perfection is unchangeable. God, being perfect, cannot change, since any change from perfection would necessarily be toward imperfection. It is the lot of fallen man that is beset by chance and change, he being imperfect. Thus, the perfection of the fruit in the garden. And thus the perfect clearness of the waters, and the fact that they do not have their source in the chance changes of evaporation and condensation, but flow at a constant (unchanging) rate from the fountain of the Will of God.

97–99. *When vapors of the earth and water meet:* This is Dante's basic conception of the origin of storms in the clash of earthy (fiery) and watery vapors (see *Inferno* XXIV, 145–147). *toward heat:* Toward the Sun. These vapors (evaporations) are produced by heat and seek, by natural affinity, to rise to the Sun that called them forth.

103–108. *Now since the air revolves in one conjoint . . . :* The earth is conceived as standing still while the atmosphere moves from East to West at the constant rate imparted to it, as to the heavenly spheres, by the Primum Mobile. On the earth's surface the air is deflected by many obstructions (surface turbulence) that make it flow in all directions, but at the altitude of the Earthly Paradise one experiences only the air's unperturbed original motion. This is the "mild wind" Dante felt (lines 8–9), as it is the wind that makes the whole wood murmur (lines 17–18).

109–120. (See also note to line 69.) The phrasing here seems to suggest that all earthly plants have their origins in "virtues" or "powers" (somehow distinct from seeds). They impart these virtues to the wind that bears them around the world as wind-borne gifts of Heaven. On earth, if soil and climate favor, these "virtues" cause new species to spring up (which then reproduce themselves from their own seeds). But since no earthly soil and climate is perfect (unchanging), no zone on earth can raise all plants, whereas in the Earthly Paradise *all* created plants may be found, including species unknown to mankind since the Fall.

130. *Lethe:* In classical mythology, a river of Hades from which the souls of the dead drink forgetfulness of their first existence. Dante, with his usual readiness to adapt ancient mythology to his own purposes, places it in the Earthly Paradise, and gives it the power (directly related to its original power) of washing from the souls who drink of it, every last memory of sin. Note, too, that Dante's Lethe (*Inferno* XXXIV, 133) flows down to the bottom of Hell, bearing down to Satan, to be frozen into the filthy ice around him, the last lost vestiges of the sins of the saved.

Eunoë: Having adapted Lethe to his purpose, Dante invents as its complement Eunoë (the name meaning, literally, "good memory") and gives it the power to strengthen every memory of good deeds done. The powers of the two rivers will not operate, however, unless one drinks from them in the right order. So drinking from them is surely an allegory of the way to Heaven: one must first drink of Lethe (leave all evil behind) and then of Eunoë (reawaken and strengthen every good in the soul).

146–147. *the poets:* Virgil and Statius would be two of the poets to whom Matilda refers. Dante turns around to see how they have taken her remarks about their errors. Finding them smiling at the re-

CANTO XXIX

The Earthly Paradise—The Banks of Lethe

THE HEAVENLY PAGEANT

Chanting a blessing on those whose sins are forgiven, Matilda moves upstream along one bank of Lethe, and Dante keeps pace with her on the other side. A glorious light and a sweet melody grow on the air, filling Dante with such rapture that he cries out against Eve's daring, through which such joys were lost to mankind.

Soon thereafter he sees the approach of *The Heavenly Pageant.* It is led by *Seven Golden Candelabra* that paint *A Seven-Striped Rainbow* on the sky. Behind them come *Twenty-Four Elders* (the Books of the Old Testament), and behind them *Four Beasts* (the Four Gospels), who guard *A Triumphal Chariot* (the Church), drawn by a *Griffon* (Christ). At the right wheel of the Chariot dance *The Three Theological Virtues;* at its left wheel, *The Four Cardinal Virtues.* This group is followed, in order, by *Two Elders* representing Luke as the author of *Acts* and Paul as the author of the fourteen epistles; by *Four Elders* representing James, Peter, John, and Jude as authors of the four Catholic epistles; and finally by *A Single Elder* representing John as the author of *Revelation.*

When the Chariot reaches a point directly across from Dante, a thunderclap resounds, and the entire pageant halts upon that signal.

Her words done, she began her song again—
  Beati quorum tecta sunt peccata—
  as if in love when love is free of pain.   3

As nymphs of old went wandering alone
  through the deep-shaded woodlands, some pursuing,
  and others seeking to evade, the Sun;   6

so, then, she started up the riverside
  and, on my own bank, I kept pace with her,
  matching her little steps with shortened stride.   9

Some fifty paces each we moved this way,
  when both banks curved as one; and now I found
  my face turned to the cradle of the day.   12

Nor had we gone as far again, all told,
  beyond the curve, when she turned to me, saying:
  "Dear brother, look and listen." And behold!—   15

through all that everlasting forest burst
  an instantaneous flood of radiance.
  I took it for a lightning-flash at first.   18

But lightning comes and goes. The light I saw
  not only stayed on but grew more resplendent.
  "What can this be?" I asked myself in awe.   21

And a sweet melody filled the bright air—
  so sweet that I reproached in righteous zeal
  Eve's fatal recklessness. How could she dare?—   24

one woman alone, made but a moment since—
  all heaven and earth obedient—to refuse
  the one veil willed by High Omnipotence;   27

beneath which, had she stayed God's acolyte,
  I should have known before then, and for longer
  those raptures of ineffable delight.   30

My soul hung tranced in joy beyond all measure
  and yearning for yet more, as I moved on
  through those first fruits of the eternal pleasure;   33

when, under the green boughs that spread before us
  the air became a blaze, and the sweet sound
  we had been hearing grew into a chorus.   36

O holy, holy, Virgins, if for you
  I ever suffered vigils, cold, or fasts,
  occasion spurs me now to claim my due.   39

Empty all Helicon! Now is the time!
  Urania, help me here with your full choir,
  to bring things scarce conceivable to rhyme!   42

I saw next, far ahead, what I believed
  were seven golden trees (at such a distance
  and in such light the eye can be deceived);   45

but in a while, when I had drawn so near
  that chance resemblances confused by distance
  no longer made false images appear,   48

that power that reaps for reason's mill could see
  that they were candelabra; and in the chant
  it heard that word *Hosanna!* ringing free.   51

Above the gold array flamed seven times seven
  candles more lucent than the mid-month moon
  at midnight in the calm of clearest heaven.   54

I turned about, amazed at what I saw,
  to my good Virgil, and he answered me
  in silence, with a look of equal awe.   57

I turned back then to those sublimities
  that were approaching at so slow a pace
  that new brides might outdistance them with ease.   60

The lady cried: "Why have you set your mind
  so fixedly upon those living lights
  that you do not observe what comes behind?"   63

Then I saw people walking like attendants
  behind their lords, and clothed in robes so white
  earth has no snow of such a pure resplendence.   66

Upon my left the polished river shone
  bright as a mirror, and when I looked in
  I saw my left side there, perfectly drawn.   69

And when I had moved close enough to be
  kept at a distance by no more than water,
  I halted my slow steps, better to see.   72

I saw the flames advance, leaving the air
  painted behind, as if by massive strokes,
  or by bright pennons they were trailing there;   75

thus, all the trailing heavens were aglow
  with seven bands of light of the same color
  as Delia's girdle or Apollo's bow.   78

Those bands stretched back further than I could see,
  and the distance separating side from side
  came to ten paces, as it seemed to me.   81

And there, advancing two by two beneath
  that seven-striped sky came four-and-twenty elders,
  each crowned in glory with a lily-wreath.   84

And all sang with one voice, triumphantly:
  "Blessèd art thou among the daughters of Adam!
  Blessèd thy beauty to eternity!"   87

And when those souls elect, as in a dream,
  had left behind the flowers and the new grass
  that shone before me, there across the stream,   90

as star follows on star in the serene
  of heaven's height, there came on at their backs
  four beasts, and these wore wreaths of living green.   93

Each had three pairs of wings, and every pair
  was full of eyes. Were Argus living yet,
  his eyes would be most like what I saw there.   96

I cannot spend my rhymes as liberally
  as I should like to in describing them,
  for, reader, other needs are pressing me: 99

but read Ezekiel where he sets forth
  how they appeared to him in a great storm
  of wind and cloud and fire out of the North;   102

and such as he recounts, such did I see;
  except that in the number of their wings
  John differs with him, and agrees with me.   105

Within the space they guarded there came on
  a burnished two-wheeled chariot in triumph,
  and harnessed to the neck of a great Griffon   108

whose wings, upraised into the bands of light,
  inclosed the middle one so perfectly
  they cut no part of those to left or right.   111

Higher than sight its wing-tips soared away.
  Its bird-like parts were gold; and white the rest
  with blood-red markings. Will it serve to say   114

Rome never saw such a caparison,
  no, not for Africanus, nor yet Augustus?
   The Sun's own would seem shabby by comparison;   117

yes, even the Sun's own chariot, which strayed
  and was destroyed in fire by Jove's dark justice
   that day the frightened Earth devoutly prayed.   120

Beside the right wheel, dancing in a gyre,
  three maidens came. The first one was so red
   she would be barely visible in fire.   123

The second looked as if both flesh and bone
  were made of flawless emerald. The third
   seemed a new snow no slightest wind has blown.   126

And now the white one led the dance, and now
  the red: and from the song the red one sang
   the others took their measure, fast or slow.   129

Beside the left wheel, dancing in a flame
  of purple robes, and led by one who had
   three eyes within her head, four glad nymphs came.   132

Behind these seven came on, side by side,
  two elders, different in dress, but both
   by the same massive bearing dignified.   135

One showed he was a follower of the art
  of great Hippocrates, whom Nature made
   to heal the creatures dearest to her heart.   138

The other, his counterpart, carried a blade
  so sharp and bright that at the sight of it,
   even across the stream, I was afraid.   141

Next I saw four who walked with humble mien.
  And last of all, one who moved in a trance,
  as if asleep but his face was firm and keen.   144

These seven were robed like the first twenty-four
  in flowing robes of white, but, for their crowns,
  it was not wreaths of lilies that they wore,   147

but roses and whatever blooms most red.
  One would have sworn, seeing them at a distance,
  that they were wearing flames about the head.   150

And when the chariot had reached the place
  across from me, I heard a thunderclap
  that seemed a signal to those souls in grace,   153

for there, in unison with the exalted
  first flaming standards, all that pageant halted.

NOTES

2. *Beati quorum tecta sunt peccata:* This is Dante's elision of Psalm XXXII, 1: "Blessed are they [whose transgression is forgiven] whose sins are covered."

11. *both banks curved as one:* Note the regularity (constancy, perfection) of the river's curve.

12. *the cradle of the day:* The East.

23–30. *so sweet that I reproached . . . :* For having thrown away the glory of the Earthly Paradise by refusing to endure the one veil (of ignorance) under which, had Eve been dutiful, Dante would have known his present bliss since birth (hence, "before then, and for longer").

33. *the eternal pleasure:* The joys of Heaven. The joys of the Earthly Paradise are the first fruits of the great harvest to come.

37–42. INVOCATION OF THE MUSES. Dante is about to

describe the entrance of the Heavenly Pageant, a spectacle of such
splendor that it is difficult to conceive, let alone put into rhyme. For
his great effort, therefore, he summons all the Muses from Helicon,
calling upon Urania to preside, since she is the Muse of Astronomy,
hence of heavenly things. (Her name in Greek means, literally, "the
heavenly one.") *O holy, holy Virgins:* The Nine Muses. *with your full
choir:* With all the other Muses.

43 ff. THE HEAVENLY PAGEANT. The Pageant Dante now
describes is an allegory of the Church Triumphant in the form of a
religious procession or a formal masque in which devout mummers
present themselves in allegorical guises. The center of the Pageant is
the Chariot of The Church Triumphant, guarded by the Four
Gospels, and attended on the right by the Three Theological Graces
and on the left by the Four Cardinal Virtues. The Chariot itself is
drawn by the Griffon, who represents the twofold nature of Christ
as Man-and-God. Before this central group walk twenty-four Elders
representing the books of the Old Testament. Behind the central
group walk seven Elders representing the books of the New Testa-
ment. The entire procession is led by seven enormous Candelabra
whose candles trail a rainbow canopy across the sky representing the
Seven Gifts of the Spirit under which the Church moves.

Dante has not presented any allegory of such formality up to this
point, and some readers have thought the allegory of the Pageant stiff
and lifeless. One should bear in mind, however, that Dante is begin-
ning to deal, now, not with reason but with revelation, and that the
increased formality of his allegory here is apt to its content, and apt
again in its resemblance to the rituals of the Church whose triumph
he is representing. Note too, as distinct from the rest of Dante's alle-
gory, that these figures do not enter as themselves (St. John, for ex-
ample, appears in three guises) but as heavenly beings made up to
represent others.

43–51. *I saw next . . . :* Dante sees in the distance what he takes
to be seven trees of gold. Drawing nearer, he sees they are, in reality,
enormous candelabra. At that point, too, he is close enough to make
out that the word being sung by the chorus (line 36) which was first
heard as a distant melody (line 21) is "Hosanna!" *chance resemblances:*

Of the bases of the candelabra to tree trunks. *that power that reaps for reason's mill:* The discernment of the senses through which reason draws the data of nature from which it derives its concepts.

50. THE SEVEN CANDELABRA. On the Mountain the Lord specified to Moses the exact form of the seven-branched candelabrum of pure gold which was to be an essential part of the tabernacle (*Exodus* xxv, 31–37). In *Revelation* i, 12, John had a vision of seven candelabra and interpreted them as seven churches (i, 20). Later (iv, 5) he interprets them as the Seven Gifts of the Holy Spirit (wisdom, understanding, counsel, might, knowledge, piety, and fear of the Lord). As the Candelabra advance in the van of the procession, their candles paint the sky overhead with a seven-striped rainbow that represents these Gifts. Thus, the Candelabra may be taken as the light and glory of God from which issue the Seven Gifts of the Holy Spirit. The Church follows where the Candelabra lead.

51. *Hosanna!:* (Literally, "Save, we pray!") On Palm Sunday as Christ was about to enter Jerusalem, he was hailed at Bethphage on the Mount of Olives with the words "Hosannah to the son of David!" (*Matthew* xxi, 9.) The chant is especially apt in that Christ, as the Griffon, is about to enter in triumph.

56. *my good Virgil:* A new and much more familiar form of address signifying Dante's new state. Dante has always referred to Virgil with titles of honor and superiority.

57. *a look of equal awe:* Allegorically: Dante, out of old habit, turns to Reason for an explanation, but finds that Reason itself is overawed. Virgil has already explained (XXVII, 129) that he has passed the limit of his understanding.

60. *new brides:* Walking back from the altar. Hence, at a very slow pace. But even that pace would easily outdistance this procession.

64. *I saw people walking:* These are the figures made up as four and twenty elders who represent the books of the Old Testament as counted by St. Jerome in his *Gallican Psalter* (the twelve minor prophets are counted as one book, and so are *Ezra-Nehemiah, I* and *II Kings, I* and *II Samuel,* and *I* and *II Chronicles*). Thus the elders represent all Revelation before Christ. They wear white robes and wreaths of lilies as symbols of the purity of their faith. John has a vi-

sion of them in *Revelation* iv, 4–5, and explains them, there, as the Twelve Patriarchs and the Twelve Apostles. In his vision they wore crowns of gold. Their song (lines 86–87) is an adaptation of the words used by Gabriel and Elisabeth in addressing Mary at the time of the Annunciation. (*Luke* i, 28, 42.)

78. *Delia's girdle:* The rainbow-colored halo round the moon. Delia was another name for Diana, the moon goddess. *Apollo's bow:* The rainbow. Apollo was, of course, the Sun.

79–81. *stretched back further than I could see:* Allegorically, the Gifts of the Holy Spirit stretch further back into time than any man can reckon. *ten paces:* May certainly be taken as the Ten Commandments in which the Seven Gifts of the Holy Spirit were revealed, and through which they may be enjoyed.

93–105. THE FOUR BEASTS. They represent the Four Gospels of Matthew, Mark, Luke, and John that follow immediately upon the Old Testament. Their wreaths of living green signify Hope. The wings may be taken as signifying the speed with which the Gospels spread through the world. The fact that there are three pairs of wings obviously suggests the Trinity, and the eyes may be taken as Omniscience which is able to see past, present, and future. That much stated, Dante refers the reader to *Ezekiel* i, 4–14, for a detailed description, except that they are there described as having only four wings, and Dante follows John (*Revelation* iv, 8) in giving them six.

95. *Argus:* Jove made love to Io. Juno, in wifely jealousy, turned Io into a cow and set Argus of the hundred eyes to watch her. Mercury, sent by Jove, caused Argus to fall into an enchanted sleep and cut his head off. Juno set Argus' eyes in the tail of the peacock. Dante makes the point that the peacock's eyes, bright as they are, are dead, whereas the eyes in the feathers of these beasts are alive.

106 ff. THE CHARIOT OF THE CHURCH TRIUM-PHANT. Within the square guarded by the Four Gospel Beasts the Church is represented by a chariot so splendid that Rome never saw its equal, not even in the triumphs of Scipio Africanus or of Augustus. The very chariot of the Sun could not compare with it.

Its two wheels may best be taken as representing the Old and the New Testament. It is drawn by the Griffon that represents

Christ, and it is flanked by the Theological Virtues and the Cardinal Virtues.

108 ff. THE GRIFFON. A mythical figure with the fore parts of an eagle and the hind parts of a lion, here meant to represent the dual role of Christ as God and Man, his birdlike part divine, his lionlike part animal, hence human, and the unity of the two a symbol of his incarnation as the Word. His upraised wings, their tips soaring higher than the sight of man can follow, extend into the seven-striped heaven and inclose the central stripe representing MIGHT as the central Gift of the Holy Spirit and as a symbol of His triumph. The Griffon's coloration is probably suggested by *Song of Solomon*, v, 10–11: "My beloved is white and ruddy, the chiefest among ten thousand. His head is as the most fine gold."

118–120. *the Sun's own chariot, which strayed . . . :* The Chariot of the Sun was driven by Apollo. One day Phaëthon, Apollo's son, tried to drive it, but could not manage the horses. The chariot swerved from its path, scorching the sky and threatening to destroy the Earth. In terror Earth prayed to Jove for deliverance, and Jove destroyed the chariot with a thunderbolt. The scar left on the sky by Phaëthon's course became the Milky Way.

121–129. THE THREE THEOLOGICAL VIRTUES. They are Caritas (Christian Love), Faith, and Hope. Caritas is so red she could scarcely be seen in a fire. Hope is green, and Faith pure white. They dance in a ring at the Chariot's right wheel, and Faith and Caritas take turns leading the dance, while Hope (who cannot move except as Faith and Caritas direct) follows. Note that it is Caritas ("And the greatest of these is Charity") that sings the song to which they dance.

130–132. THE FOUR CARDINAL (OR NATURAL) VIRTUES. They are Prudence, Justice, Fortitude, and Temperance. They are dressed in the Imperial Purple, for they represent the Classical Virtues. Prudence, who leads them in their dance, has three eyes symbolizing that it is her duty to look at and consider the past, the present, and the future. Note, too, that the Classical and the Theological Virtues *must* go together if the soul is to develop.

133 ff. THE SEVEN ELDERS. These represent the remaining

books of the New Testament (aside from the Four Gospels). Note that it is the books, not the persons, that are represented, for John appears three times in this procession; first as the Gospel, next as the Epistles, and finally as *Revelation*. Thus the first two are *Acts* and the Fourteen Epistles. The next four are the Catholic Epistles. And the final single figure is *Revelation*. They wear wreaths of brightest red to signify the ardor of Caritas.

136–137. *One showed he was a follower of the art of great Hippocrates:* Luke, as the author of *Acts*. In *Colossians* iv, 14, Paul describes him as "the beloved physician." He is the doctor of souls, as Hippocrates was the doctor of bodies.

139–141. *The other, his counterpart:* The figure is Paul. The sword he carries may symbolize his martyrdom by a sword, or more aptly "the sword of the Spirit, which is the word of God." (*Ephesians* vi, 17.) Thus he is here the taker rather than the healer of lives, as presented in the Epistles.

154–155. *the exalted first flaming standards:* The candelabra that led the procession like pennons. *in unison:* The rear and the van of the procession stopped at the same instant.

CANTO XXX

The Earthly Paradise—Beatrice

VIRGIL VANISHES

The procession halts and the Prophets turn to the chariot and sing "Come, my bride, from Lebanon." They are summoning *Beatrice,* who appears on the left side of the chariot, half-hidden from view by showers of blossoms poured from above by *A Hundred Angels.* Dante, stirred by the sight, turns to Virgil to express his overflowing emotions, and discovers that *Virgil Has Vanished.*

Because he bursts into tears at losing Virgil *Dante Is Reprimanded by Beatrice.* The Angel Choir overhead immediately breaks into a Psalm of Compassion, but Beatrice, still severe, answers by detailing Dante's offenses in not making proper use of his great gifts. It would violate the ordering of the Divine Decree, she argues, to let Dante drink the waters of Lethe, thereby washing all memory of sin from his soul, before he had shed the tears of a real repentance.

When the Septentrion of the First Heaven,
   which does not rise nor set, and which has never
   been veiled from sight by any mist but sin,   3

and which made every soul in that high court
   know its true course (just as the lower Seven
   direct the helmsman to his earthly port),   6

had stopped; the holy prophets, who till then
   had walked between the Griffon and those lights,
   turned to the car like souls who cry "Amen."   9

And one among them who seemed sent from Heaven
   clarioned: *"Veni, sponsa, de Libano,"*
   three times, with all the others joining in.   12

As, at the last trump every saint shall rise
  out of the grave, ready with voice new-fleshed
  to carol *Alleluliah* to the skies;   15

just so, above the chariot, at the voice
  of such an elder, rose a hundred Powers
  and Principals of the Eternal Joys,   18

all saying together: *"Benedictus qui venis";*
  then, scattering flowers about on every side:
  "Manibus o date lilia plenis."   21

Time and again at day break I have seen
  the eastern sky glow with a wash of rose
  while all the rest hung limpid and serene,   24

and the Sun's face rise tempered from its rest
  so veiled by vapors that the naked eye
  could look at it for minutes undistressed.   27

Exactly so, within a cloud of flowers
  that rose like fountains from the angels' hands
  and fell about the chariot in showers,   30

a lady came in view: an olive crown
  wreathed her immaculate veil, her cloak was green,
  the colors of live flame played on her gown.   33

My soul—such years had passed since last it saw
  that lady and stood trembling in her presence,
  stupefied by the power of holy awe—   36

now, by some power that shone from her above
  the reach and witness of my mortal eyes,
  felt the full mastery of enduring love.   39

The instant I was smitten by the force,
  which had already once transfixed my soul
  before my boyhood years had run their course,   42

I turned left with the same assured belief
  that makes a child run to its mother's arms
  when it is frightened or has come to grief,   45

to say to Virgil: "There is not within me
  one drop of blood unstirred. I recognize
  the tokens of the ancient flame." But he,   48

he had taken his light from us. He had gone.
  Virgil had gone. Virgil, the gentle Father
  to whom I gave my soul for its salvation!   51

Not all that sight of Eden lost to view
  by our First Mother could hold back the tears
  that stained my cheeks so lately washed with dew.   54

"Dante, do not weep yet, though Virgil goes.
  Do not weep yet, for soon another wound
  shall make you weep far hotter tears than those!"   57

As an admiral takes his place at stern or bow
  to observe the handling of his other ships
  and spur all hands to do their best—so now,   60

on the chariot's left side, I saw appear
  when I turned back at the sound of my own name
  (which, necessarily is recorded here),   63

that lady who had been half-veiled from view
  by the flowers of the angel-revels. Now her eyes
  fixed me across the stream, piercing me through.   66

And though the veil she still wore, held in place
  by the wreathed flowers of wise Minerva's leaves,
  let me see only glimpses of her face,   69

her stern and regal bearing made me dread
  her next words, for she spoke as one who saves
  the heaviest charge till all the rest are read.   72

"Look at me well. I am she. I am Beatrice.
  How dared you make your way to this high
                              mountain?
  Did you not know that here man lives in bliss?"   75

I lowered my head and looked down at the stream.
  But when I saw myself reflected there,
  I fixed my eyes upon the grass for shame.   78

I shrank as a wayward child in his distress
  shrinks from his mother's sternness, for the taste
  of love grown wrathful is a bitterness.   81

She paused. At once the angel chorus sang
  the blessèd psalm: *"In te, Domine, speravi."*
  As far as *"pedes meos"* their voices rang.   84

As on the spine of Italy the snow
  lies frozen hard among the living rafters
  in winter when the northeast tempests blow;   87

then, melting if so much as a breath stir
  from the land of shadowless noon, flows through itself
  like hot wax trickling down a lighted taper—   90

just so I froze, too cold for sighs or tears
  until I heard that choir whose notes are tuned
  to the eternal music of the spheres.   93

But when I heard the voice of their compassion
  plead for me more than if they had cried out:
  "Lady, why do you treat him in this fashion?"   96

the ice, which hard about my heart had pressed,
  turned into breath and water, and flowed out
  through eyes and throat in anguish from my breast.   99

Still standing at the chariot's left side,
  she turned to those compassionate essences
  whose song had sought to move her, and replied: 102

"You keep your vigil in the Eternal Day
  where neither night nor sleep obscures from you
  a single step the world takes on its way;   105

but I must speak with greater care that he
  who weeps on that far bank may understand
  and feel a grief to match his guilt. Not only   108

by the workings of the spheres that bring each seed
  to its fit end according to the stars
  that ride above it, but by gifts decreed   111

in the largesse of overflowing Grace,
  whose rain has such high vapors for its source
  our eyes cannot mount to their dwelling place;   114

this man, potentially, was so endowed
  from early youth that marvelous increase
  should have come forth from every good he sowed.   117

But richest soil the soonest will grow wild
  with bad seed and neglect. For a while I stayed him
  with glimpses of my face. Turning my mild   120

and youthful eyes into his very soul,
  I let him see their shining, and I led him
  by the straight way, his face to the right goal.   123

The instant I had come upon the sill
  of my second age and crossed and changed my life,
  he left me and let others shape his will.   126

When I rose from the flesh into the spirit,
  to greater beauty and to greater virtue,
  he found less pleasure in me and less merit.   129

He turned his steps aside from the True Way,
  pursuing the false images of good
  that promise what they never wholly pay.   132

Not all the inspiration I won by prayer
  and brought to him in dreams and meditations
  could call him back, so little did he care.   135

He fell so far from every hope of bliss
  that every means of saving him had failed
  except to let him see the damned. For this   138

I visited the portals of the dead
  and poured my tears and prayers before that spirit
  by whom his steps have, up to now, been led.   141

The seal Almighty god's decree has placed
  on the rounds of His creation would be broken
  were he to come past Lethe and to taste   144

the water that wipes out the guilty years
  without some scot of penitential tears!"

NOTES

1. *the Septentrion of the First Heaven:* The Septentrion is the seven stars of the Big Dipper. Here Dante means the seven candelabra. They are the Septentrion of the First Heaven (the Empyrean) as distinct from the seven stars of the dipper which occur lower down in the Sphere of the Fixed Stars.

2. *which does not rise nor set:* The North Star does not rise or set north of the equator, but the Septentrion, revolving around the North Star, does go below the horizon in the lower latitudes. This Septentrion of the First Heaven, however, partaking of the perfection and constancy of Heaven, neither rises nor sets but is a constant light to mankind. So these unchanging lights guide the souls of man on high, as the "lower Seven" (line 5), in their less perfect way, guide the earthly helmsmen to their earthly ports.

7. *the holy prophets:* The twenty-four elders who represent the books of the Old Testament. (See XXIX, 64, note.)

10. *one among them:* The Song of Solomon.

11. *Veni, sponsa, de Libano:* "Come [with me] from Lebanon, my spouse." *Song of Solomon* iv, 8. This cry, re-echoed by choirs of angels, summons Beatrice, who may be taken here as revelation, faith, divine love, hence as the bride of the spirit, to Dante (man's redeemed soul).

17–18. *a hundred Powers and Principals:* Angels.

19. *Benedictus qui venis:* "Blessed is he who cometh." (*Matthew,* xxi, 9.)

21. *Manibus o date lilia plenis:* "Oh, give lilies with full hands." These are the words of Anchises in honor of Marcellus. (*Aeneid* VI, 883.) Thus they are not only apt to the occasion but their choice is a sweetly conceived last literary compliment to Virgil before he vanishes.

31. *a lady:* Beatrice. She is dressed in the colors of Faith (white), Hope (green), and Caritas (red).

34. *since last it saw:* Beatrice died in 1290. Thus Dante has passed ten years without sight of her.

36. *stupefied:* Dante describes the stupor of his soul at the sight of the living Beatrice in *La Vita Nuova* XIV and XXIV. Then, however, it was mortal love; here it is eternal, and the effect accordingly greater.

54. *washed with dew:* By Virgil. I, 124.

55. *Dante:* This is the only point in the *Commedia* at which Dante mentions his own name. Its usage here suggests many allegorical possibilities. Central to all of them, however, must be the fact that Dante, in ending one life (of the mind) and beginning a new one (of faith) hears his name. The suggestion of a second baptism is inevitable. And just as a child being baptized is struck by the priest, so Beatrice is about to strike him with her tongue before he may proceed to the holy water.

64. *that lady:* There are thirty-four Cantos in the *Inferno* and this is the thirtieth of the *Purgatorio,* hence the sixty-fourth Canto of the *Commedia.* This is the sixty-fourth line of the sixty-fourth Canto. In Dante's numerology such correspondences are always meaningful. Six plus four equals ten and ten equals the sum of the square of trinity and unity. Obviously there can be no conclusive way of establishing intent in such a structure of mystic numbering, but it certainly is worth noting that the line begins with "that lady." The Italian text, in fact, begins with *vidi la donna,* i.e., I saw the lady [who represents the sum of the square of trinity plus unity?]. The lady, of course, is Beatrice.

68. *wise Minerva's leaves:* The olive crown.

80. *his mother's sternness:* Beatrice appears in the pageant as the figure of the Church Triumphant. The Church is the mother of the devout and though she is stern, as law decrees, her sternness is that of a loving mother.

83–84. *In te, Domine, speravi . . . pedes meos:* In mercy the angel chorus sings Psalm XXXI, 1–8, beginning "In thee, O Lord, do I put my trust" and continuing as far as "thou hast set my feet in a large room."

85–90. *the spine of Italy:* The Apennines. *the living rafters:* The trees. *the land of shadowless noon:* Africa. In equatorial regions the noonday sun is at the zenith over each point twice a year. Its rays then fall straight down and objects cast no shadows.

101. *compassionate essences:* The Angel chorus.

106. *greater care:* For his understanding than for your intercession.

109–11. *the working of the spheres . . . :* The influence of the stars in their courses which incline men at birth to good or evil ends according to the astrological virtue of their conjunctions.

114. *our eyes:* Beatrice is still replying to the plea of the Angel choir. Hence "our eyes" must refer not to mortal eyes, but to the eyes of the blessed. Not even such more-than-human eyes may mount to the high place of those vapors, for that place is nothing less than the Supreme Height, since Grace flows from God Himself.

124–126. *my second age:* Beatrice's womanhood. When she had reached the full bloom of youth Dante turned from her and wrote to his *donna gentile.* Allegorically, he turned from divine "sciences" to an overreliance upon philosophy (the human "sciences"). For this sin he must suffer.

144–145. *were he to come past Lethe:* In passing Lethe and drinking its waters, the soul loses all memory of guilt. This, therefore, is Dante's last opportunity to do penance.

CANTO XXXI

The Earthly Paradise—Lethe

BEATRICE · MATILDA

Beatrice continues her reprimand, forcing Dante to confess his faults until he swoons with grief and pain at the thought of his sin. He wakes to find himself in Lethe, held in the arms of Matilda, who leads him to the other side of the stream and there immerses him that he may drink the waters that wipe out all memory of sin.

Matilda then leads him to *The Four Cardinal Virtues,* who dance about him and lead him before *The Griffon* where he may look into *The Eyes of Beatrice.* In them Dante sees, in a *First Beatific Vision,* the radiant reflection of the Griffon, who appears now in his human and now in his godly nature.

The Three Theological Virtues now approach and beg that Dante may behold *The Smile of Beatrice.* Beatrice removes her veil, and in a *Second Beatific Vision,* Dante beholds the splendor of the unveiled shining of Divine Love.

"You, there, who stand upon the other side—"
  (turning to me now, who had thought the edge
  of her discourse was sharp, the point) she cried   3

without pause in her flow of eloquence,
  "Speak up! Speak up! Is it true? To such a charge
  your own confession must give evidence."   6

I stood as if my spirit had turned numb:
  the organ of my speech moved, but my voice
  died in my throat before a word could come.   9

Briefly she paused, then cried impatiently:
  "What are you thinking? Speak up, for the waters
  have yet to purge sin from your memory."   12

Confusion joined to terror forced a broken
  "yes" from my throat, so weak that only one
  who read my lips would know that I had spoken.   15

As an arbalest will snap when string and bow
  are drawn too tight by the bowman, and the bolt
  will strike the target a diminished blow—   18

so did I shatter, strengthless and unstrung,
  under her charge, pouring out floods of tears,
  while my voice died in me on the way to my tongue. 21

And she: "Filled as you were with the desire
  I taught you for That Good beyond which nothing
  exists on earth to which man may aspire,   24

what yawning moats or what stretched chain-lengths
                              lay
  across your path to force you to abandon
  all hope of pressing further on your way?   27

What increase or allurement seemed to show
  in the brows of others that you walked before them
  as a lover walks below his lady's window?"   30

My breath dragged from me in a bitter sigh,
  I barely found a voice to answer with;
  my lips had trouble forming a reply.   33

In tears I said: "The things of the world's day,
  false pleasures and enticements, turned my steps
  as soon as you had ceased to light my way."   36

And she: "Had you been silent, or denied
  what you confess, your guilt would still be known
  to Him from Whom no guilt may hope to hide.   39

But here, before our court, when souls upbraid
  themselves for their own guilt in true remorse,
  the grindstone is turned back against the blade.   42

In any case that you may know your crime
  truly and with true shame and so be stronger
  against the Siren's song another time,   45

control your tears and listen with your soul
  to learn how my departure from the flesh
  ought to have spurred you to the higher goal.   48

Nothing in Art of Nature could call forth
  such joy from you, as sight of that fair body
  which clothed me once and now sifts back to earth.   51

And if my dying turned that highest pleasure
  to very dust, what joy could still remain
  in mortal things for you to seek and treasure?   54

At the first blow you took from such vain things
  your every thought should have been raised to follow
  my flight above decay. Nor should your wings   57

have been weighed down by any joy below—
  love of a maid, or any other fleeting
  and useless thing—to wait a second blow.   60

The fledgling waits a second shaft, a third;
  but nets are spread and the arrow sped in vain
  in sight or hearing of the full-grown bird."   63

As a scolded child, tongue tied for shame, will stand
  and recognize his fault, and weep for it,
  bowing his head to a just reprimand,   66

so did I stand. And she said: "If to hear me
  grieves you, now raise your beard and let your eyes
  show you a greater cause for misery."   69

The blast that blows from Libya's hot sand,
  or the Alpine gale, overcomes less resistance
  uprooting oaks than I, at her command,   72

overcame then in lifting up my face;
  for when she had referred to it as my "beard"
  I sensed too well the venom of her phrase.   75

When I had raised my eyes with so much pain,
  I saw those Primal Beings, now at rest,
  who had strewn blossoms round her thick as rain;   78

and with my tear-blurred and uncertain vision
  I saw her turned to face that beast which is
  one person in two natures without division.   81

Even veiled and across the river from me
  her face outshone its first-self by as much
  as she outshone all mortals formerly.   84

And the thorns of my repentance pricked me so
  that all the use and substance of the world
  I most had loved, now most appeared my foe.   87

Such guilty recognition gnawed my heart
  I swooned for pain; and what I then became
  she best knows who most gave me cause to smart.   90

When I returned to consciousness at last
  I found the lady who had walked alone
  bent over me. "Hold fast!" she said, "Hold fast!"   93

She had drawn me into the stream up to my throat,
  and pulling me behind her, she sped on
  over the water, light as any boat.   96

Nearing the sacred bank, I heard her say
  in tones so sweet I cannot call them back,
  much less describe them here: *"Asperges me."*   99

Then the sweet lady took my head between
  her open arms, and embracing me, she dipped me
  and made me drink the waters that make clean.   102

Then raising me in my new purity
  she led me to the dance of the Four Maidens;
  each raised an arm and so joined hands above me. 105

"Here we are nymphs; stars are we in the skies.
  Ere Beatrice went to earth we were ordained
  her handmaids. We will lead you to her eyes;   108

but that your own may see what joyous light
  shines in them, yonder Three, who see more deeply,
  will sharpen and instruct your mortal sight."   111

Thus they sang, then led me to the Griffon.
  Behind him, Beatrice waited. And when I stood
  at the Griffon's breast, they said in unison: 114

"Look deep, look well, however your eyes may smart.
  We have led you now before those emeralds
  from which Love shot his arrows through your
                           heart."   117

A thousand burning passions, every one
  hotter than any flame, held my eyes fixed
  to the lucent eyes she held fixed on the Griffon. 120

Like sunlight in a glass the twofold creature
  shone from the deep reflection of her eyes,
  now in the one, now in the other nature.   123

Judge, reader, if I found it passing strange
  to see the thing unaltered in itself
  yet in its image working change on change.   126

And while my soul in wonder and delight
  was savoring that food which in itself
  both satisfies and quickens appetite,   129

the other Three, whose bearing made it clear
  they were of higher rank, came toward me dancing
  to the measure of their own angelic air.   132

"Turn, Beatrice, oh turn the eyes of grace,"
  was their refrain, "upon your faithful one
  who comes so far to look upon your face.   135

Grant us this favor of your grace: reveal
  your mouth to him, and let his eyes behold
  the Second Beauty, which your veils conceal."   138

O splendor of the eternal living light!
  who that has drunk deep of Parnassus' waters,
  or grown pale in the shadow of its height,   141

would not, still, feel his burdened genius fail
  attempting to describe in any tongue
  how you appeared when you put by your veil   144

in that free air open to heaven and earth
  whose harmony is your shining shadowed forth!

NOTES

1. *the other side:* Of Lethe. But also the other side of the immortal life, i.e., still living.

2–3. *edge . . . point:* The image of the sword (of Justice) is carried over from lines 56–57 of the preceding Canto. It is continued in line 42, below. So far the sword has only cut, now it pierces.

11. *the waters:* Of Lethe.

16 ff. *arbalest . . . snap . . . diminished blow:* The figure is a bit confusing. Dante seems to say that the bolt (corresponding to an arrow) of a crossbow strikes the target with less force when the bow snaps. He does not stop to consider that the bolt may miss the target entirely. Nevertheless, the intent of his figure is clear enough.

25. *moats . . . chain-lengths:* These were, of course, defensive military measures. The moats guarded castles. The chains were strung to block roads, bridges, and gates. Both measures imply great labor forces. Thus the point of Beatrice's question: "What enormous forces blocked your way?" The block was, of course, within Dante himself.

42. *the grindstone is turned back against the blade:* Turning the grindstone away from the blade sharpens it. Turning it back against the blade dulls it. Thus Beatrice is saying that when a soul openly confesses in true repentance what could not in any case be hidden from God, the sword of Justice is blunted, i.e., no longer cuts as deeply.

49–60. DANTE'S FOLLY. If the beauty of her earthly body was Dante's supreme joy and still decayed to mere dust, says Beatrice, how could Dante have placed his trust in any other earthly thing? *love of a maid:* Dante mentions another maiden in some of his songs but in an indefinite way. No specific reference can be attached to these words.

62. *nets:* Were sometimes used for trapping birds.

68–75. *your beard:* Beatrice means "your face," but the word choice is especially cutting. She has been accusing Dante of acting like a child or a fledgling bird. To refer to his beard, therefore, is a sarcastic way of reminding him that he is, presumably, a full-grown man. *a greater cause for misery:* The sight of her accompanied by the guilty knowledge that he had turned away from so much beauty and perfection.

80–81. *that beast which is one person in two natures:* The Griffon. He is the masque of Christ and represents His two aspects as man and God.

83. *first-self:* Her mortal self.

92. *the lady who had walked alone:* Matilda.

94. *She had drawn me into the stream:* Dante wakens to find Matilda bending over him. She has already pulled Dante into Lethe and he is in the water up to his throat, but Matilda walks *upon* the water. The fact that this particular miracle is attributed specifically to Christ cannot fail to suggest an allegorical meaning.

97. *the sacred bank:* The far bank, the other side. One bank of Lethe is nearer the world, the other nearer Heaven. The sacred bank, moreover, lies the other side of the absolution of Lethe's water. On the near side sin may still be said to exist; on the sacred side, even the memory of sin has been washed away. Contrast Beatrice's words in line 1.

99. *Asperges me: Asperges me hyssopo, et mundabor; lavabis me, et super nivem dealbabor.* ("Purge me with hyssop, and I shall be clean; wash me, and I shall be whiter than snow.") *Psalms* li, 7. These are the words the priest utters when he sprinkles holy water over the confessed sinner to absolve him. Matilda, that is to say, is performing the office of absolution. Her action, therefore, must be seen as being directly connected with Dante's confession and repentance, for nothing else could prepare him for absolution.

104. *the Four Maidens:* The Four Cardinal Virtues: Justice, Prudence, Fortitude, and Temperance. In their present manifestation they are nymphs. In another manifestation they are the four stars Dante saw above him when he arrived at the base of the mountain. (I, 23, note.) As the Cardinal Virtues (i.e., the best man can achieve without the revelation of Christ's church) they cannot themselves bring the soul to the Second Vision (of Divine Love receiving the soul) but they can lead to the First Vision (of the Two Natures of

Christ), and thence to the Three Theological Virtues, through which the Second Vision may be received.

Since Beatrice, in one of her present manifestations, represents the Authority of the Church, lines 104–105 must mean that the Four Cardinal Virtues were ordained to be the handmaidens of the Church even before it was founded, working in the virtuous pagans, and in all men, to prepare the way for the triumph of the Church.

110. *yonder Three:* The Theological Virtues: Faith, Hope, and Charity (i.e., *Caritas*).

116. *those emeralds:* The eyes of Beatrice. Dante may have intended to describe them as green (hazel) but more likely his choice of words here is meant only to signify "jewel bright." Green is, of course, the color of Hope, and an allegorical significance may be implied in that.

118–126. THE EYES OF BEATRICE. Led by the Four Cardinal Virtues, Dante takes his place before the Griffon and receives a first beatific vision of its nature, seeing now the lion (the human) and now the eagle (the divine); now one, now the other, constantly shifting, though the Griffon itself remains immovable (i.e., constant, perfect). He does not, however, see the two natures as one. For that revelation he must wait till he reaches the top of Paradiso.

Note that Dante does not achieve his revelation by looking at the Griffon itself, but rather by looking at its reflection in the eyes of Beatrice (as the Church). Thus he achieves here the first fruits of Faith, seeing as much of the nature of God as is perceivable in the first life. The final revelation can happen only in Heaven, in the rapturous presence of God.

129. *both satisfies and quickens appetite:* "They that eat me shall yet be hungry, and they that drink me shall yet be thirsty." (*Ecclesiasticus* xxiv, 21.)

138. *the Second Beauty:* The smile of Beatrice (Divine Love). Dante was led to the First Beauty by the Four Cardinal Virtues. Now the Three Theological Virtues, as higher beings, lead him to the second, and higher beauty, which is the joy of Divine Love in receiving the purified soul.

140. *Parnassus' waters:* The fountain of Castalia. To drink from it

is to receive poetic gifts. To grow pale in the shadow of Parnassus signifies to labor at mastering the art of poetry. Note that Dante makes no effort to describe the smile of Divine Love, but only his rapture at beholding it.

145–146. *that free air:* Dante has earlier made the point that the Earthly Paradise possesses an atmosphere that is entirely unconstrained by earthly influences, but moves only in perfect harmony with the primal motion. That harmony is, however, no more than the shadow of the shining of Perfect Love.

CANTO XXXII

The Earthly Paradise—Beatrice Unveiled

DEPARTURE OF THE HEAVENLY PAGEANT · TRANSFORMATION OF THE CHARIOT

Beatrice unveils and for the first time in ten years Dante looks upon her face. When he recovers from that blinding sight, Dante finds the Heavenly Pageant has wheeled about and is heading east. Dante and Statius follow the Chariot to *The Tree of Good and Evil,* which rises to vast heights but bears neither leaves nor flowers. The Griffon ties the pole of the Chariot to the Tree, and the Tree immediately breaks into leaf and flower. The Heavenly Pageant greets this wonder with a hymn unknown to mortals. Overpowered by the singing *Dante Sleeps.*

He awakens to find himself, as he believes at first, alone with Matilda. The Heavenly Pageant has, in fact, departed, but as Dante soon learns, Beatrice has remained behind to guard the chariot and the Seven Nymphs have remained to attend her. She is seated upon the ground, on the roots of the tree and under its shade.

Dante then witnesses an allegorical masque of *The Corruption of the Church Through Wealth.* First *An Eagle* (the Roman Empire) attacks the tree and the chariot. Then *A Fox* (heresy). Then the Eagle returns and covers the chariot with its feathers. Immediately *A Dragon* (Satan) rips at the chariot's foundation. The chariot then covers itself with the feathers (riches) and is converted into *A Monstrous Beast* on which rides *A Harlot* (the corrupted Papacy) attended by *A Giant* (the French Monarchy) that beats the harlot and drags the monster into the woods and out of sight.

My eyes were fixed with such intensity
　　on quenching, at long last, their ten years' thirst
　　that every sense but sight abandoned me.　　　　3

Tranced by the holy smile that drew me there
  into the old nets, I forgot all else—
  my eyes wore blinders, and I could not care.   6

When suddenly my gaze was wrenched away
  and forced to turn left to those goddesses:
  "He stares too fixedly," I heard them say.   9

And as a man is blinded by the light
  when he has looked directly at the sun,
  just so I found that I had lost my sight.   12

When I could make out lesser (I mean, of course,
  "less sensible objects") as compared to the greater
  from which I had been called away by force,   15

I saw the legion of those souls in grace
  had turned right-wheel-about, and marched back now
  with the sun and the seven torches in its face.   18

As forward troops when they are giving ground
  turn under their shields, and their standards face about
  before the rest of the column has turned round—   21

just so the vanguard of that heavenly force
  had all gone by before the chariot
  had swung its pole around to the new course.   24

Then to their wheels the ladies turned together,
  and the Griffon once more pulled the sacred car,
  not ruffling so much as a single feather.   27

Statius and I followed across that park
  with the lady who had led me through the ford,
  behind the wheel that turned the lesser arc.   30

We marched across the sacred wood which she
  who heeded a forked tongue had left deserted,
  our steps timed by angelic melody.   33

We had moved on, I think, about as far
  as three good bowshots, end to end, might reach,
  when Beatrice descended from the car.   36

"Adam!" I heard all murmur, censuring him.
  Then they all formed a circle round a tree
  that bore no leaf nor flower on any limb.   39

It soared so high that even in woods like those
  the Indians know it would have seemed a wonder;
  and the crown spread out the more the more it rose. 42

"Blessèd art thou, Griffon, whose beak hath rent
  no morsel of the sweet wood of this tree,
  for it grips the belly with a raging torment!" 45

—So shouted all the others as they stood
  about the tree. And the two-natured being:
  "Thus is preserved the seed of every good!"   48

Then he drew up before the widowed mast
  the chariot's pole, and what came from the tree
  he gave it back, and tied the two stems fast.   51

As in the spring on earth, when the great light
  falls mingled with the rays of those sweet stars
  that follow Pisces into Heaven's height,   54

the trees begin to swell, then burgeon full,
  each one in its own hue, before the Sun
  harnesses his team beneath the Bull—   57

just so the boughs that had been bare before
  took color, turning something less than rose
  and more than violet as they bloomed once more.   60

The hymn I heard those blessèd souls sing then
  is not sung here, nor did I understand it;
  nor did I hear it through to the Amen.   63

Could I portray the eyes of Argus here,
  lulled one by one by drowsy tales of Syrinx,
  that time their pitiless watch cost him so dear,   66

as a painter paints his model, I would try
  to show exactly how I fell asleep.
  But who can imagine drowsiness? Not I.   69

Therefore, I pass to my waking, and declare
  a radiance tore the veil of sleep; a voice
  cried out: "Arise! What are you doing there?"   72

When they were shown the flowering of that Tree
  that makes the angels hungry for Its fruit
  and sets a feast in Heaven eternally,   75

Peter, John, and James, awe-stricken, fell
  into a sleep from which they were recalled
  by the same word that broke a greater spell;   78

and saw their company reduced, as both
  Moses and Elijah vanished from them;
  and saw the Master's robe change back to cloth.   81

Just so did I awaken from my dream
  to find, bent over me, the compassionate lady
  who had conducted me along the stream.   84

Fearful I cried out, "Beatrice! Where is she?"
  And the lady: "She is seated on the roots
  of the new foliage, as you can see,   87

encircled by the seven shining Graces.
  The others mount to Heaven behind the Griffon,
  intoning sweeter and profounder praises."   90

If she said more, her words were lost on me,
  for now my eyes were fixed once more on Beatrice,
  my senses closed to all that was not she.   93

She sat on the bare earth alone, left there
  to guard the chariot that the Biformed Beast
  had fastened to the tree with such great care.   96

A living cloister ringing her about,
  the Seven Nymphs stood, holding in their hands
  those candles no wind ever shall blow out.   99

"Here briefly in this forest shall you dwell;
  and evermore, with me, be of that Rome
  in which Christ is a Roman. Hence, look well   102

there at the great car, and that you may be
  a light to the dark world, when you return
  set down exactly all that you shall see."   105

Thus Beatrice; and I, devoutly bent
  at the feet of her commands, turned mind and eye
  as she had willed, in all obedient.   108

No flash from densest clouds when the rains fall
  from the remotest reaches of the sky
  ever shot down as fast out of the squall   111

as did the bird of Jove that I saw break
  down through the tree, ripping the flowers, the leaves,
  even the bark, with its fierce claws and beak.   114

He struck the chariot a tremendous blow,
  at which it lurched like a storm-battered ship,
  now rolled to port, now starboard, to and fro.   117

Next came a fox, so gaunt and angular
  it seemed to know no fit food; and it pounced
  upon the cab of the triumphal car.   120

But threatening all its filthy sins with woe
  my lady sent it reeling back from there
  as fast as such a bag of bones could go.   123

Then, through the tree, I saw the bird descend
  once more into the car, and shed its plumes
  to feather it in gold from end to end.   126

And from the sky, as if a heart let slip
  all of its grief in one sound, a voice cried:
  "O what a load you bear, my little ship!"   129

Then, as I watched, I saw a fissure split
  the earth between the two wheels, and a dragon
  rise to the car and sink its tail in it.   132

Much as an angry wasp draws back its stinger,
  it drew its tail back, ripping the car's floor,
  and wandered off as if it meant to linger.   135

Like rich soil left to weeds, what then remained
  covered itself with feathers, which no doubt
  had been intended to burnish what they stained.   138

And both the wheels and the pole were overgrown,
  and all the car to the last part, and all
  in less time than the lips part for a moan.   141

So changed, the holy ark began to sprout
  heads from its various parts: three from the pole,
  one from each corner. Seven in all grew out.   144

The three were horned like oxen, but the four
  were each armed with a single evil horn.
  No one had seen the monster's like before.   147

Secure as a great fortress on a crag,
  an ungirt harlot rode the beast, her eyes
  darting with avarice. Beside that hag,   150

and ready to risk all to keep her his,
  a giant strode erect, and as they passed,
  from time to time the two exchanged a kiss.   153

But when she turned her hungry eyes on me,
  her savage lover in a bestial rage
  whipped her from head to foot unmercifully.   156

Then in a jealous fit the brute untied
  the monster from the tree, and dragged it off
  into the woods, far toward the other side,   159

until between me and the doxie queen
  on her weird beast, he made the trees a screen.

NOTES

1–9. DANTE'S RAPTURE ADMONISHED. Beatrice had
died in 1290. Dante has not, therefore, seen her for ten years, and the

sight of her unveiled face so draws him into the old nets (of love) that he loses track of all else until he is brought to his senses by overhearing the Three Maidens charge him with overdoing. For it is immoderate (*non è bello,* i.e., it is not an Aristotelian means of good conduct) to stare so intensely, even at the vision of eternal beauty, if in so doing a man loses sight of the other gifts of God. Bear in mind, too, that Dante is staring with his earthly memory of the other Beatrice. The Heavenly Beatrice has not yet been truly revealed to him. That revelation will take place in the next Canto.

16–18. The Heavenly Pageant came originally from the east. It passed Dante, executed a right-wheel-about, and is now returning, face to the east. Accordingly, it now has in its face the light of the sun as well as that of the candelabra.

20. *under their shields:* Troops turning in retreat within range of the enemy held their shields over their heads for protection.

22. *the vanguard of that heavenly force:* The twenty-four elders.

30. *the wheel that turned the lesser arc:* The right. In making a right turn, it would swing through the lesser arc. The poets, therefore, are walking behind the Three Theological Virtues.

36. *when Beatrice descended:* In this masque, Beatrice has entered in a chariot that represents the Church Triumphant. The procession is now moving to the tree that represents the Civil Authority of the Holy Roman Empire. Her descent in order to approach on foot signifies the humility the Church should display before civil authority, as commanded by Paul (*Romans* xiii, 1): "Let every soul be subject unto the higher powers. For there is no power but of God: the powers that be are ordained of God." To this, as Dante's image of the ideal Church, contrast his lament for the evils that befell the Church when it grew rich and arrogant (*Inferno* XIX, 109–111, and note), and the final allegory of the present Canto.

37–60. THE TREE OF GOOD AND EVIL. This passage contains an elaborate conception, difficult in itself, and made more difficult by much of Dante's phrasing in what is certainly his least attractive style.

The tree, to begin with, is instantly recognizable, by its resemblance to its offshoot on the ledge below, as the original Tree of

Good and Evil. It is for this reason that all souls murmur against Adam at the sight of it.

Then, in a second symbolism, the tree is made to represent the Holy Roman Empire, towering so high (and spreading wider as it soars) that no tree in the Indian forests (the comparison is from Virgil) could equal it. (The comparison to Indian forests implies, of course, the superiority of the Christian empire.) But though enormous, the tree is, by itself, barren.

When Christ (the Griffon) approaches the tree, all praise Him for not having eaten (peculiar diet) the sweet-tasting wood (the material riches of the Empire), for by His holy poverty in this world, He escaped the bellyache of corruption (with which the Church has been plagued ever since it grew rich). The Griffon replies that only so (in holy poverty) can the seed of goodness be preserved.

To understand the Griffon's next action, it is necessary to know that the true cross, according to legend, had been cut from the Tree of Good and Evil. The Griffon draws the Chariot (the Church) to the tree and binds fast to the tree "what came from it," i.e., the pole of the chariot. Thus one may understand that the pole the Griffon has been pulling (and what draws the Church forward) is the true cross. This interpretation is disputed but does have the virtue of being coherent.

Now with the Church securely bound to the Empire by the true cross, the tree that had been barren breaks into bloom, turning (lines 59–60) something less than rose and more than violet (i.e., the Imperial purple).

For good measure, Dante throws in a legendary reference and several astrological ones. Sense of lines 52–57: "As in the spring on earth when the great light falls mingled with the days of those sweet stars [of Aries, the sign in which the sun rides from March 21 to April 19] that follow Pisces [the zodiacal sign immediately preceding Aries] the trees begin to swell, then burgeon full . . . before the Sun [Apollo, the charioteer of the Sun] harnesses his team [to bear the Sun across the sky] beneath the Bull [Taurus, the sign the Sun enters on April 20]."

64–65. *Argus . . . Syrinx:* Argus (called Panoptes or "the all-seeing") had a hundred eyes all over his body. When Jupiter was smitten by Io, Juno changed the girl into a cow and sent Argus to keep watch over her. Jupiter, in his turn, sent Mercury to lull Argus to sleep either by the magic of his flute or, in the version Dante follows, by a kind of Arabian Nights series of tales about Syrinx, who was loved by Pan, and who was changed into a reed by her sisters to save her from Pan's pursuit. His watch cost him dear because Mercury, after lulling him to sleep, cut off his head. Juno set the eyes of her dead gamekeeper into the tail of the peacock, the bird sacred to her. (See XXIX, 95, note.)

70 ff. DANTE'S DREAM AND AWAKENING. The strains of the heavenly hymn lull Dante into a blissful sleep, which may be taken as symbolizing the serenity of the Kingdom. A radiance reaches through his closed eyes and he awakens to hear a voice cry "Arise!" This is the word with which Christ called Lazarus, among others, from the "greater spell" of death. Obviously, therefore, Dante's awakening symbolizes one more release from mortal error into eternal life. Opening his eyes, Dante finds Matilda bending over him. It was she who cried to him, and at first Dante thinks that all the others have left and that he is alone with her.

Dante then compares his experience to that of Peter, John, and James at the Transfiguration. "And after six days Jesus taketh with him Peter, and James, and John his brother, and bringeth them up into a high mountain apart, and he was transfigured before them: and his face did shine as the sun, and his garments became white as the light . . . they fell on their face, and were sore afraid. And Jesus came and touched them and said, Arise, and be not afraid. And lifting up their eyes, they saw no one, save Jesus only." (*Matthew* xvii, 1–8.) And see also *Luke* ix, 28–36, especially, "Now Peter and they that were with him were heavy with sleep: but when they were fully awake, they saw his glory, and the two men that stood with him."

Basing his account on these two passages, Dante adds his own allegory. The vision that is shown to the disciples becomes a vision of Christ as the Mystic Tree of Heaven (which is, of course, another aspect of the Tree of Good and Evil). The vision, however, is not of the fruit of the tree but of its flowers (line 73). It is, therefore, the vision of the flowering promise of Christ, from which will follow the fruit of eternal rejoicing. The vision is especially apt since, during Dante's sleep, Christ (the Griffon) has reascended to Heaven with most of the Heavenly Procession. There Dante shall follow him in the *Paradiso,* and there the fruit of felicity awaits.

73. *that Tree:* Christ.

81. *and saw the Master's robe change back to cloth:* I.e., back to its mortal state, as it was before the Transfiguration.

83. *the compassionate lady:* Matilda.

85. *Fearful:* Seeing only Matilda by him. Dante is afraid that Beatrice has left.

86–90. *She is seated on the roots of the new foliage:* As Christ, after his Transfiguration, resumed his earthly appearance, so Beatrice, having entered as the figure of revelation aboard the triumphal chariot, is now seated upon the ground.

Beatrice is seated *on* the ground and *under* the new foliage (that sprang from the touch of Christ—the Griffon). Let the tree in this aspect symbolize the Holy Roman Empire, and the roots Rome. The chariot, of course, represents the Church. It rests on the roots (Rome) and is tied to the tree (the Empire). Beatrice (Divine Love) is left on earth to guard the chariot under the protective shade of the tree, while the Griffon (Christ) ascends to Heaven followed by the rest of the Heavenly Train, which is singing a hymn that is sweeter and profounder than earth can understand. Beatrice is left on earth encircled and attended by the Seven Nymphs (the Three Theological Virtues and the Four Cardinal Virtues).

109–111. Dante's meteorological figure here is based on the belief that the highest reaches of the sky are the domain of fire. The highest clouds, therefore, being closest to the sphere of fire would be especially subject to fiery influences and would give forth the most powerful lightning flashes.

112. *the bird of Jove:* The eagle. See *Ezekiel* xvii, the Parable of the Eagles and the Cedar. There, the eagle represents the Babylonian persecution of the Jews. Here, Dante clearly enough intends its attack to symbolize the Roman persecution of the early Christians.

118. *a fox:* Is most usually taken to represent the heresies that threatened the early Church and that were repelled by the divine wisdom of the Church Fathers.

124–129. THE GIFT OF THE EAGLE. The Eagle of Imperial Rome returns and covers the car (the Church) with its feathers (riches) and a voice from Heaven cries out in grief. The grief is clearly for the evils that descended upon the Church when it grew rich. Dante must certainly have had the Donation of Constantine (see *Inferno* XIX, 109–111, and note) in mind in the first feathering of the car. The second gift of the eagle would then symbolize the whole process whereby the temporal wealth of the Empire passed so largely into the hands of the Church.

131. *a dragon:* Satan.

135. *as if it meant to linger:* Having broken the floor of the car (the foundation of the Church, once it has been weakened by wealth), Satan would certainly not run away, but rather remain to see what other mischief he could do, wandering off only very slowly.

142–147. THE CAR TRANSFORMS ITSELF INTO A SEVEN-HEADED MONSTER. "And I saw a woman sitting upon a scarlet-colored beast full of the names of blasphemy, having seven heads and ten horns." (*Revelation* xvii, 3.)

The Seven Heads have been interpreted in endless ingenious ways. Let them be taken as representing the Seven Deadly Sins. They thus took root in the Church as soon as it covered itself with wealth. The first three of the seven are Pride, Wrath, and Avarice. Being the worst sins, they sprout from the pole (i.e., they come before the others). And since they represent offenses against both God and one's neighbors, they are represented as having two horns. The four lesser sins (Acedia, Envy, Gluttony, and Lust) offend God but not necessarily one's neighbors and they are, therefore, represented as having single horns. Thus the total of ten horns.

149–150. *an ungirt harlot:* She represents the Papacy as it existed under Boniface VIII and Clement V, the two popes Dante most charges with corruption. (See *Inferno* XIX, and note to 77–79.) "Ungirt" (Dante uses *sciolta,* "untied, unbound") should be understood to imply both lewdness (immodesty of dress) and lack of restraint (knowing no bounds). *her eyes darting with avarice:* looking everywhere for plunder.

152. *a giant:* The French monarchy, and especially Philip the Fair (Philip IV, 1268–1314, crowned in 1285), who made the Papacy his puppet.

154. *But when she turned her hungry eyes on me:* The question here is why the giant beats the harlot for looking at Dante. Again, many answers have been suggested, but two seem most to the point.

If Dante is taken here as representing Italy, the whipping can only refer to Philip's humiliation of Boniface VIII (see Canto XX, 85–93, note), and the harlot's covetous glance at Dante-as-Italy would represent Boniface's intrigues with various rulers. It was these intrigues that put him most at odds with Philip.

On the other hand, Dante may be taken to represent the typical Christian who looks to the Church for guidance. The allegory would then be saying that every time the corrupt Church is stirred by a wish to return to its true pastoral mission, the French kings whip her and drag her back to sin.

158. *and dragged it off:* In 1304 Philip engineered the election of Clement V and transferred the Papal Seat (dragged it off) to Avignon.

CANTO XXXIII

The Earthly Paradise —Eunoë

DANTE'S PURIFICATION COMPLETED

The Seven Nymphs sing a hymn of sorrow for the grief of the Church, and Beatrice answers with Christ's words announcing his resurrection. All then move onward, Beatrice summoning Dante to her side as they walk on.

Beatrice begins her discourse with an obscurely worded prophecy of the Deliverance of the Church. In much simpler language, she then utters her *Final Reproach to Dante* for having so lost sight of the truth.

Just as she finishes, the train halts before *The Great Spring* from which flow the waters of both Lethe and Eunoë. At Beatrice's command, the Seven Nymphs lead Dante forward and he *Drinks the Waters of Eunoë.* By drinking the waters of Lethe, Dante has already forgotten all sin and error; now every good is strengthened in him. Thus is his *Final Purification* completed, and Dante rises "perfect, pure, and ready for the stars."

"*Deus, venerunt gentes*"—the Holy Seven,
　in alternating chorus through their tears,
　first three, then four, raised a sweet chant to Heaven;　3

and Beatrice, when she heard them mourn such loss
　sighed with a grief so deep that even Mary
　could not have changed more at the foot of the cross.　6

But when the other virgins in their choir
　fell still for her reply, she rose erect
　in holy zeal, and said, as if afire:　9

"*Modicum et non videbitis me;*
　et iterum, dearly beloved sisters,
　modicum, et vos videbitis me."　12

Then placing the Seven before her, she moved ahead
  with a nod to me, to the Lady, and to the Sage
  that had remained, to follow where she led.   15

So she strolled on, and she had not yet laid
  her tenth step on the sward, when she turned round
  and struck my eyes with her eyes as she said   18

with a serene tranquillity: "Draw near,
  that you may, if I wish to speak to you
  as we move on, be better placed to hear."   21

When I was, as I should be, at her side,
  she said: "Dear brother, why are you not moved
  to question me as we move on?"—Tongue-tied,   24

like one who knows his station is beneath
  that of the presences in which he stands,
  and cannot drag his voice across his teeth,   27

so did I, with a voice almost choked through,
  manage to say: "My Lady, all my need
  and all that is my good is known to you."   30

And she to me: "My wish is that you break
  the grip of fear and shame, and from now on
  no longer speak like one but half awake.   33

The cart the dragon broke was, and is not;
  let him whose fault that is believe God's wrath
  will not be calmed by soup, however hot.   36

The eagle you saw shed its plumes back there
  to make the cart a monster and a prey,
  will not remain forever without heir;   39

for certain as my words, my eyes foresee,
  already nearing, the unstayable stars
  that bring the time in which, by God's decree,   42

five hundred, ten, and five shall be the sign
  of one who comes to hunt down and destroy
  the giant and his thievish concubine.   45

My prophecy, being obscure as those
  of Themis and the Sphinx, may fail to move you,
  since all such words hide what they should disclose;   48

but soon now, like an Oedipus reborn,
  events themselves shall solve the dark enigma,
  and without loss of either sheep or corn.   51

Note my words well, and when you give them breath,
  repeat them as I said them, to the living
  whose life is no more than a race toward death.   54

And when you come to write them down, make clear
  what you have seen of the Tree, now twice-despoiled
  since all-creating God first raised it here.   57

All those who rob or break those boughs commit
  a blasphemy-in-deed, offending God
  who sacred to Himself created it.   60

For just one bite, the First Soul's tears were spilt
  five thousand years and more, yearning for Him
  who suffered in His own flesh for that guilt.   63

Your wits must be asleep not to have known
  that a particular reason must account
  for its great height and its inverted crown.   66

Had not your idle thoughts been to your brain
  an Elsan water, and your pleasure in them
  a Pyramus to the mulberry's new stain,   69

those two facts surely should have made you see
  the justice of God's interdict shine forth
  as the moral meaning of the form of the Tree.   72

It is my wish—because I see your mind
  turned into stone, and like a stone, so darkened
  that the light of what I tell you strikes it blind—   75

that you bear back, if not in writing, then
  in outline, what I say, as pilgrims wreathe
  their staffs with palm to show where they have been." 78

And I to her: "As pressed wax will retain
  a faithful imprint of the signet ring,
  so is your seal imprinted on my brain.   81

But why do your desired words fly so high
  above my power to follow their intent
  that I see less and less the more I try?"   84

"They fly so high," she said, "that you may know
  what school you followed, and how far behind
  the truth I speak its feeble doctrines go;   87

and see that man's ways, even at his best,
  are far from God's as earth is from the heaven
  whose swiftest wheel turns above all the rest."   90

"But," I replied, "I have no recollection
  of ever having been estranged from you.
  Conscience does not accuse me of defection."   93

And she then with a smile: "If, as you say
  you lack that memory, then call to mind
  how you drank Lethe's waters here today.   96

As certainly as smoke betrays the fire,
  this new forgetfulness of your wish to stray
  betrays the sinfulness of that desire.   99

But I assure you that I shall select
  the simplest words that need be from now on
  to make things clear to your dull intellect."   102

Now with a brighter flame and slower pace
  the sun was holding its meridian height,
  which varies round the world from place to place,   105

when suddenly—as one who leads a line
  of travelers as their escort will stop short
  at a strange sight or an unusual sign—   108

so stopped the Seven at an edge of shade
  pale as a shadow cast by a cold peak
  on a cold stream deep in an Alpine glade.   111

And there ahead of them, in a single flow,
  Tigris and Euphrates seemed to rise
  and part as friends who linger as they go.   114

"O light and glory of mankind," I cried,
  "what is this flood that pours forth from one source
  and then parts from itself to either side?"   117

In answer to that prayer I heard the name
  "Matilda" and "ask her." Who spoke up then
  as one does who absolves himself of blame: 120

"This, and much more, I have this very day
  explained to him, and Lethe certainly
  could not have washed that memory away."   123

And Beatrice: "Perhaps a greater care,
  as often happens, dims his memory
  and his mind's eye. But see Eunoë there—   126

lead him, as is your custom, to the brim
  of that sweet stream, and with its holy waters
  revive the powers that faint and die in him."   129

Then as a sweet soul gladly shapes its own
  good will to the will of others, without protest,
  as soon as any sign has made it known,   132

so the sweet maid, taking me by the hand
  and saying in a modest voice to Statius,
  "Come you with him," obeyed the good command.   135

Reader, had I the space to write at will,
  I should, if only briefly, sing a praise
  of that sweet draught. Would I were drinking still!   138

But I have filled all of the pages planned
  for this, my second, canticle, and Art
  pulls at its iron bit with iron hand.   141

I came back from those holiest waters new,
  remade, reborn, like a sun-wakened tree
  that spreads new foliage to the Spring dew   144

in sweetest freshness, healed of Winter's scars;
  perfect, pure, and ready for the Stars.

NOTES

1. *Deus, venerunt gentes:* Psalm LXXIX, the lamentation for the destruction of Jerusalem. "O God, the heathen are come into thine inheritance; thy holy temple have they defiled; they have laid Jerusalem on heaps." So have the later unbelievers despoiled and defiled the Church.

3. *first three, then four:* The Seven Nymphs sing the psalm antiphonally, the Three Theological Virtues singing first (they being higher in the scale of things), and then the Four Cardinal Virtues.

5–6. *even Mary could not have changed more:* The comparison is not a hyperbole. Beatrice, mourning for the crucifixion of the Church, would endure the same grief Mary suffered at the crucifixion of her son, Christ and the Church being one.

10–12. *Modicum et non videbitis me . . . :* "A little while and ye shall not see me; and again a little while, and ye shall see me [because I go to the Father]." (*John* xvi, 16.)

These are Christ's words to his disciples, announcing his resurrection. Beatrice speaks them afire with her holy zeal in reply to the mournful psalm. She is saying, in effect, that the triumph of the True Faith shall be seen again. On one level her words may be taken to mean that the pure in heart shall rise above the corruption of the Church to see Christ again in Heaven. More likely, Dante meant that the Church shall be purged until Christ is once more truly visible in its workings.

14–15. *the Lady:* Matilda. *the Sage that had remained:* Statius. The other Sage, Virgil, has departed.

17. *her tenth step:* Every number mentioned by Dante invites allegorical conjecture, and many have taken the "ten" here to refer to the Ten Commandments. The interpretation seems doubtful, however, especially since the actual steps taken were not yet ten.

18. *struck my eyes with her eyes:* Dante takes this forceful way of emphasizing the power of her eyes. (The Lamps of Heaven?)

19. *serene tranquillity:* The Change in Beatrice is not a matter of feminine mood. When Dante still had upon himself a stain of ne-

glect, Beatrice berated him for it. But he has now done fit penance and the stain has been removed, thereby removing all cause for anger.

22. *When I was, as I should be, at her side:* Dante's whole progress up to this time has been, as it should be the object of every soul, to stand beside Divine Love.

27. *and cannot drag his voice across his teeth:* It is characteristic of Dante that a certain pungency should creep into his phrasing even at such sublime moments.

31–33. *like one but half awake:* Dante has achieved purification, and all memory of sin has been washed from him by the waters of Lethe. He must yet drink of the waters of Eunoë, which will strengthen every good memory in him. Because he has not yet been so strengthened, he still speaks, partly, with the habituated fears and confusions of his former ways. It is these fears and confusions Beatrice is telling him to put by.

34–36. Beatrice now refers to the allegory that concluded Canto XXXII, assuring Dante, as in her answer to the psalm, that a dawn of righteousness is approaching. *was, and is not:* These are the words of John, *Revelation* xvii, 8: "The beast thou sawest was, and is not." *soup:* In some parts of ancient Greece a murderer could protect himself from all vengeance if for nine successive days he ate soup on the grave of his victim. In Florence it became a custom to stand guard for nine days over the grave of a murdered man to see that no one ate soup upon it. The reference is a strange one, but Dante's intent is, clearly, that no such simple rite will ward off the vengeance of God.

37–39. *the eagle . . . will not remain forever without heir:* The eagle is, of course, the Roman Empire. The true heir of the Caesars, who will restore order and goodness, will come at last. Dante thought of Frederick II as the last real heir of the Caesars.

41. *the unstayable stars:* Nothing can stay the stars in their courses. Beatrice foresees propitious stars already near at hand. (God's wrath will not be stayed: *cf.* lines 35–36.)

43. *five hundred, ten, and five:* As Beatrice says in the next tercet, she is speaking in the veiled tongue of prophecy, and her words hide what they should disclose. Whatever the numerological significance